Steven Berkoff
Plays Two

Decadence, Kvetch, Acapulco, Harry's Christmas, Brighton Beach Scumbags, Dahling You Were Marvellous, Dog and *Actor.*

Steven Berkoff is an actor, director and playwright. His plays include *East, West, Sink the Belgrano!, Decadence, Kvetch, Acapulco, I am Hamlet* and an adaptation of Kafka's *Metamorphosis.* His film credits include *A Clockwork Orange, Octopussy* and *Beverly Hills Cop.* He lives in London.

STEVEN BERKOFF
Plays Two

Decadence
Kvetch
Acapulco
Harry's Christmas
Brighton Beach Scumbags
Dahling You Were Marvellous
Dog
Actor

faber and faber

This collection
first published in 1994 as *The Collected Plays* Volume II
by Faber and Faber Limited
3 Queen Square London WC1N 3AU
Reissued in 1996 as *Steven Berkoff: Plays Two*

Decadence was first published privately by the author in 1981 and then in 1982
by John Calder (Publishers) Ltd, London
Kvetch was first published in 1986 by Faber and Faber Limited
Acapulco was first published in 1986 by Faber and Faber Limited
Harry's Christmas was first published in 1985 by Faber and Faber Limited
Brighton Beach Scumbags was first published in 1994 by Faber and Faber Limited
Dahling You Were Marvellous was first published in 1994
by Faber and Faber Limited
Dog was first published in 1994 by Faber and Faber Limited
Actor was first published in this version in 1994 by Faber and Faber Limited

Photoset in Plantin by Parker Typesetting Service, Leicester
Printed in England by Mackays of Chatham plc, Chatham, Kent

British Library Cataloguing in Publication data is available

ISBN 0–571–17102–8

6 8 10 9 7 5

CONTENTS

DECADENCE

CHARACTERS

HELEN
STEVE
SYBIL
LES

AUTHOR'S NOTE

Decadence is a study of the ruling classes or upper classes, so called by virtue of strangulated vowel tones rather than any real achievement. The voice is caught in the back of the throat and squashed so as to release as little emotion as possible. Consonants are hard and biting, since emotion is carried on the vowel. The upper class slur the vowel or produce a glottal stop, which by closing down of the glottal creates an impure vowel – like 'hice' for 'house'. They move in awkward rapid gestures or quick jerks and sometimes speak at rapid speeds to avoid appearing to have any feeling for what they say. They achieve pleasure very often in direct relation to the pain they cause in achieving it. Particularly in causing intolerable suffering to achieve exquisite pâtés; boiling lobsters alive with other crustaceans, and hunting down defenceless animals to give them (the hunters) a sense of purpose on Sundays.

These activities can be achieved only by dulling the emotions that spring from awareness, and increasing sadomasochistic activity. Emotion for others, feelings of altruism and generosity, have to be suppressed in order to be able to tolerate the life-style they have adopted. Public schools help to foster the image of superiority without merit and the repression of sensuality. The emphasis being on imposing your will on lesser and junior colleagues, which in turn breeds the future masters and officers class. Upper-class people often regress when in groups to behaviour of simple infantilism, since this is the only time they can escape into their childhood, which was cut off by boarding school at an early age. They are very often seen to be anally fixated, having never made a natural progress into maturity. Equality is an awkward feeling whereas being ruled or ruling produces fluency in speech or actions. Equality suggests that giving should be on an equal par and makes demands that they have not been equipped to deal with. So they make bad lovers but are known to be very decent to servants and extremely loyal to royalty, which to them represents the pinnacle of achievement and the sum total of Englishness.

Decadence was first performed at the New End Theatre,
Hampstead, London, on 14 July 1981. The cast was as follows:

HELEN	Linda Marlowe
STEVE	Steven Berkoff
SYBIL	Linda Marlowe
LES	Steven Berkoff
Director	Steven Berkoff

A new production of *Decadence* was presented at Wyndham's
Theatre on 25 February 1987.

ACT ONE

SCENE I

Black floor. A white set. Woman in black. Man in black and white. A woman sits on a white leather sofa. Music plays, a forties Ambrose record. A man in tails and wing collar stands near her in a pose of frozen upper-class glee. He remains frozen until he speaks, apart from lighting her cigarette. All cigarettes and drinks are mimed with great emphasis to extract the greatest amount of absurdity from the physical response. Acting should be sensual, erotic, flamboyant.

HELEN: How sweet of you to come on time / bastard! sweet
   darling! my you do look so divine. I've been so bored / have a
   drink / what . . . ? / Of course! a Drambuie with soda and a
   splash of Cinzano . . . with masses of ice / I've been so bored
   tearing round to find just what would enchant you to eat me
   for breakfast (*Raising skirt*) *charmant n'est-ce pas* / does it
   make you go all gooey / does it send spasms up and down
   your spine / enough ice! sweety you do look nice. Do you like
   my legs? / aren't my frillies sweet / does it make you get just a
   little on heat / kiss me / gently / don't smudge now / just a
   touch / a graze won't be a trice / I'll get ready / so late I
   couldn't find a fucking taxi / oh I hate to miss the first scene
   the first embrace / what's that we're seeing / the name of the
   play! / taxis were thin on the ground / outside Harrods there
   were none around / I stretched out an arm / I felt like Moses /
   what did he do / raise his arms to heaven for the Hebrews /
   the longer he kept his arm in the air the better would his
   armies fare, but when it fell wearily down / bloody nosed
   moishers and crunch smash and pound / you've not said a
   word / but you do look dishy / a bird in the ice floes / or
   chilled meringue frappé / you look simply gay / got a fag . . .
   hmm! Smoke gets in your eyes! Shit! Oh sorry / tit! Ready
   heart? Where for dinner after / surprise me then, give me a

thrill / so long as I gorge on some juicy meat / I'm as hungry
as a vampire / if I don't eat soon I'll simply expire / did you
have a nice day / little wife all safe and tucked away / come
open your mouth and dazzle my ears / come love . . . / you
look troubled / close to tears / what have I done . . . shit . . .
you look bad / what's the matter hone(y)?

STEVE: So bleeding dextrous / wouldn't you know / too much
bloody ice love / tastes like a crow / you ask me the cause for
my down face / wait till you hear what I have to say / unzip
your ears and let me flood them with verbs and make your
mind a jangle of nerves / the bloody slut got cute / decided for
a hunch to hire a dick with a nose like a Jew / a private
detective in case you're not yet clued / to follow me here / and
now I fear the game's up my dear / the bloody bitch got wise
when too many spunkless nights rolled by / it made her think
that I was not emptying my tea pot in her old kitchen sink /

HELEN: Oh fuck darling /

STEVE: You've said a mouthful there /

HELEN: Don't worry darling / you've nothing to fear / say your
hard on's taking a small holiday this year / the work and
strain of conning your way in this world sends the cock to the
brain / her jealousies are painted shadows / relieve her pain /
and drop a morsel or two in your old dame / but a private
dick / that's a hell of a game!

STEVE: Too bloody true Helen / my god you're a beaut / a
fabulous sight / I could feast my eyes on you day and night /
let's go out on the town / fuck this dick / let's go and get
tight / but damn this greasy bleeder if he's outside he'll
follow us / there's nowhere to hide / then it's all out / the
evidence clear / he'll tell her all there is needed to hear.

HELEN: Is Chartreuse with pink just too too much / my head is
spinning darling / what did you say / are you sure you're not
fantasizing / did you have a bad day / I don't know what to
wear / help me darling don't just stand there.

STEVE: Let me make it clear / let me shake up the slop that tries to
pretend it's a brain not a mop / my dearest wife Sybil, this
morning she said / if I don't stop whoring I'm just as well

dead / now try and get that in your fucking head! A divorce
and it's ample she has all the clues / photos no doubt / it will
make all the news / cut off / not a penny / as broke as a
mouse / no fortune no wages / and she keeps the house / got a
light?

HELEN: So what shall we do? Oh Stevie / it's beastly what she
does to you / is my seam straight / oh come on darling we
mustn't be late /

STEVE: You don't seem to realize this beast is trailing my scent / I
can't think / my hard on's getting quite bent / to feel this
creature so close on my back / spying, reporting my every
track / I can just see him now / can't you / putting two and
two together to the bloody cow /

SCENE 2

LES *and* SYBIL (*same actors change attitude and positions*).

LES: So, I followed him to this sumptuous flat / a conspiracy is
what I make of that /

SYBIL: Wadya mean a conspiracy? To fucking wot? /

LES: Wak your treasure! Your old man's sticking his nasty in
some horrible / birds of a fucking feather ducky stick to
fucking gether / these ex-public schools well grounded in
making fools of us / the country's pus that welts up from the
blood and guts of me and you / you married the runt / when
your old dad at the time / he's just a cad / just after your
considerable dough / which dad's sweated his balls off for
and now you bunged it to some male whore / set up no doubt
in pad / contributed by your not inconsiderable swag / it
makes you double choke / this ponce swishes you off your
feet / your plates of meat / down Blakes or Tramps or other
swishy hole / where half-assed bastards and criminals go / the
foul / ignoble mob / odd judge MP and law sniff round the
seamy door / liking what's on the other side of the swamp /
have a romp / Incognito and hope that what's for dough will
taste better than old Flo in curlers / rancid in East Cheam /

and when they've had their bit of fun / head home again all
nice for Flo / who's lying in a heap of cream and wax /
clutching *Cosmopolitan* or other crap / with overfed pussy on
her lap.

SYBIL: And I don't want to get like that / thanks love / I feel a
little better now / when I found out / I'll kill the fucking cow
I thought / at first / you know how you do / I cried for days /
right broke up / never dreamed that my dear Steve would do
that to me / the big question is why / ours is not to reason but
to die / that's how I felt / but now I'm calmed and like the sea
all tempest tossed / you're thrown this way and that / like
being screwed if you like by some big black cat / you can't
think for the storm shoved up / but after in the trough of
calm / thoughts that seem wise gather round / counsel me to
nothing rash / be clever Sybil / don't go mad / the taste is
sweet when you're stabbing guts in heat / but later in cold
cell / there's too much time to dwell / but do it neat / cut off
his money and you may as well cut off his feet / he won't
move / he can't / he's helpless like his kind / no drive within /
no chin to take the blows that come at him /

LES: Attagirl / that's how I like to see you chat / like some fucking
great jungle cat / claws withdrawn ready to pounce and rip
apart this paltry mouse / quiet as death still as a stone / then
pow! Tear his flesh off his bones / that's what we do / take
our time / don't frite the bastard he'll shit his pipe / let him
be forgiven / don't do it again darling / slip powdered glass in
his gin / I seen a guy who swallowed glass / I seen the blood
pour out of his ass and out of his ears / vomit it up in cups of
mashy red / the simple conclusion / he's better off dead!

SYBIL: You're crazy Les I swear / don't do nothing daft / he
knows about you dear /

LES: What! You've told him about me / shit! Now you've blown
my little fantasy!

SYBIL: He only thinks I hired a private dick / but one familiar for
whom I lick his prick / but I disturbed one day by ill
concealed traces of some sexual play / some love tattoos left
in his flies / he thinks I hired a pair of eyes / not realizing that

I was on to anything more strong than a vibrator when he's
on his trips so long / and now I know that those business trips
were dirty business to see his trick / greasy joints and my
dough to help cream the way / they say money's the best
lubricator / no need for K-Y.

LES: You sound just great / I could eat you up / you look like a
lioness / I feel like your cub / take your knickers off I wanna
fuck /

SYBIL: Tell you the truth / I'd rather have a suck!

SCENE 3

STEVE *and* HELEN (*they melt into the characters as before*).

STEVE: (*Smoking*) Do you know I never saw my old dad / maybe
on weekends sometime / or end of term / he'd come over with
mum in a Toni perm / prize giving / that was it / I never got
nothing / a prize nitwit / then we'd go to lunch / sit in a
bloody restaurant / a tight horrid bunch of us / all quite like a
church and all the other kids with dads and mums
pretending it was such fun to see your mum once in three
months / a fiver in your pocket and chin up Steve / write to us
Colin / work hard Pete / give us a call when you feel the
need / cheers love / the Jaguar bites the gravel and tears away
in the dust / hands wave from the back / you bite and gulp /
feel tears about to start / they're off to somewhere hot / to
Monte Carlo for the season / dad's a whiz at bridge and both
of them like to dance but never taught me a game of cards
that I might join them in their nights of laughs / that I heard
from other rooms / when I in bed all alone would moan /
these were the days before public school darling or poofs
palace for the sons of fools / when I was still a thing to be
shunted around / don't make a sound / don't spoil their play /
just laughter from other rooms and wet long days / and then
the drive to bloody P. school and farewell home for ever
really / you'll love it here he said / rugger, cross-country
runs / will make the man of me / he wants so much to be / see

you / spring summer autumn winter / and each time the
absence makes the heart grow colder / more restrained and
still the bloody mid-term restaurants / you are looking older
Steve / and how's the game / you still wing three quarters? /
Here's a fiver / shove it in your pocket / so when the PT
master showed a friendly eye I warmed to him / and when he
put his hand on my thigh / it didn't feel so bad 'cause I
missed dad / or man / or somehow had / to unite with
someone not to feel sad / so at first it's just a little wank / all
friendly / just a dirty prank / start looking forward to it now
and getting good at it myself / and then one day he asked me
to stick it in / right up his ass / I felt a little queer I must
confess but after it felt fine / just like a cunt / funny that /
could be a juicy tart / if you shut your eyes and put your
mind on snatch well after I opened flies like sardine cans /
and public school / it taught me this / that buggery can be
total bliss / some poor small frightened fag / protect him and
you've got his bum for life / well, so one day headmaster
strolls in when I'm giving head / and says Forsyth / you're
dead / get out this school you filthy scum / I won't have these
things going on / just pack your bags / this is not a school for
fags / he wrote to dad / to say your son likes nothing better
than a schoolboy's bum and would he come up and collect
the scum / you see the school was rife / so thick in queers you
could have cut it with a knife / but dad was too ashamed to
think he sired a bloody poof / and sent instead the chauffeur
down to pick me up / who must have got wind somehow of
my deed / since after driving for some time / he stopped along
a country lane / and said / you're not to blame / these schools
are cesspits of male vice / but I suppose it is sometimes rather
nice / it doesn't make you bent as a hairpin / to indulge
sometimes in a little sin / I've got two kids your age myself he
said / and put his hand right on my prick / and when it got as
hard as rock / he winked and gave it a bit of a lick / bloody
hell he turned me round and shoved it right up my Khyber
pass / fuck you I thought / I've had enough / so dad said when
at home / you disgust me / you perve / dirty little homo /

reptile and foul bandit for turds / take that / and with his fist delivered a mighty whack / which missed / since I boxed somewhat at school and knew a thing or two about Queensberry rules / I didn't just hold prefects' tools / I had enough somehow from me / and all my hate welled up for him / don't do it dad I said / and smashed a right hand on his nose / which forthwith began to sprout a rose / I then curled hard my other fist and put it on his jaw / mother screamed and dad looked very ill / but do you know / it gave me quite a thrill to beat my dad up / suddenly my pain just went away / and that was the last time I was gay / I don't regret it though I'm glad to say / I think the dads of this world carry a lot of blame . . .

HELEN: So darling / what's new? / You lay back like a cow / all fat and cuddy and relate the news of your distant past / of your distress at home with nasty old pa / the tape unwinds / the story starts afresh / and as you speak you seem to lay back in a bath / you wallow in a trouble of all your suffering and woe / prattle on / take out a cigarette and . . . go! / And dad did this to me and that / and he said this to me and that / and he **never** gave me this or that / when I was young and needy / little wretch more like and greedy / with an ego like a hole that never can be filled / until it sucked the very air from out their mouths / and on and on the never-ending tape of dad and mum / and why you're like you are / the scars from wounds that open fresh showing their tincts of blood / whenever I or other by mishap should graze that precious weal / that you are not too keen to heal / that you so covetously keep so you can whine afresh and weep my dad did this to me / he never took me to the football match / deprived you pet and mum gave you a hiding / so you kept your little treasure chest of grief / that you would open when you want to peck at your old little pains / and multiply a little grief that lasted seconds into a bible of woe is me / makes us all read the boring text and thus excuse yourself of all your crimes / just because life's been so unkind / when you can't think, or grow a little bored with how or what to do / the

unused precious energy now feeds on you / frustrated in
other words / starts fishing out dead herrings of past hurts /
and waves them hot and smelly from their long sojourn. /
Throw out these stinking fish / don't use another soul to
listen to your ancient threadbare woes / you crave for new
fresh birds that can fill chock full / unroll again your scroll of
agony for them / and then you want new talents / new
assaults to taste because you've nothing more to say / how
many ways of cooking that old stew / get on your stomach
darling (*She starts massaging his back.*) but live now in the
present / perceive what's outside you bring home your tales
of raw today / and what I'm feeling now / all the hurts
accept / nay welcome since they are fresh fish from the
ocean / cut off the past that you drag by a rope like some old
ship carrying cargoes of junk and waste then you'll be light,
weightless and fast not tied like Ulysses to a mast / afraid to
hear unchained the Sirens' blast / afraid of the unknown / kill
off the kid and be full grown / with me your sack is empty /
so feverishly you scratch at some other unsuspecting pair of
ears / till they say ow! Enough! I can't take any more / then
on you go / the ancient mariner or wandering Jew who must
unload his slops and spew / live in the now / and pain and
past will crumble fast in sweet fresh air / like ancient
mummies dead for years in darkened vaults just fall apart
when light and air expose their fetid lair / don't drag your ma
and pa from out their graves to bail you out for all the shit /
it's you now boy / if the shoe fits . . .

STEVE: Wear it / it's so true (*He starts to grope her.*)
HELEN: Stop it!
STEVE: Darling . . .
HELEN: Stop it!
STEVE: Darling . . .
HELEN: Stop i i i it!!
STEVE: OK darling.

   (*They both sit on couch – he looks suitably abashed.*)
   Truce?
HELEN: (*Silence*)

STEVE: Love you!
HELEN: (*Silence*)
STEVE: Lurve you!
HELEN: (*Silence*)
STEVE: Luurrve yoouu!
HELEN: OK. Love you.

> (*This continues for a moment more –* STEVE *sits back happy and contented.*)

STEVE: Mustn't feel sorry for myself / but I do get bored darling waiting for you / to come home and cheer me up / give me a laugh / you're super jolly good at that / not bloody half / a sense of humour / that's a treat / that's what is vital to our love / I think / can't bear humourless people / the ones who think, the ones who think their shit don't stink / still you're right about me love / you've hit it on the nail I do repeat the same old tale / I think I told that story every time / to every different woman of mine / and like a player on the stage / repeating the same life every day / repetition wears the brain away / what's my stars say? Any fortune or some fame along the way / some foreign travel . . . what! My love life is so perfect so there's nothing there / couldn't be better poppet / love you darling / my super wondrous piece of dolly arse / my dishy lovely slice of peach Melba / pour me a gin and it / no make it a Scotch and dry / I fancy that / and then / no parties anywhere tonight / ring Alex would you or old Keith / he'll have a rubber or gin rummy going / bless him, he's a card / raced his Ferrari last week 'gainst Claude's Lamborghini and both bloody collided / pissed myself laughing / you think Keith gave a fart / no fear / that's fucking fixed that one / let's go and get another / and damn me if the blighter didn't just go and buy a bloody new one / what a card / there's too much bloody ice in here you wicked nymph / it takes so long to train them nowadays / what's for dinner darling / something new / surprise me / I'm so bloody bored with filet / tastes like rubber nowadays / what's in the bloody feed I wonder, plastic chippings I've no doubt / oh let's book up at Fred's / that's very you / a sole *bonne femme* or Strogonoff or even a

fondue / another drink my sweet / love you darling / you
OK? / You seem a little pinched / what's up my lollipop eh? /
What's a-matter little lollipop / does you want papa to take
your little drawers down and pin you to the sofa / oh don't
look like that / like I'm something just brought in by the cat /
OK I'm off the beam tonight but feel a little twitchy down
there / thought to pass the time . . . *n'est-ce pas* / *petit
divertissement* / no? / That's just fine with me / lovely legs
you've got / they go right up and up and get lost up your
bum / oops mustn't get a hard on / just when we are going
out / eh love / fancy a tickle with the old giggle stick / no,
OK / you used to get weak at the knees just at the
suggestion / cream your jeans / you used to say / I suppose
you take me now for granted, eh! / But I'm so bloody bored
tonight / don't know the cause / maybe I'm reaching male
menopause / what do you think? I'm only joking dear / don't
look like you smell some awful stink.

SCENE 4

Lights fade. Come up on SYBIL *and* LES.

SYBIL: So how's the plot / what's happening / what's the plan / are
you still with me my desperate Dan / powdered glass or
poison in his drink / what's better / what do you think? /

LES: It's hard to tell / fuck only knows / poison leaves traces in his
gut / and clues that may point back to you my pet / don't
make things worse by sewing seeds that may sprout later as
evil deeds that tend to boomerang and whack you down /
kick out the bastard / get rid of the clown / that's my advice /
get your mouth round that.

SCENE 5

Mood is from prior scene. Lights fade – come up on HELEN *and*
STEVE.

STEVE: I don't know why I'm so bored /

HELEN: Oh let me cheer you up.

STEVE: Would you?

HELEN: It's very simple – you're a pup who needs a game to keep his spirits all /

STEVE: Yeees!

HELEN: I'll tell you a story – once upon a time / you just lie there and I'll be Scheherazade / let me beguile your eyes with tales to ravish you my dear /

STEVE: Let's have a cigarette first.

HELEN: OK.

(*They light cigarettes and they both have hysterical fun blowing smoke rings.*)

The morning's sun was high up in the sky / a great big orange in a sea of blue / and caw caws from the fluffy floating gulls, and yachts were thick as icing in the breathless still and crispy morning / the wind as soft as shantung whispers / the windows from my hotel room lay open and the curtains softly waved from time to time / the bed as white as arctic snows and little bells would tinkle from the yachts to tickle in your ears and wake you up / the servants softly tread down corridors thick pile with chink of coffee cups and clutching morning papers thickly folded / little gentle taps on doors / the knuckle's light morse code to wake the wealthy from their night-long doze, while swallowed in silk sheets and thick duvets in darkened curtained rooms they lay / fat and white giant slugs, stirring with parched and furry mouth anxious for their morning cups / the room still drenched in the stale cigar smoke while their stomach's lining burn in torment still from last night's bloated fill / mignon stuffed with oysters / cavier and crêpe Suzette, lobster Thermidor and poisoned liver of wild ducks / the brains of pigs in aspic laced with the tongue of sheep in the blood of nightingales / garlic crushed in veal whose occupants were shut in boxes from their birth and fed with milk to be more tender / their flesh so soft it hurts / so in their fat cocoons they lay in half somnolent daze / the bathroom scattered like jewels with multitudes of coloured pills / the clothes lay in a heap, my watch from Cartier. Good time it keeps / lay on the side / with a glass of champagne, half drunk, warm and tacky now / all that had been so sweet the night before / looked in the morning like death and gore / the plates not gathered by room service looked a foul and fetid mess / and then the servant bless him all crisp and white came like an angel / a blessed sight / a soft tap on the door / like a whisper / like a plea / to be allowed to serve the tea / and not disturb / come in I said and lay your treasures by my bed / your silver tray and pot all steaming hot / and croissants crisp and soft and twirls of butter / coloured sugar like broken glass / honey and the *Paris Match* / he gathered up the last night's dregs and cleared the room / made it sweet and clean again / removed the clues of last night's greed when guts were stuffed with sensual things / and then I breathed / to pay him for his chore / to give a tip I turned around to wake the bore / the beast I came with / but he was dead asleep / I could not find a franc for the young and pretty man / so there he stood like some Apollo waiting to be dismissed but still stood near the bed / like he was waiting for a gentle kiss / the tray he held so tight / his knuckles went quite white / stood in humble supplication / ready to spin on his heel and exit at my will / I raised a hand / just enough to say / don't go yet / please stay / he caught something that I had planted in my eye / an inclined arch of eyebrow gently raised suggested . . . something / something sweet / I could almost feel his body's heat. At last I fumbled in my purse and found a franc / the corpse next to me snored and turned around / the body stood still / as stiff as rock / the thing that I had planted from my eyes to his / he now returned / it gave me a tiny shock / but not too much to stop my hand from wandering up / I placed it like a breath upon the inside of his leg / which felt like marble angels carved by Donatello / still he held the tray / and since the beast was snoring deep I opened the servant's flies and put my hand down deep inside until I found a large warm penis which couldn't hide / he withdrew a touch, not

much / a trifle scared perhaps of monster waking and then
scenarios of losing needed job / but then I flashed a pleading
look / as if to say it's fun / the old man will not wake / he
caught my look and bravely stayed / and gently began to
squeeze his hips and buttocks / so when I took him in my
mouth it was a gorgeous thrill to do it there with bastard still
snoring in his lair / and then he thrust and squirted fine silk
jets of come and nearly dropped the tray / the beast next door
me waked / but slowly like a drunken pig / surfacing through
mud / the boy retrieved his shrunken shark / turned on his
heel / and made a quick depart / I meanwhile swallowed fast /
then Harry woke / 'Good morning darling' I sweetly slurred /
Did you sleep well? he said like bliss and fastened on my
mouth a faggy kiss / my god I thought he tastes like hell.

STEVE: How decadent darling / how simply fab divine and rare to
gobble the waiter with your husband lying there / how
splendid spiffing whizzo fab and gear / it's the most
enchanting story that ever I did hear / you amaze me, stun,
astound / Oh! Wait till this story goes around / what a plot,
what an amazing scene / let's put it in a play / no one would
believe it anyway / no you can't say those / those nasty words
on stage / you'll have the Tory mothers in a spitting rage / oh
shit, *regardez l'heure* / we simply mustn't be late / the play
starts at a quarter to eight.

HELEN: What are we seeing darling / what's my treat tonight?

STEVE: A play about some filthy soldiers sticking their ends up
some poor tyke.

HELEN: How fabulous / how simply great / I want to see that / I
just can't wait / all those dishy soldiers in the raw with cocks
a-flashing everywhere / how simply shocking / how awfully
bizarre / to train at RADA then at last when you're a full
fledged actor / 'what speech will you do today' / you turn
around and bare your arse / he'll do / a three-year contract at
Waterloo / I love all that / that blood and gore / to shock us
pink and crave for more / do they do it for real darling / eight
times a week?

STEVE: No stupid / or their asses would be sore / they **act** the buggering / it's an Equity law /

HELEN: Oh darling what a bloody bore / give me realism that's
what I'm paying for!

(*He throws her on sofa and dives on top.*)

(*Light fades and they come up from clinch as* SYBIL *and* LES.)

SCENE 6

(*As they come up from their embrace*)

LES: Was that all right for you?

SYBIL: Yeah – it was great. Was it all right for you?

LES: Yeah – lovely . . . do you enjoy it?

SYBIL: Yeah . . . it was . . . nice . . . did you?

LES: Wo?

SYBIL: Enjoy it!

LES: Yeah – it was handsome.

SYBIL: Les . . .

LES: Wo?

SYBIL: You don't love me no more.

LES: Why say that?

SYBIL: It's a fact.

LES: If I cut off his head, is my love intact?

SYBIL: It shows a willingness, it shows a fact.

LES: A mug an all / a dozy git to put himself right in the shit / kick
out the cunt / cut off his gelt / put him in limbo / set him
loose in the world / stained, dishonoured / a con man known
by all / not a leg to stand on / not even a ball / he won't even
show his mug to mum as she sits in shame in the bingo hall.

SYBIL: It don't satisfy me / it chokes me to here (*throat*) to think of
that pig out in the strasser dear / stealing more dough /
conning some sweet / sucking on her innocent white teat / till
he's drained her dry the cunning thief / the bloated vampire /
let's extinguish the creep /

LES: You are a one / you are a hag / a right vicious tough old slag /
but give me time and then I'll prove I'm twice the bloke you

20

think / kiss me you luscious dolly pink and bouncy / you're a doll / you make me randy.

SYBIL: You're getting back your desperate dan so don't be mean / you know how much I love you so / you're big and strong / ooh your arms are huge / then hold me tight and make me ooze you filthy bastard / touch me doll / stick your hand inside me coat / feel my nipple / hard as rocks / oh sugar I'm just aching for your . . .

LES: Cor blimey, shuch / you're putting me off / my mind's ablaze with violent acts inspired by your need for facts / I'll prove I love you / I'll make you see just how wondrous thou art to me / I'll measure my love in deeds so cute / I'll make de Sade go back to school / first of all one night / he comes home / stops the car, alights / my car's just behind and rams him down and pastes him to the side / he needs unpeeling so intense will be my hard caress / in bed one night / he's with his whore / there'll be a little tapping on the door / he, careful as a skunk thinking his trail has left no trace of stink / peeps through the spyhole / and sees me / costumed as a telegram boy / all safe he thinks and opens up / a ten-inch blade dives in his gut / at his squash club / he's had his game / all sweaty in his shower / innocent and tame / in the steam no one sees a furtive me drop a tarantula in his pants / he dries off / dresses and suddenly shrieks / there's something up his Kyber pass and it feels to me like broken glass / 'cause tarantula bite is a vicious sight / or a bomb under the lovers' bed / ready to go off as she or he comes / a neat device so sensitive / that extra pressure will blow them to shreds / they'll fly / that's an orgasm that will send them to paradise / gun's too messy and far too noisy / let's leave that out and choose a poison / we'll send him Christmas cake juiced up with cyanide / lots of sherry to help disguise the bitter acrid taste that burns his guts / she'll scream in pain / they'll wait as death starts digging inside their brain / or, excuse me, what's the time? hydrochloric acid in his eyes / he screams / then in the dark / a fine needle penetrates his heart / he didn't see it / so in his dying breath he cannot identify Mr Death / a minute atomic

bomb the size of a pearl / a present in a ring from his golden
girl timed to go off whenever you will / as the mood takes you
ka boom ka blast ke pling! In Africa from leper colony I
extract from a native a deadly smear / then lace his shaver /
one morning you'll hear / Oh I've scratched myself darling /
smile and count down the minutes my dear / best of all I'll
loose some rats whose fangs have been dipped in a deadly
unction / one small bite and the cunt won't function / longer
than it takes to drop down dead / it also saves disposing of the
corpse since the rats will eat the lot of course / so
whatyathink – you make your choice dove / it's just to show
you what I feel **is love**!

SYBIL: Ah darling now I know you care / a little attention makes a
girl all yours / kiss me sweetheart.

LES: Pull off your drawers.

(*Fade out and come up on* STEVE *and* HELEN.)

SCENE 7

STEVE: What are you doing tomorrow darling?

HELEN: Hunting.

STEVE: How absolutely super / marvellous and fabulous – can I
come!

HELEN: Just me and the horse!

STEVE: I bet you're a jolly good rider.

HELEN: You want to practise with me . . . be the horse? . . .

STEVE: What! Can I?

HELEN: Of course. You get down on the carpet . . . (*He does so
and she smacks his bum a few times before she starts speech.*)

The Chase.

HELEN: The morning hung crisp over the village like a Chanel
voile gown or a bouclé ruffle / hunting is so fucking thrilling /
if you haven't done it / it's like explaining a fuck to the pope /
do you know what I mean? it's the togetherness / the meeting
at the morning pub / the stomp of horses and that lovely

bloody smell / the preparation, pulling those fucking
jodhpurs on / bloody hell they can be tight after a binge the
previous night hello Claude and what ho Cecil! There's
Jeremiah and Quentin / Jennifer / Vanessa darling you do
look fab / that jacket fits you like a glove / the asses of the
men look small and pretty bouncing on their steaming
steeds / snorting from their sculptured snouts / what a sight /
off we go, we shout / the leader of the hounds sounds his
horn / they're straining hard 'gainst the curbing leash / a pack
of hate / bursting to get free / dying to get that nasty little
beast / yoiks and tally ho and onwards we shall go / the
bloody fox let loose he scampers out all keenly in the bush /
he has a bloody good time / a jolly taste of pure excitement /
who doesn't like a smashing race? / The leader sounds the
horn the scent's been picked up / dashed good form/heels dig
in ribs the horses swing to face the direction of the horn's
sweet ring / on we go over hill and dale / watching for the
bloody foxy fox's tail / gosh Cynthia's fallen in the muck /
bloody bad luck! / over the brook / dash over the stream / my
pounding steed's just one with me / it's hard / the saddle
chafes / it's tough / my pussy feels delightful though with
each successive thrilling dash / it heaves up huge between my
thighs / this hot and heaving sweating beast / it tugs my hips /
it heaves me on / on to the golden hills of Acheron / I grip
him hard / my knees dig in I soar up high / I float / I flow /
I'm thrown into the sky and then thud down / the air is
singed in smells of mud / crushed grass / horse shit and
sweat / mixed up in one divine and bloody mess / we've lorst
the fucker / oh bloody balls the nag's confused / the scent is
lorst / the dogs go searching / now confused / now whining /
now all cross / oh shit and piss! The fucking league of love
the bloody foxes sabotaged the scent! / The careful thread,
the ribbon of fear that leads us on to the bloody kill / those
left-wing bastards jealous as hell / to see their betters
enjoying themselves / threw scent to confuse / those rotten
sods / I'd thrash them black and blue I'd have them flogged /
those dirty, poofy, Marxist, working-class yobs / wait!

Pluto's found the scent again! Oh fab. We're off! Tarquin
bloodies one of their noses! Oh heavens, it's just raining
roses / he's on the ground and Tarquin's ready to drive his
horse into the bugger / Jeremy says nay / restrains hot
Tarquin / they'll come another day! He says / Oh bravo!
Dashing! Super! Wow! I'm going now / look at meeeeeee! /
The day's spun rich in magenta to auburn / the hounds
shriek louder / the scent grows strong / the fox is tired / my
cheeks are red / my eyes are bright / blood will be shed / oh
god it's getting fucking awful thrilling / the flesh *is* weak but
the spirit is willing / my pants have come galore / and my ass
is deliciously bloody sore / we're close / the fox has gone to
ground / we'll find the little beastly hound / yes! It's trapped
down in some gully / horses crash through the farmer's land /
all in a hurry / tear up the crops / oh dear / we'll pay later
never fear / oh fuck! Some kid's pet cat is torn to shreds in
the wake of the enthusiastic chase / never mind there's plenty
more / ah, we've got him now / I see it caught / it's trapped /
its breath is pounding out in horrible short stabs / its fear
setting each hair on end / the hounds all teeth and smiles as
they go in and sink their fangs into its throat / the blood was
one long jet / just fabulous / I'm sure the fox was pleased to
make his end this way / the fury / the chase / the ecstasy / the
embrace / the leader dismounts / cuts off its tail / bloodies the
kids / oh they were thrilled / oh what a day / let's have a gin
and tonic / whadya say / lovely life / wouldn't have it any
other way /

STEVE: I must say you've made me thirsty / let's have a drink
OK / I enjoyed that / shame about the cat.

HELEN: Ice?

STEVE: Masses (*She mimes handing him the glass.*) I like getting
pissed / like the sound / the crisp crunched feel of bursting
ice / crushed diamonds melting in the acid of your vice / I'll
have a tequila / a frozen glass / grind it into a salt sea bath /
squeezed lemon sharp as a razor / as a spinster's tongue, a
gob of Cointreau adds the dash of fun shake it hard then pour
it out / into your icy salt-licked glass / the first tastes nice and

bitter sweet / grips the tip of your tongue / like the mouth of a baby on a mother's teat / well have another / that chases through / warms the furnace / rattles a window or two / the third one slides along the avenue / well lined by now and gets to work / a glow appears / your inhibitions crumble and your fears, they take a gentle tumble / number four drags from the cupboard your other self / the Jekyll to your Hyde / watch yourself bloom as four pours blood into the withered you. No. Five / proves the fact that you're alive after all / and not a dreary fucking bore / it knocks on other doors down deep / out come the demons from their wretched sleep / so pleased at last to be set free / let's have some fun he! he! he! here comes your past / persecution mania opens his door / the alcohol prises open a few more / paranoia, guilt / jealousy and hate / ready to rehearse the message of agro and bile / you feel good / number six adds fuel to the fire / there's a party down there raging within / your best friend now you hate worse than sin / you and you / piss off you splat / I don't give a shit / accuse and slag / it's all coming out now / like an acid bath / it unpeels the old varnish / removes the old scabs / the wounds now feel fresh, alive and they sting / I throw down number seven / gis another I sing / insults are woken from some ancient time / spit out again / some antediluvian forgotten crime / but I wanna 'nother / I'm having a great time / I'm dragging out the dirty linen and all the grimes / and too much / it dampens the fire / rather than blaze / the one over the edge / the door slams shut in your brain / the demons return to their old domain / Pandora's Box is shut again / you grab another in the hope that you can entice rather than drown but all you've got is slush and sentiment / tears in the eye and howl! Forgive me darling / I didn't mean it / you cry / the party's over / you're left with the mess and your pain / old newspapers lashed by rain / fuck it, I wanna 'nother drink / you've had nine! I don't care no more / it's my second wind / I feel fine / shit it's good / but as the sunset scorches a blazing exit from the skies and just as quickly lays down and dies / so my good feeling pissed off just as fast and left me with an empty glass / gimme – I slurp my number ten / it's late / the light snaps off inside your skull / darkness falls / I feel like hell / and then the next thing then you will espy is the lav staring you in the eye / up come your guts / lurch / past, acids through in one hot stinking steaming stew / your mouth a cesspit of rotting food / it reeks, like shit flows out your head / you just can't wait to get inside your bed.

HELEN: If that's a good time / I'd rather be dead!

(*Fade out.*)

SCENE 8

Scene appears with SYBIL *and* LES *on top of her: same dialogue to begin it as earlier scene.*

LES: Was that all right for you?

SYBIL: Yeah – it was great. Was it all right for you?

LES: Yeah . . . lovely . . . do you enjoy it?

SYBIL: Yeah . . . it was . . . nice . . . did you?

LES: Wo?

SYBIL: Enjoy it!

LES: Yeah it was handsome!

SYBIL: So with all the thrills and all the spills in the end you're over the hill / you are no further, no, in the exploit than when I first discovered my painful plight / you shift your plates of meat from side to side, plan murder, death, cyanide. But in the end we watch TV and larf at arse holes making mugs of all our class / you sit / swill down a jug of gin / play with your balls / say ''ark at him'! Football and darts, the mind boggles at the space that runs between your ears / the working classes ruled always by their peers / 'cause daft you are and thick / that's why you live like pigs / she, chained to a sink / and my old man / that ponce! you can't face with your empty bonce / 'cause you're afraid – his accent frightens you away /

LES: Don't make me laugh / do me a turn / fink his dialogue will make me squirm / fink a chatter with his nibs will set old Les a-trembling on his pegs / 'cause he can utter 'olesome tones.

It's content, what goes in to make his bones / it's there the marrow mate! Eff off you stupid come-pot. Slag-stained hag / you filthy load of ancient slag / why should I enunciate to him the dirty fink I hate / it's him that I'll annihilate / without the chatter / with no threat of tongue wobble banter / like two poofs ready to tear each other's wigs off. No screaming heebie jeebies no! When I k'blast him / watch me go!

SYBIL: Yeah tell me another / six months it's been my Les / you can't make up your mind / like Hamlet in a tizz / you come all over heavy like a Patton tank / but when it comes to deeds / your chat is merely wanks / you've lost me Les / I'll find some geezer new / who will do for me what I do do for you / some hard determined lad that will not me disgrace / not lay a single finger on his rotten face! / not volunteer a bunch of fives to show him your love's alive / let alone / the murder, death and dark revenge you swore / when you were in my minge / once there you would swear all / and like the famous rat / that in escaping from the claws of some fat cat / falls in a vat of wine / cries out, 'save me! Save me cat! I'd rather be eaten alive than drown, oh horror in that vat of wine.' The cat concurs and flips the rat out on his paws / whereupon seeing himself on steady floors, rat scarpers to safe hole inside the wall. The cat now flaming mad to see he'd been so badly had says 'you said I could eat you rat if I plucked you from out that vat' to which the rat replied . . . 'you'll say anything when you're drunk' / that's you all right you punk!

LES: What a turnabout / what a double choke to suffer slagging from the slut I poke / you think I am not waiting, choosing well before consigning adenoids to hell / don't make me piss my pants / don't make me laugh / death takes its time / it stalks a lonely path. Conditions must be good / the hour right / don't mess it up and make me rush it / right! I'll have him sure, I swear I will / but do it all careful like / now – here's the spiel / I got a plan / now listen to your Desperate Dan. I'll destroy him with **telepathy!** By my magic powers I turn on that heat / I concentrate with all my strength / tune into his wave length and crumble goes his brain's network,

cells and nerve centre go berserk / like radios jamming
enemies' airwaves / my mind will send him in a rave / he'll
freak, twitch and explode when senses he my vicious probes.
I read it in a book how you can work the spell or spook some
geezer into living hell / by concentration / thinking on his
boat / or staring hard at his mug that's in a phot / fix on his
eyes and pour a thousand evil thoughts inside / he'll cop the
message every night like needles in his brain and burning
bright / 'til sickness claim him like a bride – so much cleaner
than cyanide /

SYBIL: Where do you cop that pile of shit / I fink he's doing it to
you, you twit.

SCENE 9

STEVE *and* HELEN.

STEVE: Cigarette?

HELEN: Thanks darling. Nearly killed someone with my car last
night.

STEVE: Oh really darling. Were you pissed?

HELEN: Couldn't see the bugger.

STEVE: Oh, why was that?

HELEN: He was so damn black.

STEVE: Couldn't you see the whites of his eyes?

HELEN: His back was towards me.

STEVE: I hate the bastards. No no no no no. I won't say that / just
find them different to us / white is white and brown is brown
and black is black / you know what I mean? / they're
fabulous, in their place / in Jamaica I found them just ace / a
gas / great sense of humour / and move like a dream / they're
all instinct is what I mean / whereas we think / to create and
rule / they feel all the time / like children and play with their
tools / they want before their time / they want the taste of
power / but their minds are no higher than their stomachs /
even lower / my God what do they put in the shit that they
gobble / I can't imagine / it makes my knees just wobble /

You can't give in to the kaffir / to the wog / just because they demand it / my God, what would they do to us / they must be trained not to rebel / but to use their brain as well / if we gave in to every tinpot black / they'd be throwing spears and hurling threats / even atomic bombs / yes! / It could come to that / they're thick / good natured / more like a dream / but don't feel pain / not like us is what I mean / they're tough / more like the animals / they kill and chop each other up / life's not worth a fig / a string of beads and they'd sell their mum / of course we're all brothers under the sun / but I hate my fucking brother even if we've got the same mum / don't persecute the fuckers / they're all-right blokes / there's one down at the club / he takes in the coats / don't kill or hurt them / just put them on the bloody boats / please Maggie put your money where your mouth is / don't be all talk and no fuck / stick up for us – have a little pluck. My God she's a handsome woman / I bet the man who gets inside her pants had a lot to answer for / oh don't look at me like that / we're all the same / there's not a man in England who wouldn't drop his Y-fronts for that dame / still look at the unemployment and sponging in the name of socialism / half of them are on the game / could you touch one love / I mean could you / it's rumoured that they're hung like bloody mules / well it's not such a rumour actually / one day at the club they let in one / the laws that make us do these things / so anyway, in the shower I caught a glimpse of the bugger / I just couldn't believe it darling (*Mimes*) it was simply obscene / it made me feel like a shrimp and you know I'm quite well endowed.

HELEN: (*Fast*) Yes yes darling, of course.

STEVE: He should have it covered up or at least require a yearly licence for it / so I threw down my card at the club office and said / shove that up your jack if you let in any more of that / he's the Prince of Morocco they replied / oh well, I said, that puts a different complexion on the face / of course they have to travel / our royals do it for the trade / they have to shake hands even eat with the bloody spades / they do it for the

cash / the foreign office tells them to / you wouldn't catch
them with the buggers otherwise / not after work / not in the
house / why – they wouldn't get past the dogs who have
never seen one in the house / wouldn't know a bloody wog /
what! we must preserve what's English / or British if you
must, though it's very hard to think of paddy quite like us /
there is no place like England / you can't sing there'll always
be a Great Britain / it doesn't have the taste / or there'll
always be an England . . .
(*Sings, and* HELEN *accompanies. They get through two verses.*)
Sorry darling, it brings a tear to my old face whenever I hear
that good refrain / let's keep it clean love / let's keep it white /
kick out the Pakis, blackies, paddys and kikes / go back to
the jungle / Belfast and Israel / don't turn our happy haven
into a rancid hell.

SCENE 10

HELEN: We mustn't be late, you mustn't dip your spoon into the
cup of hate / it's the first night / the audience will be sheer
delight, and I assure you, they will be absolutely white! I'll
wear something stunning / I'll just astound / the important
thing darling is to make you proud (*She mimes the following.*)
I'll wear a fulsome daring Chanel robe / slashed to the thigh /
in black cashmere / gathered from the bellies of baby goats /
it hugs every line every detail made clear / every vale of my
body / every genital contour will amplify itself on my
exterior / arms gathered and arranged in gossamer ripples
that float in waves / belt by Fiorucci from the skin of snakes
that slither round glistening lakes / the gown weighted down
at the hem which flares allowing a flash of golden thigh as I
climb the stairs / so demure on the outside / such a whore
within / fashion is so divine it makes dressing up a sin / a rash
display of silver filigree curls round my cheeks / and makes
my bum two silver moons that I display for fun / the gown
now draws my flesh down from those swelling curves

tapering at the thigh / then up it rushes scooping my tits like
tasty cherry pies / they softly float inside their silken net like
two blancmanges wanting to be ate / a pair of shoes in satin
with five-inch heels forged from Venetian glass / opaque and
hollow / here small glow worms shine in the dark / my
stockings must be silk and finish at the thigh / tops grasped
by black suspender belt / like lizard's teeth held tight / my
knickers, sheer opaque and thin made from crushed water
silk / within, the gusset tiny pleats will hold my special
midnight treats / soft and crushy / nice and sweet / my hair is
gathered up in waves / is spun and twisted into furls / is
plaited, combed and arranged in precious curls / it's
modelled on Utrillo's nymph rising from the sea / Sassoon
spent many sleepless nights creating this dream for me / my
arms, my love will be as long white snakes beneath
transparent tulle / sewn in with chrysoprases and tiny pearls /
I'm ready now darling / let's swirl /
(*Opera music comes on,* STEVE *mimes eating chocolates with*
HELEN, *opera concludes, grand applause which turns into* LES
and SYBIL *slagging each other which then turns back to* STEVE
and HELEN *applauding once more*.)

STEVE: Then after the opera.

HELEN: The supper.

STEVE: Is it at the Savoy?

HELEN: Is it Rules?

STEVE: Kettners is now a hamburger joint.

HELEN: The Caprice is over too.

STEVE: We'll go to the Zanzibar, that will do.

HELEN: My lover holds out my coat / my wrap of pink ermine / he
opens the door / the air smells like wine / that special time
when the evening is yours / gone to bed are the swine /
outside, the porter / the cab is hailed /

STEVE: Taxi!

HELEN: The air crisp and tangy / my lover in tails / expectancy
hangs like some fine perfume / he squeezes my shoulder / he
says /

STEVE: How are you?

HELEN: I'm lovely darling I must reply / we watch the big red buses go sludging by / heaving their cargoes of workers and aged.

STEVE: Here's our cab darling.

HELEN: The porter is paid.

STEVE: Great Queen Street please. (*They get in taxi.*) Cigarette?

HELEN: Thank you my sweet / my hands find your prick / I feel somewhat shy / as cabby in mirror steals sneaky spy the world is closed to us / wrapped in our love and wealth / I snuggle up close / your coat is rough / you feel manly and tough / and smell of musk / your shiny powdered chin and brilliant teeth / you're a blade all right / you make me weak at the knees / you sparkle / you thunder / your hat sits just right / a trilby snapped brim / a Bogart or a Flynn / I like my man tough / I like to be ruled by an iron fist but a velvet tool within / I love you opening the doors and getting the bills / make yourself broke including my sins / being the master / ruling me / a genius in bed / an expert driving me crazy / weak as a kitten up a tree / let me wait for your call / let me pine / let me fret / and when the phone rings / my heart goes pitta-pat / send me an orchid ply me with perfume / from Givenchy, Chanel and Cardin as well / say how pretty you look tonight / say how swell / I can't have enough of that / grab my elbow / squeeze it tight / guide me darling into the light / like I was helpless / without my sight / let me blaze like a meteor shower / you make me feel good / you have the power / I gleam for you / I sparkle / I'll effervesce display me like a proud conquest / like a trophy like an animal from the jungle tamed / wild cat to others / for you love a lamb / you'll be proud / you'll look suave in your black and white / you devil from hell / you Lucifer / anti-Christ / you hypnotize me with your blazing eyes / your adamantine personality / let's go lover / oh! I must have a pee!

SCENE II

STEVE: We escape to the restaurant / at last some repose / throw
off your coat darling / powder your nose / put on some lip
gloss / I'll splash my toes / hello Giovanni / 'How is M'sieur
and Madame tonight?' / his bright teeth assure us that all is
quite normal and right / all is quite safe / the window's
double barred / 'gainst the dreaded IRA / our table is ready /
how simply hooray / elated wide-eyed / we view the sight / a
river of lords, barons and knights / a stream of gold,
diamonds and pearls / a torrent of lawyers, judges and earls /
a splatter of royalty on top / (*Aside*) (hallo Charles, hallo Di)
just the sauce that lends a perfect flavour to all / a small royal
sprinkling seems to draw from the rest a flavour that's
absolutely the best / Aperitif? Cinzano and bitter lemon / a
crunch of ice / it tastes like heaven / What would Monsieur
and Madame like? Some salmon fumé / smoked just perfect /
its flesh tears like silk / was spawned in Scotch lakes / hung to
be cured by those that know the secret of salmon / the ones
with the nose / to follow avocado stuffed with prawns / garlic
to taste / crushed in a paste / pear as soft as the bellies of
babes / prawns crisp as ice / champagne Perignon washes all
away in its tide / the mashed hors d'oeuvres / all clean inside /
the mouth is pink and raw once again / to receive like
Gargantua its morsels of fun / what now, oh love decide /
steak au poivre or le boeuf sur le toit, noisette d'agneau or
poached turbot / crab freshly dropped in a boiling scream so
its flesh is sunset pink and taste a dream / filet mignon with
oysters crushed with sauces / that sounds a must / we'll have
two of those / some escargots on the side / they taste so
divine / cooked in sweet herbs and wine / a Mouton
Rothschild chilled to a thaw / wash it down / hmm!
Delicious / let's have some more / I slice the steak / its blood
runs free / raw as a wound / soft as a kiss / I embrace it / I
swallow the last ecstatic piece / it flows like lava into me / a
mountain of spinach and acre of mushroom / we shove it all
in and still there's room / more champagne! It showers away

the fish and the garlic / the slightly acid taste / the burp, the silver of nausea that starts to grow / from compound of prawns, salmon, beef, oysters, the sparkly flows / we're fresh again darling / order / what did you say? More champagne / my god you're stacking it away / more champagne / dry cold and wild / what – you've got no more Mouton Rothschild / well, give us the best, the best that you've got / get fucking moving you Italian git / no, sorry! What did I say? I was joking, what / you're my friend / (*Aside*) fucking waiter pretending he's the bloody end / just 'cause he had Charlie and Diana to dine / he thinks his piss now tastes like wine / yes, we'll have some cheese / we'll have some Armontal, Gruyère, fine herbs and some Brie / it must be dead ripe / it must ooze gently / just enough / no more / if it's runny I'll hurl your fucking cheese through the door / I'm joking you cunt / now don't get sore / more champagne / I said more / now caviare to finish / taken at the end it's perfect when you think you can't shove more in your head / a spoonful of caviare will slither around and find a space there you hadn't found / more champagne darling? Feeling all right? Yes! Crêpe Suzette / brandy éclairs / rum babas and liqueur pears / hmm! That's gurgly / that's rich and oozy / God it squelches past / my guts are on fire / more champagne I gasp / I can hardly breathe / give me a cigar / a brandy / something that doesn't take the remotest inch of any more space / I couldn't bear to think there's any more space left / the remotest chink that might house some morsel / some unexplored delight / that might put the cap on the perfect night / so now I feel fine / I need a shit / oh shit, I can't move / I want to be sick / I want to heave up / be back in a tick / I'll shit and I'll piss and I'll blow the house down / Ha! Ha! Ha! Oh fuck it's coming up / can you sick, shit and piss all at once? It must be a record / see you darling / sorry I'm such a sight /

HELEN: Darling, don't apologize / it's been a wonderful night!

SCENE 12

LES: It's no good / this geezer's got me by the balls / can't seem to work my little plan / I'm not really a desperate man or dan / so what he's off with his high-class dame / so what, for them life's just a game / not like us / working for our bread / get up / alarm clock near our bed / a bunk up when we're not too tired from slog / hustling down the highest. For the cheapest flog / can we afford the trip this year / we're overdrawn / oh fuck / the kids need more socks / look what they took for tax this week love / no meat today, we'll look for scraps / they make a lovely soup / OK / petrol's up and smokes are dear / it's much cheaper to be a ginger beer these days it really is / 'cause there's no hope / no none with kids / in the pub / kicked out at time / 'let's have your glasses / there's always tomorrow' / but not for them with clubs / and out all night 'cause they don't have to graft at break of light / they can lay abed till ten / have coffee rolls sent in to them / fiddle / screw the state / form companies and liquidate / they do it legal like, like all of them / but if we do a straight thieve they shove us in the pen / at least our thieving's honest / break and enter / armed robbery / a good old-fashioned thieve / but those bastards do it legally / lawyers, companies, minutes and fraud / and end up in the House of Lords / she's right / whenever I hear his voice I go weak at the knees / it's not from choice / it's something ingrown like a toenail / the neverhads have always doffed their hats to those wot have / it's the voice / the style / the polite smile / with millions at their beck and call / they can still hold us in thrall / it's like a pyramid / us at the base / pile of stupid trash / fed by all that's worst in life / *Daily Mirror* / football, Wimpy bars and darts / to make sure the workers stay working class / artless pile of muck / fit only for a piss-up and Fray Bentos heated up when we get in / and keep your noses down / here's the boss / here's the police / here's the judge / here's the royals / ooh! ain't she sweet / what dress will she wear this week / brain-washed workers waving flags at coronation dressed in rags / the cost of war is going up / the bear is on the move again / I do not wish to fight and kill to satisfy some other pervert's will / when if I take my vengeance private like / I get ten years / but do it wholesale / kill a lot in uniform to make it legal / they pin a medal and make it regal / so my hate's not hot enough / to shove a knife in this ponce's guts / I'll let him fade out like the dinosaur / and kick out this bitch my whore.

SCENE 13

SYBIL: Coward like all his kind / why should I fucking care / when men are two a penny fuck him / snap my fingers, I'll find some more / they're sitting ducks / all they want to do is . . . need I say it twice / they're all so easy such a bore / a bit of titillation and they're yours / a hard-on makes him soppy as a kid / drooling for his candy / they think of nothing else, and when they're randy / why, it's like taking from a kid his candy / we fuck the bastards / but not quick / just trap them with a tender kiss / sus out the guy and check his bankability / his standing in the world / be careful dear / don't cast your pearls before bankrupt swine / don't fuck for love for fuck's sake / cast your net and wag your tail / they'll soon be slobbering for you / never fails / the child / man heroes think they claim you as pussy hovers in their dreams / dash that image / or you're just a dustbin for his passion's lust / receptacle for spunk / give him a taste and then withdraw a while / he'll crave for more and more / think your pussy's made of gold and myrrh / he'll write poems to your asshole the pathetic cur / tantalize / don't be too keen / like dope pushers, give the first lot free / hook him first with your sweet sting / then play the game / don't be around when hard-on rings / so then the drug has bit / you're in his blood you won't be so damn free the next time / let him crawl, he'll think you're just the end / you'll be nirvana / a goddess, Aphrodite, perfect divine and rare / to what my love shall I compare thy hair / he'll think he's Shakespeare and go

36

fucking spare / since he thinks that he's found grace / the
perfect elusive face / then let him back / be sweet and let the
cunt relax once more / even be his little whore / then whack!
withdraw!! 'You don't love me any more.' He's hanging on
just by his nails / just be unsure / 'I don't know if we're right
my dear' / make him grovel, sleepless nights / this bit is very
tricky girls and risky too / he may decide he's better without
you / if he's got strength / one ounce too much / you may lose
him and start at square one all again / but chances are, like
Pavlov's dogs, the jerk's confused / you now seem, if it works /
immortal to the Burke / you're gold-dust, opium, exotic fruit /
he's on his knees then kick him in the teeth / then hold on fast /
he's weak / go for the dough / a wife comes next / then in for
the kill / house, protection and at last his will / and not the one
he leaves / the one that keeps his brains in place / dislodge that
and you're made / dangle him a while then snuggle up / be his
sweet bride / and then he thinks **he's** conquered in the world
the only one that fate for him has squired / he's proud / it's
been a chase / an easy game not so laced in danger with that
smell of fame / reputation goes up / high-class dame / to trap
an animal cunning is necessary but if you trap a lion it's more
tough / the going's hard and lonely, but on your wall he makes
a smashing trophy / but then it's all the same / beast and
human man / they're just big game / you do not get them by
being nice / you get them by cunning skill and shrewd device /
or else be sweet and honest girl and be well fucked, four kids
and end in hell / liberation?? This is it girl!

SCENE 14

They come together for the final dance.

STEVE: I like to dance.

HELEN: I like tea in the Ritz.

STEVE: I like to fly / sipping champagne in the sky.

HELEN: I like to wriggle my hips to the beat in my heart / turn and
twist.

37

STEVE: I like to Fred Astaire and Gene Kelly / I like to lick absinthe off your belly.

HELEN: I like to smell like a wild garden after rain.

STEVE: I like the pleasure I derive after pain. I like holding your waist seeing red rubies glance off your face.

HELEN: Dance under stardust whirling in the sky.

STEVE: Glittering lights / diamonds shattering your eye.

HELEN: Violets, thick carpets and cocktails.

STEVE: Invitations on embossed cards / to rub shoulders with the rich and special.

HELEN: Long fingers bejewelled with art nouveau.

STEVE: Like fireworks burning bright.

HELEN: Pearls and amethysts crushed in white. I like to wake with the sea licking my ears cocooned in silken sheets / my dreams dissolving in the morning dawn so sweet.

STEVE: Like butter melting over hot meat / your ass as round as warm doughnuts.

HELEN: Your cock sliced between my bum.

STEVE: Like a hot dog nestled in a bun / your hair like a soft meadow over the lacy white pillow.

HELEN: The soft knock on the door.

STEVE: The coffee and rolls and first steaming piss.

HELEN: The shower and broiling in a mist.

STEVE: The morning papers white and crisp. Murders and rape . . .

HELEN: Taken with cheese and grapes . . .

STEVE: Stabbings and bombs . . .

HELEN: More coffee my love . . .

STEVE: Earthquakes and deaths . . .

HELEN: Toast and poached egg . . .

STEVE: Starvation and famine . . .

HELEN: Sausages and gammon.

STEVE: You arise like Venus striding out of the skies.

HELEN: We leave the murder and crime in crunched newspapers never to begrime the spotless lives that are yours and mine.

STEVE: They belong in the other place where people walk in arsenic and hate.

HELEN: Where envy follows greed and becomes the seed that seeks to flower in our pot.

STEVE: No hope of that / we're protected at the top / from our exalted eyrie we float like eagles over the predators below.

HELEN: Who do the pools or any other hype that cons your greedy minds that you may be the one that fortune finds.

STEVE: When the chances are greater that you'll be killed than achieve your fortune by fate's will

HELEN: So in your beehive metropolis you breathe and hope.

STEVE: Turn on the telly.

HELEN: And go to bed when the weather forecast is read.

STEVE: Your eyes will squint and grow crows' feet staring at the fine print and the lowest price.

HELEN: We have no thought of cost damn it but only what is nice.

STEVE: Your eyes my darling will only read the make and no price tag will ever forbid you to take.

HELEN: You will never arise.

STEVE: No never surmise a better life as long as beer doesn't rise by more than two pence a pint.

HELEN: You'll be all right Jack.

STEVE: Let's go darling it's getting light.

HELEN: Let's watch the dawn arise in its vast magic palace of light.

STEVE: Thanks Giovanni, it's been a wonderful night.
Cigarette? . . .
(*They both light cigarettes and inhale deeply and as the light fades they age in the results of their debauched lives.*)

KVETCH

An American Play About Anxiety

We all live under the shadow of the bomb – cancer – carcinogens – illness – unemployment – impotence – fear of fear – blacks – whites – police – rates – income tax – parking tickets – forgetting our lines – losing money – making too much money – losing hair – getting fat – getting ugly – being stupid – being unwitty – being shy – being foolish – worry about which stereo speakers – how to fix a car – a bike – learning the piano – fear of failing – not impressing – fear of others' strength – fear of weakness – fear of being exposed – not getting to work in time – not having a pension – security – old age – dying – war – injury in road accidents – fear of blindness – deafness – of not understanding the joke – fear of tough people – fear to take risks – fear to swim – to jump – to dive off a board – fear of disease – fear of moving – fear to sell – fear to buy – obsessional fear of spiders – dark cupboards – knives – muggers – fear of people – parties – crowds – clever people – fear of speaking your mind – fear of women – fear of men – fear of police – fear of anxiety – so this play is dedicated to the afraid.

CHARACTERS

FRANK
DONNA, Frank's wife
HAL, Frank's friend
MOTHER-IN-LAW, Frank's mother-in-law
GEORGE, a wholesaler Frank sells to

Note
Much of the speech is 'aside'. For simplicity, these passages are shown in italic.

The play was staged in front of a large painted wall depicting the freeways of Los Angeles as a surreal multi-laned jam of cars. There must have been about twenty lanes and one saw them all converge in the distance. Half-way up the wall was an impervious blue sky. Downstage was a table and four chairs around which the players performed.

The movement was generally sharp and dynamic. The declarations to the audience meant as confessions and given their full value. When a character was speaking his or her thoughts the action was frozen in the last position they were in and held for the duration, almost like a freeze-frame. For the scene in the bedroom we merely threw a giant bedspread on the table and, since the characters were already behind the table, they appeared with a little adjustment to be in bed. The piece of cloth used for the scene in the office became a tablecloth in the subsequent restaurant scene. Scenes should flow easily into each other much as a dissolve in a film.

AUTHOR'S NOTE

Kvetch is a study of the effects of anxiety on the nagging kvetch that keeps you awake. It is the demon that wishes to taste your blood and sucks at your confidence. For many who can't live in the now, this is a real and terrible problem. We are beset by an array of problems that don't always sit and wait in the queue to be solved, but are liable at any instant to jump out of line and shout for your attention and kvetch you or kvetch at you until you have paid them some attention, even though in the meantime your present task may be ruined. They are the neglected children born of some distant anxiety. You may want them to go away and shout at them, confess them to shrinks or drown them at birth in drugs, but they will always return in some form or other. How often when we speak we have some background dialogue going on, sometimes to guide us and sometimes to protect us. Sometimes, though, the dialogue in the back of the head is truer than the one in the front. If only we could always speak the thoughts in the back; how much truer our communication would be. We are like icebergs slowly moving through life and seldom, if ever, showing and revealing what is underneath.

N.B.
This is my first 'American' play but its theme can be played anywhere and, with a few changes of idiom and brandnames, has successfully replanted in London. In fact London gave it a resounding success where it was crowned *Evening Standard* Comedy of the Year 1991! I have a feeling that British critics have a sharper sense of humour than their American counterparts.

Kvetch was first performed on 15 March 1986 at the Odyssey Theatre, Los Angeles, California. The cast was as follows:

FRANK	Kurt Fuller
DONNA	Laura Esterman
HAL	Mitch Kreindel
MOTHER-IN-LAW	Marcia Mohr
GEORGE	Ken Tigar

Director	Steven Berkoff
Producer	Ron Sossi
Set Designer	Don Llewellyn
Costume Designer	Ruth Brown

Kvetch was first performed in Britain on 3 September 1991 at the King's Head Theatre, London. The cast was as follows:

FRANK	Steven Berkoff
DONNA	Anita Dobson
HAL	Henry Goodman
MOTHER-IN-LAW	Thelma Ruby
GEORGE	Stanley Lebor

Director	Steven Berkoff
Production Manager	Natasha Carlish
Designed by	Silvia Johnsons
Stage Manager	Tim Allwright

ACT ONE

SCENE I

DONNA: *I'm afraid . . . I'm afraid if he comes home late the cooking will be spoilt . . . I fear his wrath . . . not physically . . . but his scowling tongue . . . his looks . . . his moods. I get in a sweat. I know it's not my fault he is late, but I can't adjust . . . I can't be flexible and half cook it and then when he comes in finish it off. Have a glass of wine, darling – soon ready . . . I can't half do it – I think he'll be home and it won't be ready and he'll scowl and say . . .*

FRANK: For God's sake, I've been on the freeway for an hour then an hour back – I shlepp my guts out and you can't have a meal waiting at least . . . For God's sake, I've been on the freeway for an hour then an hour back – I shlepp my guts out and you can't have a meal waiting at least . . .

DONNA: *Sometimes he comes home even later and so I start the spinach on a small light . . . I keep the roast simmering – the potato latkes, that I can do on the spot. But if he's on time I rush around to get ready.*

FRANK: Can't you keep still, or at least prepare it, anticipate a bit . . . must you run around like a chicken with its head cut off . . . take it easy . . . other wives I know . . . you go in . . . 'Hello, darling,' they say to their husbands, 'have a Martini' . . . 'I brought a friend back,' he says, 'Sure, why not?' she replies easily and in a relaxed fashion . . . not phased out . . . plenty of food for a surprise guest . . . you sit . . .

DONNA: *If I prepare it too early I keep it in a dish over some boiling water and keep it hot but then he complains it's overcooked . . . it's mushy – the greens are soaking . . . it's like paste. I worry what to cook each night . . . I vary it – one night a roast – one night spaghetti – one night cauliflower* au gratin *and a salad . . .*

FRANK: The cauliflower's like a mush . . . it's like a milk shake

49

. . . suppose I brought a friend home . . . for a surprise . . . since I want to be a mensch sometimes and say, 'Hal, do yourself a favour . . . Coupla beers, Charley . . . Come home to my place – why should you go home to an empty apartment? . . . what life is that? Nu? You go home and who welcomes you . . . the cat? So come for a nosh . . . Listen, gorden blurr it's not . . . you know what I'm saying . . . we'll have a homely meal and put our feet up and watch a movie . . . sure we got cable . . . have a beer . . .'

MOTHER-IN-LAW: You're buying cheap oil, it burns the latkes.

DONNA: Ma, I use the same oil you use.

HAL: You sure it's be OK?

FRANK: Of course I'm sure . . . I'm positive . . . I'd like you to . . . why not? . . . you'd like her . . . it'll make a change . . . a new face spices the evening . . . we'll exchange kvetches . . . I mean stories about our anxieties . . . ha! . . . ha! . . . then we'll watch Paul Newman killing a few people . . . wadya say? . . . *Oh God . . . I hope he says no . . . I don't know what we'll talk about . . .*

MOTHER-IN-LAW: A little pepper goes a long way . . .

DONNA: Ma!

FRANK: *Suppose the bitch hasn't enough food . . . suppose she has overcooked it 'cause we're late . . . or even worse gone to bed because her ulcers are playing up . . . Gavolt or shit . . . or maybe her mother's there who belches . . . Of course it's Friday . . . her fucking mother will be there belching and the food will be overcooked and I smell the stinking cabbage twenty floors down . . .*

HAL: You sure you want me to come?

FRANK: Look I'm not forcing you . . . you're your own man so make it another night . . . when you're free . . . you say, 'Frank . . . how's tonight?' We don't stand on ceremony . . . any time . . . our house is an open door . . . you say the day . . . next week . . . next month . . . when you like . . . if it's not convenient tonight . . .

HAL: Well . . . hell, why not? . . . You're right, you know since Betty left I must say I hate to go home . . . I hate it, you're

right . . . an empty place . . . the breakfast dishes still there
from last week . . . Are you sure your wife will have enough?

FRANK: Look . . . when she buys she doesn't buy for one – like a
shrivelled-faced vstinkiner that maybe asks for scraps for the
cat . . . for a regiment she buys. You open the fridge . . . you
can't shut it . . . Have enough!! When she shops at Vons the
shares go up!

MOTHER-IN-LAW: You shouldn't be so stingy with the garlic!

DONNA: Ma, it's enough.

FRANK: But listen, don't come for us . . . don't put yourself out
just because I asked . . . I won't be offended . . . you do what
you want . . . listen, who makes a deal out of it? . . . I sense a
certain reluctance . . . when you *really want* to come . . . you
say . . .

HAL: You mean we should make it another night?

FRANK: Hell, no! Tonight is great . . . you're welcome . . . my
life, it makes no difference . . . every night's the same . . .

HAL: OK, I'll come.

FRANK: *Oh shit!* . . . good!

HAL: *I don't know . . . should I go there? . . . At home it's quiet and I
know who I am . . . why should I sit with them? . . . what can I
say? I'll choke up . . . they'll find me boring . . . He's happily
married . . . two kids . . . I'm forty . . . separated . . . can't hold
a wife . . . living alone like a monk with a cat, and I should
watch them with their kids . . . warm laughter, gaiety . . .
fulfilling hours . . . growth . . . struggle . . . achievement . . .*

MOTHER-IN-LAW: You bought such skimpy chops, will it be
enough?

HAL: *I'll sit there and feel like a lump . . . like a leech on society . . .
incomplete . . . fruitless . . . dull. I'll choke . . . she'll ask me
what I do at nights . . .*

DONNA: Oh God, the latkes are burnt . . .

MOTHER-IN-LAW: I told you, cheap oil.

HAL: *What do I do? . . . Sit and watch TV . . . sit in the local bar . . .
visit a hooker . . . or sit in with Ma . . . What do I do, she'll ask
me . . . Oh god! . . .*

(DONNA sets out plates and forks, and mimes serving pie.

FRANK and HAL switch pieces. DONNA switches them back.)

DONNA: I'm sorry if it was a bit overcooked . . . I was expecting you earlier . . . I had it perfect . . . it was just right . . . I expected you by seven o'clock and by seven-thirty I put it on the light . . .

FRANK: *Oh, for God's sake shut that stupid hole.*

DONNA: Next time call and tell me you're bringing home a friend and I would have gotten more chops from Vons . . .

FRANK: But darling, I did call . . .

DONNA: Call earlier . . .

FRANK: What, I have to call in April for a dinner in May?
(DONNA and HAL speak fast, overlapping.)

DONNA: You're sure?

HAL: I'm stuffed, no.

DONNA: You're sure now?

HAL: I just couldn't eat another thing.

DONNA: You're not hungry?

HAL: No . . . thanks very much, it was great.

DONNA: Just a little bit . . .

HAL: No, really.

DONNA: Have some more pie.

HAL: I'm full . . .

DONNA: You're sure?

HAL: I had plenty . . . really . . .

MOTHER-IN-LAW: He's got a mouth . . . if he was hungry, he'd open it.

FRANK: *Don't embarrass me . . . I'm sweating in shame . . . Oh God!*
(MOTHER-IN-LAW belches.)
Oh God, may the earth open up . . . may a bomb drop on this house!
(Pause. Eating sounds.)

DONNA: You know my husband is so unpredictable . . . he says one thing and does another . . . lives for his work . . . so can you get a straight answer when he'll come home? . . . if he can take another order he will . . .

MOTHER-IN-LAW: He wants to look after his family . . . a wonderful worker . . . and a wonderful son-in-law . . . a great provider . . . what more can you ask? . . . Listen . . . they won't starve . . . that you can assure yourself of . . . my life, he's a jewel . . . you know what I'm saying, what's-your-name . . . Hal?

HAL: Yeah . . .

MOTHER-IN-LAW: Yeah, Hal . . . he's a provider . . . like you won't see him drinking it away in a bar, God forbid . . . like those bums at the end of the road . . . gavolt, you can hear them . . . You don't drink, do you . . . er, Hal?

HAL: Er, not too much . . . you know sometimes . . . with a friend . . . Christmas ha! ha! . . . but not much . . . no . . . don't like to lose control . . . glass of wine . . . maybe . . . you know with a meal . . .

MOTHER-IN-LAW: He's the jewel of my life, they don't come better.

(MOTHER-IN-LAW belches.)

FRANK: *I wish they were dead. Both of them. I married the mouth and inherited the belch. Could I have done better, I ask myself. I'd like to leave . . . I haven't got the guts . . . I swear I could leave right now . . . yes, right this minute, I could scream and jump out of the window . . . closed or not . . . go screaming down the street . . . me screaming and running shouting . . . fuck fuck fuck fuck fuck . . . shit and fuck . . . you stupid fucking belching cunt . . . shut up . . . but I can't . . . I sweat and squirm instead.*

(HAL and DONNA – improvised overlap:)

DONNA: Are you sure you're not hungry? There's more pie, I know it was scorched, let me get you some . . .

HAL: (With DONNA) I'm fine, really . . . no, thank you, I couldn't eat another thing, really . . . I'm stuffed . . . thank you . . . Can't eat another bite . . .

DONNA: *He's scowling at me . . . he's ashamed of me. I do what I can but I'm afraid all the time . . . What must his friend think? . . . The dinner was ruined but the apple pie was nice . . . with cream that was nice . . . I've got a stomach ache . . . my ulcer's killing me . . . I want to go to the bathroom and mix some Milk of Magnesia, but I'm afraid to go . . . in case it looks funny . . . My make-up is runny . . . His friend must think I'm stupid . . . he looks so intelligent . . . Why didn't Frank phone? . . . Just a quick call to warn me . . . Am I sweating? . . . What shall I say now? . . . Now that you're separated, Hal . . . what do you find to do at nights? . . .*

HAL: *Oh God . . . at nights . . . well . . . I . . . Sit indoors and cry . . . smoke myself to death . . . pick my nose . . . watch TV till I fall asleep with a bottle of Scotch . . . count the hairs on the comb when I go into the bathroom . . . ring a call girl . . . or jerk off in front of my favourite centrefold spread . . . pace up and down . . . fall asleep and wait for the morning so that I can do something . . . scream or take Valium . . . think about overdosing . . . at nights . . . well . . .*

FRANK: *What a stupid question to have asked a man who's separated . . . what a stupid question to ask him. Now what does she think he does . . . throw dinner parties for movie stars?*

MOTHER-IN-LAW: *That's a question to ask a single man . . . yech!*

HAL: At nights . . . well . . . *I don't know what to say . . . I feel sick . . . Look at them . . . they don't have to do anything at night. They sit and enjoy each other . . . have a dinner together . . . talk about the day . . . comfort each other . . . read and be silent in each other's support . . . lean on each other . . . What can I do? At nights . . . they go home and there's a light on . . . a golden light that attracts you like a moth to the warmth . . . at nights . . . well . . .*

FRANK: *I wish I'd never asked him . . . I should have shut my mouth . . . I want to be like other men with families . . . be a mensch . . . friends pop in . . . always something on the stove . . . plays a game of rummy . . . tell jokes . . . have my wife cook something succulent . . . be witty . . . make them laugh . . . I wish I could tell a joke . . . I must know one . . . now what joke can I tell? . . . But suppose it falls flat . . . suppose I forget the tag line . . . suppose they look or feel embarrassed . . . but one has to try . . . do it . . . go for it . . . What's the worst that can happen? . . . You won't die . . . break the ice . . . be a bit bold . . . Have I told you . . .*

HAL: What I do at nights . . . sorry . . . you were saying . . .

FRANK: No, no, sorry, go on . . . I interrupted *you* . . . please . . .

HAL: Sure I can wait . . .

DONNA: Honey, he was just telling us what he does . . .

HAL: At nights!

DONNA: Yes, at nights . . .

(MOTHER-IN-LAW belches.)

FRANK: Oh, Ma, for God's sake!

DONNA: She can't help it . . . don't be so unkind, Frank, she's an old lady . . . don't be so mean . . . I'm sorry, Hal . . .

HAL: No, really, not at all, I don't mind . . .

DONNA: She's a sick old lady, Frank, but she's got spirit . . . she's just getting on a bit . . . Hal understands, Frank . . . you got to make allowances for older people . . . you'll be old one day, Frank, and I hope our kids are more understanding than you . . .

FRANK: *This is beautiful, what an evening . . . So tomorrow it will be all over the warehouse of Frank's crazy family . . . I feel sick . . . my food wants to come up or go down and miss out the middle man . . .* I just said, 'For God's sake' – so what does that make me, Hitler? I said, 'Kill her,' didn't I? . . . 'Gas her . . . send her to the chambers.' So kill me . . . What did I say, Hal, that was such an unexcusable sin? . . . Are older people some kind of saints . . . we should hold our breath while she belches and farts? . . .

DONNA: She doesn't fart . . . For God's sake, Frank, don't be so insidious . . .

MOTHER-IN-LAW: *I'm an old lady . . . soon I'll die . . . good riddance and feh! A fine pair . . . do you think I care? . . . I'm finished . . . Give me a good book and a meal a day, or they can send me to a home. I know they want to send me to a home . . . but it's cheaper to keep me in a two-roomed pen and hire a housekeeper for a couple of hours a day . . . and once a week, big deal, I come here . . . I tell you I don't come here for the food. I come here 'cause I'm sick of the four walls. Look at them. She's become a drudge. So all she could get was him . . . worry guts. Works all his life and hasn't a pot to piss in. Still that's all she could get at thirty . . . the dregs . . .* Take no notice, Donna, I'm going to bed . . .

HAL: Well, at nights . . . I get home and you know . . . I, uh, find plenty to do . . . you'd be surprised . . . how one finds . . . so much . . . that was, er, left undone . . . yeah, you know . . . letters . . . that weren't written . . . yeah, friends you neglected . . .

FRANK: *I bet he fucks a lot, dirty bastard . . . living alone . . . lucky single fucker . . .*

HAL: And reopen . . . those old friendships . . . check out the old pals, like people you'd forgotten . . . I kind of got involved in my marriage and didn't see the old faces . . . you know how it is . . . and now I'm single again . . .

FRANK: *Single . . . even the word tastes dirty . . .*

HAL: . . . like single again . . . I thought, hey, why not look up the old pals? . . . you know, get out have a drink . . . maybe a reunion . . .

DONNA: *Friends . . . lucky man . . . seeing people . . . new people . . . friends . . . I'm so hungry for friends I can almost taste the word on my lips . . . we never see anyone . . . I hate being married to him . . . to see his miserable complaining face every day . . . I want to run away . . . I could leave tomorrow . . . if I had the guts I would . . . leave the kids and him . . . never see anyone . . . just him and his guts to fill and the inside of a supermarket three times a week . . .*

HAL: Not that marriage isn't wonderful . . . I mean it's good . . .

FRANK: *Yeah, like a pile on your anus . . .*

HAL: But it never gave me time to explore . . . and visit old friends . . . you know . . . re-acquaint yourself with the old . . .

FRANK: Frenz!

HAL: You're right, Frank, sure I miss her but then you've got to fill the gap with . . .

FRANK: *Frenz!!* . . . Friends . . . yeah, I know . . .

HAL: That's it . . . like I had a pal . . . this friend from work . . . and, hell, when he left I kind of lost touch . . . like, you know, so anyway one day I was cleaning my apartment . . .

DONNA: Ah! You have no one to clean for you? . . .

HAL: No . . . I don't . . .

DONNA: *I clean every day . . . I clean and scrub and launder and wash up for the ungrateful bastard who won't even fuck me any more . . . I would clean for him, poor guy . . . I wonder if he's circumcised?*

HAL: Yep, I clean for myself, I'm a regular housewife now . . . hahahahaha . . . now I know how she felt . . . hahahahaha!

DONNA: *He has a really sweet laugh and is a nice person . . . The evening is taking a turn for the better and during this laughter I am going to sneak out for some Milk of Magnesia 'cause my ulcer's killing me if I go out boldly now – no one will notice . . .*

FRANK: Regular housewife . . . hahahahahahahahahahahaha hahahaha! *God! The evening's taking off. I'm not sweating so much and my stomach isn't in knots . . . although I badly want to shit, but I'm afraid to now while we're just getting going, I'll get the belcher to bed and then I'll tell my joke . . .* How you doing, Ma? You OK? How was the food? . . . Good to see you . . . Isn't she sweet? . . . *Get rid of her . . . if I crap now it'll leave him with them and then they'll go silent and get uncomfortable . . . I'll tell a joke and then put on the TV . . . Shit, where'd she go? . . .* Donna? Are you doing the coffee, darling? . . .

DONNA: (Muffled from the next room) No! Do you want some?

FRANK: What are you doing, honey? . . .

(Silence.)

Are you OK? . . .

DONNA: Hmmmmmmmmmmm!

FRANK: Regular housewife, huh! Hahahahahahahahaha! Come in, honey . . . *Oh fuck and shit, come in, you idiot, while we're having a good time . . . don't leave me to hold the fort alone . . .* Honeeeey?

DONNA: Sorry, folks . . . just powdering my nose . . . haw haw . . .

(DONNA appears with white all over her lips.)

FRANK: *My God!*

HAL: *Hahahahahahaha!*

FRANK: *My God!*

DONNA: You want some coffee, everybody? . . . *What are they staring at? Do I look funny? . . .* Sorry, Hal, you were just

57

saying what you do at nights . . .

HAL: Yes . . . Yes . . . sorry . . . no . . .

(FRANK gestures to DONNA to wipe her lips. DONNA does.)
I was just saying about nights . . . yes . . . you know one
night is much like another on the whole and I was cleaning
up my room when I came across this old diary . . . you know,
with the telephone numbers in the front, so I called up this
old friend . . . I hadn't seen him for at least twenty years it
had to be . . . from school I knew him . . .

DONNA: *I hated school.*

FRANK: *He's boring me to death . . .*

MOTHER-IN-LAW: *I think I've got a bowel movement coming on,
maybe a fart will release the pressure . . .*

HAL: Yeah, twenty years at least . . . let's see . . . I last saw him
. . . in 1960 . . . yeah . . . it would be that . . .

FRANK: *I'll tell a joke . . . I've got to speak . . . say something . . .
anything . . . I never say anything . . . Once the party gets going I
say less and less and everyone else takes over . . . Look at him
talking away . . . He's getting warmed up.*

HAL: . . . and so I called and said, 'Hello . . . can I speak to Bob
Lipinski? . . .'

DONNA: A Pole?

HAL: Yes . . . that's right . . .

DONNA: I knew a Pole called Lipinski, from work.

HAL: You're kidding . . .

DONNA: Nope, the same name anyways . . .

MOTHER-IN-LAW: *I love Polish pickle . . .*

FRANK: *Now how does that joke go? . . .*

DONNA: Yeah, he had red hair and tons of freckles . . . and he had
a bulbous nose . . . like an onion at the end . . . and he had a
small gap in his teeth . . . so he had a lithp . . .

FRANK: *How come she knew him so well? . . . She never told me . . .*

MOTHER-IN-LAW: *Polish herrings are nice . . .*

DONNA: And when he spoke, he lithp . . . like that . . . 'Good
morningth . . . How are you, Thylvia? . . .'

HAL: Thylvia? . . .

DONNA: Well, my middle name is Sylvia and I went through a

58

phase of *hating* Donna . . .

HAL: Sylvia's a very pretty name . . . mind you, I like Donna . . .

DONNA: Everybody was called Donna at school but now I don't
know anybody called Donna . . .

HAL: Donna is more unusual, I think . . . it's got a kind of feel to
it . . .

DONNA: What do you prefer? . . . I mean, if you had a choice? . . .

HAL: Hell, I like both . . . but Donna is definitely more unusual
. . . you don't hear that name so often . . .

DONNA: Yeah, Sylvia's a bit common . . .

HAL: Oh, no . . . it's good name . . . I like both but Donna is more
. . . you.

DONNA: You think? . . .

MOTHER-IN-LAW: I nearly called her Barbara!

DONNA: Help! Barbara . . . can you imagine . . . at school . . .
Babs! . . . Yukky!

HAL: Do you know . . . I have a middle name . . . yep . . . I have one.

DONNA: Oh, tell us!

HAL: Ooooh, you promise to forget it immediately after I tell
you . . .

DONNA: It can't be that bad . . . not as bad as Babs! Yukky!

HAL: It's so awful . . . I can barely bring myself to say it . . .

DONNA: Go on . . . go on!!!

HAL: Promise not to laugh.

DONNA: Promise . . .

FRANK: *I promise not to throw up* . . .

HAL: OK, here goes . . .

DONNA: Oh, go on, he's teasing us now . . . you should worry . . .
do you know what Frank's middle name is? . . .

FRANK: *What . . . is she fucking crazy? . . . What's the matter with
you? . . . Idiot* . . .

HAL: Come on, Frank . . . give up the goods . . . what else do they
call you? You should know what they call him at work . . .

DONNA: Why, what do they call him?

FRANK: Aw, come on, Hal . . . *Give us a break, you prick* . . .

HAL: Can I say, Frank? . . . I thought you would have told
them . . .

FRANK: You know how it is . . . we all give each other names . . .
　　　it's a joke at work . . .

DONNA: So what do they call you? . . . What do they call you?

HAL: Can I say, Frank? . . . huh, can I tell them?

FRANK: *You stupid jerk . . . I'm sorry I ever asked you . . . You*
　　　should rot next time in hell before I offer you my home . . . Yeah,
　　　go on . . . it's no big deal . . .

HAL: Well, they call him . . .

DONNA: Go on, go on . . .

HAL: The Kvetch!!!!
　　　(All laugh.)

FRANK: *Stop having such a good time at my expense!! I haven't*
　　　spoken in hours . . . I've got to say something . . . my joke! Let
　　　me see if I remember it . . . Ah yes . . . haw haw haw haw haw
　　　haw haw . . . I hope to God I don't fuck it up. Maybe I should
　　　practise it in my head first . . . No, I'll just come out with it . . .
　　　Hey, Hal . . . listen, have you heard the one about . . . (Sniffs
　　　the air, smelling MOTHER-IN-LAW's fart.) Pooh! What's that?
　　　You haven't left the gas on, have you, Donna . . .?

DONNA: No . . . oh! . . . Oh, dear . . . maybe I did . . .

FRANK: Christ, I think you must have . . . Oh no! . . . I told you,
　　　Donna, we must get rid of that old stove . . . it's a worn-out
　　　useless piece of junk . . . it stinks . . . so let's get rid of
　　　it !!!!! . . .

MOTHER-IN-LAW: Well, I think I'm going to bed soon . . .

HAL: Heard the one about what, Frank? . . . *God I went down well*
　　　. . . I found my voice . . . it's wonderful . . . I was speaking
　　　without choking or coughing . . . without stammering or flushing
　　　. . . but clearly amusing . . . I must be making an improvement
　　　. . . this is good. I am not sweating or worrying . . . yet . . . Oh,
　　　God, I shouldn't have said that, something is bound to bother me
　　　. . . I know it will . . . any second . . . I was having too good a
　　　time . . .

FRANK: Oh, yes . . . oh, it's nothing . . . just a joke . . .

HAL: Aw, come on, Frank . . .

DONNA: Yes . . . go on, Frank . . . tell us . . . *He's not told a joke in*
　　　years . . . I have never known this to happen before . . . This is

amazing . . . because you have to remember a joke . . . you have
to take risks . . . you might not get the punch line right and then
you will be left with egg dripping down your face, and he is
actually daring to say one . . . It's giving . . . it's risking . . . it's
baring yourself and he never does that . . . This must be costing
him . . . I bet I'll have a heavy wash day tomorrow.

FRANK: No, it's nothing . . . what was it . . . a shtick . . . a piece
of nothing . . . a soupçon . . . what? . . . just a gag I heard at
work. . . . *Oh, fuck and shitass, don't make me say the bastard*
thing now . . . I can't remember, fuck it, or maybe I can . . .
The stink is still awful . . . yukk! Wish I could shoot her . . .
sometimes if I had a knife . . . (Mimes stabbing MOTHER-IN-
LAW violently.) *Horror horror horror . . . Oh, I feel a bit better*
. . . Fuck it, I'll tell the fucking joke . . . So, there was an . . .

DONNA: Darling, darling . . . what's a soupçon? . . .

FRANK: Who knows these things? . . . You hear a saying and it
sounds right . . . I forget . . . I knew but I forget but I know
that I use it right but I forget what it is.

DONNA: How can you use it right then if you forget?

MOTHER-IN-LAW: *She's right . . . when she's right she's right!*

FRANK: You sense it . . . the feeling is right although the origin
may be lost . . . *What's the matter with her? . . . She's fucking*
crazy . . . she's contradicting me with her mouth in public,
already. When she don't know from nothing, the ignoramus slut,
but hold her hand out for money, that she knows.

MOTHER-IN-LAW: Who wants coffee, who wants tea? . . .
(All begin overlap improvisation about the coffee.)

HAL: Yeah . . .

MOTHER-IN-LAW: Coffee?

FRANK: Yeah . . .

MOTHER-IN-LAW: Tea?

DONNA: Coffee . . .

MOTHER-IN-LAW: Sugar? Sugar?

HAL: No . . .

FRANK: One sugar in mine . . .

DONNA: Honey, you don't need sugar . . .

FRANK: I can have sugar . . . OK, half a sugar . . .

MOTHER-IN-LAW: Milk?

HAL: Do you have any non-dairy creamer . . .?

MOTHER-IN-LAW: No, we don't . . .

FRANK: Yeah, we do . . . we've got Mocha Mix . . .

DONNA: No, we don't . . .

FRANK: Yeah, we do . . . it's in the fridge behind the bicarb . . .

DONNA: No, I froze it . . .

FRANK: You froze the Mocha Mix?!!!

HAL: That's OK, I'll just have some milk in my soupçon . . . haw haw haw haw . . .

(End of overlap improvisation.)

MOTHER-IN-LAW: *They bring me here once a week and I'm shlepping trays . . . Next they'll want me to scrub the floors . . .*

HAL: *I am having a wonderful time . . .*

DONNA: *The dinner party is going so well and I'm so proud . . .* Haw haw haw haw . . .

FRANK: *You two fucking hyena idiots . . . sitting in your stinking mother's fart . . . I feel uncomfortable and my mouth is dry but let's get the bastard thing over with . . .* Well, there was an Englishman, an Irishman and a Jew . . .

DONNA: Haw haw haw haw haw haw haw . . .

HAL: *This is really a nice family . . . warm-hearted . . . kind . . . How nice of him to ask me . . . See, I'm warming up . . . I feel OK again . . . Maybe one day I'll have them over to me . . . Yeah, I'll make dinner for them . . . but I'm not a good cook . . . Oh, no, I've got the demons coming on . . . go 'way, go 'way!! I was happy before . . . Go away! . . . I can't be invited here again and not reciprocate . . . They may be don't expect it but how many times can I be invited before reciprocating? Once . . . twice . . . three times? . . . I could make something simple and we'll have a few drinks . . . We'll eat in the kitchen and then go in the living room for coffee . . . Must I think of it now? . . . I'll make some snacks . . . just a little soupçon of everything . . . I'll get it from the deli and then we'll have it in the living room . . . Should we start in the living room with drinks then go to the kitchen? . . . But if I'm preparing something hot, say a soup, I'll have to leave them in the living room with a drink and run in and out . . . or*

. . . why not start off in the kitchen with drinks? . . . But then the stereo is in the living room . . . Oh, shit . . . we can play some music and have a few drinks and then go in the kitchen . . . or still better . . . I'll leave them with a drink and bring the stuff into the living room . . . But why shlepp it in the living room when the kitchen is supposed to be where you dine? . . . Unless I bring the stereo into the kitchen . . . but what if we go after to the living room for coffee? . . . I can't shlepp it back again . . . Maybe I'll buy another cassette deck . . . No, I'll put all the stuff in the living room and run in and out and most of the stuff will be cold anyway, except for the soup and the coffee . . . Mind you, it's cosy in the kitchen . . . There's a big wooden table in there . . . In the living room there's small tables so I'll have to take the salad round . . . to where people are sitting at the small tables . . . There's no centre table so we couldn't all face each other with a bottle in the middle . . . I'll have to walk around with the bottle . . . but at least there'll be space . . . but it won't be so warm as the kitchen . . . Oh, fuck it, we'll eat in there . . . that's fine . . . take the consequences . . . But it would be nice for them to see the living room . . . after, with coffee . . . not before . . . no after . . . not before? Wait! . . . We could eat in the living room if I brought the table into the centre, then I could put the bottle in the middle . . . That means taking the table from the kitchen . . . but then after we've eaten we'll have to sit in the living room with all the dirty dishes or make a fuss clearing them up whereas in the kitchen you just leave it all and say, let's stretch our feet in the living room . . . No, I know what to do . . . I'll kill myself instead . . . then I won't have to do anything . . . take an overdose or get run down by a truck . . . This is why God breathed life into me . . . to decide whether the table goes in the living room or in the kitchen . . . oooohh!

FRANK: So there was an English, and Irishman and Jew . . . *Ah, they're smiling . . . like I hope we'll enjoy ourselves . . .* And they meet in a bar . . .

DONNA: You know Jews don't go to bars . . .

FRANK: I have never been to a bar!? Eh! You have never seen me in a bar?

DONNA: Yeah, but you're not a real Jew . . .

FRANK: What?

DONNA: No, no, I mean, not like those Jews . . . er . . . real ones
like . . . *Oh, shit, why does he embarrass me? . . . He knows
what I mean . . . he knows I mean the Jews like his father who
wear a hat in the house and dandruff over their coats and smell of
onions, yellow flaccid ones with round backs and beards . . .* You
know, like Orthodox . . .

FRANK: Listen to her, Hal . . . like a Jew can't be seen in a bar . . .
What do you think, they can't mix a bit? . . . You think all
Gentiles are uncircumcised anti-Semitic yid-kicking bastards
. . . where the kitchen stinks of grease and they never wash
their hands after going to the toilet? . . . What, you carry that
old legend that the goy just drink till they vomit and at
weddings you're lucky to get a hamburger and a can of beer?
. . . No . . . you're wrong . . . some of my best friends are
goyim . . . very decent people . . . 'cause they don't shtipp
lox down their guts on Sunday until it comes out of their ears
and have stomach ulcers it doesn't mean they're bad . . . so
I'll carry on . . . *I've found my voice again . . . Hal is quiet with
a new-found respect for my acid humour and the party is not so
bad . . . Wonderful, I've got the floor and no kvetch . . . I'll tell
the joke . . . this is wonderful . . .* So they were in a bar and the
Englishman says drunkenly . . . 'I've been mistaken for some
very important people in my time . . . You know, once I was
taken for Winston Churchill' . . . and then the Irishman says
. . . 'Oh, that's not such a big deal, you know, once I was
walking down Dublin High Street and a woman come up to
me, "Holy Father, if it's not the Pope himself"' . . . and the
Jew says . . . 'That's nothing . . . well, I was sitting in a
movie house and the picture was so wonderful I thought why
not see it again . . .'

DONNA: Hahahahahahahahahahaha!

FRANK: Wait a minute . . . I ain't finished yet . . .

MOTHER-IN-LAW: Here's the coffee . . .

DONNA: Shush, Ma . . . he's telling a joke . . . just a minute . . .
he's nearly finished . . .

HAL: Come on, Frank . . . go on . . . 'Vy not,' he says . . . vy not indeed . . . haw haw haw haw haw haw haw haw!

FRANK: So he's sitting in the movie house and thinks, 'So vy not see it again' . . . *Gosh, this is going really well . . . I'm excited . . . Hey, I can easily hold them there in the palm of my hand . . . I knew I could do it, so why do I hold back, why lack confidence when I'm such a marvellous story-teller? . . . I have the power . . . I know I do . . . but I always let the others do it . . . let them be funny . . . take the stage . . . impress the ladies and I go quiet and choke and then I open my mouth with a prepared speech and it sounds like death 'cause it didn't come out when it went in my head . . . I let it spoil and then when I let it out it stinks like day-old herring you forgot to put back in the fridge . . . Oh God, the joke's a prepared speech so what am I talking about? Yeah, but it's different, you got to use timing. Now timing's the gold of the comic . . . without timing, a shitty story will come across like a shitty story. But with timing a shitty story will sound like poetry . . . no, not poetry . . . but like amazing . . . like brilliant . . . A golden observation . . . but a brilliant observation will sound like drek in the mouth of a shmock! You know . . . don't laugh, but maybe I could do cabaret . . . Yeah, get up on volunteer nights in the bar down the street . . . 'Hey, ladies and gentlemen, what's a Jewish American princess's favourite wine?' . . . Gentiles love Jewish jokes . . . I could get up and tell a lot of anti-Semitic jokes and I could get away with it . . . Oh, I know a beauty . . . I'll save it for after this . . .* Yeah, vy not indeed . . . so he sees the film again, he likes it so much that he stays for the last show . . . *Why are they yawning? . . . No, it's not going down too well . . . it's terrible . . . I promise God I won't tell anti-Semitic jokes . . . Just let me get to the end . . . please . . . I wish I never started . . . Why do I want to be funny and tell jokes? . . . I hate telling jokes . . . I hate it . . . I can't tell jokes . . . I'll never be able to tell them . . . I've never told them so why did I insist? . . . I loathe it . . . I'm going hot and cold . . . why on earth do I give myself this torture? . . .*

HAL: So vat happened? *I wish I could tell jokes . . . He's so easy and relaxed in front of his wife . . . maybe I can think of one . . . now let me see . . .*

DONNA: *I wonder how much time he really spends in bars . . . Does he find shiksas in there . . . maybe, they're so easy. They drop their panties at any excuse, loose dirty sluts . . .*

FRANK: Yeah, so the Jew stays for the last show and the usherette says . . .

DONNA: *A real shiksa usherette with a short skirt and she probably made a date with him in the bar . . .*

FRANK: So the usherette says to the Jew after seeing him in there for the third showing . . . she says . . . 'Jesus Christ! You here again' . . . hahahaha –

MOTHER-IN-LAW: Yours is with the milk . . .

FRANK: Ma! Later! You see, she thought he was Jesus Christ!

MOTHER-IN-LAW: You have half a sugar . . .

FRANK: Ma! Not now! No, not really, though for the sake of the joke he pretends to believe that she thought he was Jesus Christ . . .

MOTHER-IN-LAW: . . . and yours is black . . .

FRANK: Ma!!! Later!!! . . . Or that he thought that she thought that she thought he was . . . 'cause he was there three times for the movie . . .

HAL: I think we have the wrong coffee . . . (Exchanges his cup with FRANK's.)

FRANK: . . . so she said . . . hawhawhaw . . . 'J.C., you here again!!' No! Of course she didn't think he was . . . it was an expression . . .
(Pause.)

DONNA, HAL and MOTHER-IN-LAW: Oooooohhh . . . hahahahahahahahahahahahaha . . .

HAL: *I don't get it . . . I wasn't paying attention . . . I was thinking of a joke to tell and I missed the tag line . . . And now he thinks I'm not too bright . . . Can he see the blank stare in my eyes? . . . I have to fake it . . . Hawhawhawhawhawhaw! . . .*

FRANK: *I fucked it up . . . My mind went in the middle . . . I was going well and my mind went . . . I didn't make it clear . . . and then she came in with her fucking coffee fucking milk her fucking sugar, fuck you!!! . . . Oh, God . . . my stomach aches . . . my voice is going . . .* (Cough, cough.)

HAL: Haw haw! that's good . . . *My laugh is unconvincing . . . He knows I didn't get it . . . He's looking at me like I'm a killjoy, one that spoils the party. I'm not free any more . . . I was having a good time . . . He's staring at me like he'll never have me round again . . .* Good, Frank!

FRANK: *He's looking at me like I'm crazy . . . He's thinking I'm crazy . . . I'm sweating . . . He's staring at my sweat and wondering about it . . . They're all staring at my sweat. I'll slowly take a handkerchief out and mop it casually . . .*

HAL: *He's staring at me waiting for me to do something . . . tell a joke or what I do with myself . . . I'm stuck . . . I'm stuck in life . . . I can't move or open my mouth . . . my jaw feels clamped . . .* Hahahahahahahahaha . . .

FRANK: *Can't find my handkerchief.*

HAL: *I feel like dying.*

FRANK: *What's Donna doing? . . .*

DONNA: *It's gone very quiet . . . I don't like to interfere when the men are speaking . . . I like to listen. I don't want to be the focus of attention . . . I've got nothing to say but when I do. Sometimes. When I'm being myself I've got plenty to say. But when they are talking I don't sound important . . . I sound stupid . . . But I could say something now! . . . Now is the chance . . .*

(ALL are fixed in a tense stance.)

FRANK: *For God's sake, speak, Donna!!*

HAL: *May the earth open up.*

DONNA: *Now, what can I say . . . umhf? . . .* So, Hal, what else do you do at nights? . . .

HAL: At nights! Nights! (Cough.) Sorry . . . hmmmm . . . yes, at night . . . (Cough, cough.) Yes, well, at nights . . . (Cough, cough.) Yes, well as you were saying . . . at night . . . (Cough, cough.) Yes, well, at nights . . .

DONNA: Frank . . . help me, please . . .

FRANK: . . . Yeah . . .

HAL: . . . at nights, well . . . (Cough, cough.) Nights are so . . . (Cough, cough.) The thing about nights . . . (Cough, cough.) You see, nights . . .

FRANK: *This is a beautiful evening!!!* (Smells a huge fart.) Oh, God
. . . Donna! Did you leave the gas on again? . . .
(Blackout.)

SCENE 2

DONNA: Hold me, Frank . . . don't just sleep . . . kiss me
goodnight . . . don't just lie there like a lump . . . I might as
well be alone . . .

FRANK: Hmmmf . . . hummmf . . . g'nigh' . . .

DONNA: Frank . . . kiss me goodnight . . . come on turn over . . .

FRANK: Tirrrrreeed . . .

DONNA: Then just kiss me and say goodnight, darling . . .

FRANK: G'nigh', daarrrrling . . .

DONNA: Look at me and say it . . . turn your head . . .

FRANK: *Oh, for fuck's sake . . . I just want to bury myself in sleep . . .
just want to drag sleep over me like a sack and die in it until the
morning . . . It was a terrible night but at least I did it . . . Now
sleep . . . that's what I need, but she keeps asking to be kissed . . .
'Kiss me . . . kiss me . . . kiss me' . . . It's like a goldfish coming at
you every time you stand still . . . It's kiss kiss like I was giving
resuscitation . . . What is it about the kisses? . . . It's enough
already . . . The mouth keeps coming at me followed by the face
. . . Sure I love her but tell you the truth I can't shtipp it in any
more . . . Sometimes I roll over . . . you know, I've got to make a
gesture and stick it in . . . I think of the shiksa in the bar . . . I see
her with those tits ripe to plop out like melons . . . so I roll over but
it's difficult . . . but I've got a card index to help out . . . the chick
in the bus who kept crossing her legs . . . the one who eyed me
walking down the street with the kids . . . the girl who smiled at me
on the beach all those years ago . . . What might have happened if I
made a move always fascinated me . . . so I go through it as I roll
over . . . Her legs on the beach . . . long . . . long beautiful legs . . .*
(FRANK kisses DONNA perfunctorily and climbs aboard.)
There . . . there . . . ouch . . . ow! what are you wearing? . . .
ouch! . . .

DONNA: Ouch . . . ow! . . . here let me do it . . . there . . . *I want to be raped . . . Sometimes I want the garbagemen to throw me on the bed in the morning after the lump has gone to work and just use me . . . the three of them . . . and I know they've been eyeing me . . . They empty the garbage cans and I'm still in my nightdress . . . I know they're horny for me . . . They smile and talk after they've gone about the dirty things they'd like to do to me . . . tear my nightie off . . . put their hands all over . . . grab me and tear me to pieces . . . examine and explore me . . . all hungry and sweaty and dirty . . . Sometimes the lump next to me rolls over and sticks his end in and moves it about a bit . . . big favour . . . I let him because he needs to do his duty . . . tell you the truth I'm bored . . . but I want him to do it so I can think of the garbage man . . . taking my panties off and thrusting against me . . . Oh, no . . . he's pulling them down . . . the dirty beast . . . I hope they're clean . . . who cares . . . I'm abandoned . . . I want the two but I resist . . . a bit . . . One of them has already got his cock rubbing against me and the other is kissing me furiously . . . crazily . . . unbelieving his good luck . . . furious and hard . . . passionate as if he might be dreaming all this and wants to grab it all before it evaporates . . . Oh, their faces are rough and I'm brittle and soft . . . yielding to all their terrible demands. I give in . . . I'm melting . . . OH!!!! They're doing terrible things to me . . . no . . . not that . . . Oh, it's terrible . . . You're so hungry . . . And they all come at me, each satisfying his scummy lust on me . . . oh, using me . . . ripping me apart with their hot burning lusts . . . oh . . . I'm swimming in it . . . ooh, it's wonderful . . . oh! . . . ooh! . . . ooh! . . .*

FRANK: *I excite her like mad . . . so I've got to do it . . . Sometimes even if I find it a struggle . . . I make an effort . . . Listen, she finds me exciting . . . What can you do? . . . I only wish it was reciprocated on my part . . . So I keep my story going to the very end . . . sometimes I vary the story but I always start with picking her up . . . the beach . . . I start talking . . . We slowly link fingers through the sand . . . It's like thunder . . . I have my arm around her waist . . . It feels slender and small . . . She's smiling . . . I tell her a joke . . . She laughs . . . beautiful white teeth . . .*

*and then she puts her arm around my waist and I love that . . .
We have a coffee and under the table I can feel her knee brush
against mine . . . We're in her room now and she throws herself
on to the sofa carelessly . . . He skirt rides up . . . I join her . . .
Suddenly I'm kissing her, soft slushy wet mushy kisses and her
legs are so strong and fine and she opens them slightly as I kiss her
and my hand is crawling up the inside of her thigh which feels
like satin and cool and my heart pounds like it's ready to break
and now her hand is on my thigh and her fingers gently slipping
down into my groin which is packed and now my hands are
climbing higher, higher and her legs feel stronger and the thighs
powerful and suddenly I feel this enormous . . . What's
happening here? . . . Why are you in my fantasy, Hal? . . . Go
away . . . I want the soft squishy sweet succulent . . . not this
hard thick big thing . . . go away . . . get out of my fantasy.*

HAL: *But I am your fantasy . . . Relax, don't fight it . . . No one
knows . . . only you . . . Even I don't know . . .*

FRANK: *You sure?*

HAL: *Of course. I'm only a fantasy . . . They're supposed to be good
for you . . .*

FRANK: *But only in fantasy, you understand . . . This is to go no
further . . . I couldn't even think of it in reality . . . Phahhh, it
would make me sick . . . yuk! The idea of even kissing another
man . . . let alone the other stuff . . .*

HAL: *That's why it's a fantasy . . . You don't even have to smell it . . .*

FRANK: *Don't be so vulgar . . .*

HAL: *Come on . . . Enjoy it without the pain and the guilt . . . Enjoy
my big beauty . . .*

FRANK: *God, Hal . . . It's so big . . . and firm . . . mmmmmm . . . go
on then, Hal . . . Stick it in and get it over with . . . quickly . . .
HaHmmhmmmhmmmhmmhmmhmm!*

(HAL disappears.)

Was that nice for you?

DONNA: Yes, honey . . . Was it OK for you . . . ?

FRANK: Yeeeh . . . g'night . . .

DONNA: 'Night . . .

(Blackout.)

ACT TWO

SCENE I

FRANK: *I'm afraid . . . I'm afraid of my rates going up . . . I'm afraid to go to the door and look at the bills . . . I'm afraid of brown envelopes . . . I'm afraid of not having enough money . . . Money . . . I want it and need it . . . It gives me peace of mind . . . I work* all day for money and I work hard to make more . . . I sell hard and give value . . . I've got a technique when I sell . . . *I'm not afraid . . . not so much . . .* It's a beautiful piece of cloth . . . eighteen-ounce gabardine . . . Look, no crease . . . *I'm afraid to look at the tax demand . . . I'm afraid I'll never make enough* . . . You asked to see drape, I give you drape . . . You asked for texture, how's this for texture? Here, rub this against your dick . . . I'm kidding, really – just kidding . . . *What is life but working every day and never quite doing it?* . . . I can get you as much of this as you want . . . last of the range, that's why we're knocking it out cheap . . . Listen, it's a job lot . . . we made a deal . . . What can I say? . . . We bought up a lot . . . so we sell low . . . *How do you start a business?* . . . *I'm afraid to start one because then you could lose everything* . . . Say, George, there was an Englishman, an Irishman and a Jew, and they met in a bar . . .

GEORGE: 'Jesus Christ! you here again' . . .

FRANK: You heard that one . . . oh . . . *But what's to be afraid of?* . . . *You can't die . . . Take a risk . . .* So how's Monte? . . .

GEORGE: Fine . . . fine . . . still at college . . .

FRANK: Wonderful! He's a beautiful kid . . . he's clever . . .

GEORGE: Yeah . . . he's taking his degrees in languages . . .

FRANK: No kidding . . .

GEORGE: Yeah . . . he wants to do United Nations work . . . how about that . . .

FRANK: What, like translating and meeting important people? . . .

71

GEORGE: More like relief work in distressed areas . . .

FRANK: What a kid . . . like he's got some kinda . . .

GEORGE: Moral scruples.

FRANK: Yeah . . . *Wish I had said that* . . .

GEORGE: Not interested in money . . . crazy kid . . . thinks we're all so obsessed by it and we don't look any happier for it . . . so he wants to do some good . . .

FRANK: He knows there's more to life . . . right . . .

GEORGE: That's right . . . he could make a fortune . . . brains coming out of his ears . . . take over the business . . . It's a huge turnover now that we're into ladies' underwear . . .

FRANK: You were wise . . . it's a very good line . . . always changing . . .

GEORGE: But he didn't want to end up like us two shmocks, eh!?

FRANK: No . . . that's for sure . . . Hey . . . how do you mean? Us two! . . . Haw haw haw . . .

GEORGE: Come on . . . just kill yourself for dough . . . same old talk . . . same old grind . . . What's for next season? . . . Shlepp it out . . . No time to pick up a book . . . enjoy your life . . . just money money money . . . or worry if you're left with stock . . . When did you last see an opera?

FRANK: An opera? . . . Well, to tell you the truth . . . it's not really my cup of tea . . .

GEORGE: What are you reading at the moment?

FRANK: Reading . . . reading? . . . yeah, well, I just finished a book . . . yeah I just finished one . . . a week ago . . . No, I tell a lie . . . it must be two maybe three weeks . . . yeah . . . It's essential to keep your eye on the world . . . It's not all about dough . . . you're right . . . or you'll turn into a pumpkin . . . hahahahaha!

GEORGE: Or a shmock! . . .

FRANK: That's right . . . we're a pair of shmocks!!

GEORGE: So what was the book you were reading?

FRANK: The book? Oh, it was a great book . . . a very, very good book . . . deep, mind you . . .

GEORGE: *Look at the pathetic shmock . . . He makes me grow old . . . He reminds me of what I might have become . . . so I shudder*

72

inside like I might have some of that contamination inside me . . .
Tell you the truth, he makes me sick . . . an ass-kissing slug that
creeps around . . . but I see him out of pity and to remind myself
what not to become . . . I look at his wheedling pathetic face . . .
his greasy skin and the kvetch lines ingrained into his forehead . . .
his attempts to smarten up . . . his hopes whenever he comes into the
building . . . To be a salesman is to be a wheedling ingratiating
creep . . . because you need . . . all the time you need our goodwill
so you can stay alive . . . I hate salesmen because they make you
responsible for their livelihood . . . I hate the guilt trip they lay on
you . . . Look at this fake trying to remember a book he never read
. . . Who could even bear to live with him? . . . What his poor wife
Donna must think staring at this shuffling wreck with hairs on his
collar . . . his yellow face . . . Why do I hate him so much? . . .

FRANK: *I wish I was on a beach sitting in the sun with a book and maybe a*
Martini on the side . . . I am trying to remember a book I read recently
. . . When was the last time I read a book? . . . I don't remember
. . . I come here to push my stuff and I get put on the spot . . . Fuck
him, the smug bastard . . . Where does he get off calling me a
shmock? . . . He's a shmock . . . But look at him all comfortable
. . . sitting by the Sunday pool while the kids play Pac-man in the
playroom . . . Look at his greasy face well lined in comfortable
dinners and arrogant airs like he owns me because maybe his money
buys something from me which he needs anyway . . . So I have to
kiss his ass 'cause he spends a few bucks . . . I have to suffer this
ignorant fat pig telling me I'm a shmock because his ability to be
greedy is bigger than mine . . . Who is he to make me sweat? . . .
Don't I do enough sweating? . . . Up yours, you fat greasy
bastard . . .

GEORGE: *Good, soon I'll take lunch . . . When creepo is gone I'll*
saunter down to the deli and order a juicy pastrami sandwich with
the meat hanging out and dropping down the side topped with some
cheese and some nice pickle to crunch . . . then some strong mustard
and swallow the whole thing in rye . . . My mouth is drooling . . .
Maybe I should buy to support his family . . . But then he's always
coming back . . . Then be honest . . . tell him . . . don't shove your
job lines and shmutters here . . . But then he won't have a good

lunch . . . He'll not take maybe as many orders and return home empty-handed . . . So spread a little cheer . . . Why do I have to suffer this guilt? . . . The bastard makes me sick and guilty at the same time . . .

FRANK: *I'll tell him, 'Don't give me your "What have you read lately?" bullshit . . . I don't have to listen to it . . . Shove your orders up your ass and don't lecture me from your high pulpit of inherited wealth, you fat greedy smarmy bastard . . . When was the last time you fucked your wife? . . . I bet you buy $500 tricks, you creep.'*

GEORGE: *No more guilt . . . just say no more . . . I don't want your shmutters . . . Be polite, it's down-market stuff and get rid of it once and for all . . .*

FRANK: *Right, here goes . . . Now you'll get the biggest earful you ever heard . . . God, I feel good just in anticipation . . . My heart's pumping like mad . . .* You know, George . . .

GEORGE: Yeah, Frank . . . you remember the book now . . . haw haw haw . . .

FRANK: No . . . I've something on my mind I want to say . . .

GEORGE: Oh, yeah . . . good . . . spit it out . . .

FRANK: *You fat greasy stinking lousy smug creep . . . I'd like to kick your ass into next week . . . Don't you ever dare talk to me in your patronizing manner . . . I'm a human being, you whoremonger . . . I haven't said this yet . . . I'm just practising.*

GEORGE: *If I invest a quarter-million in silver this month . . . ummmmm . . .*

FRANK: *You vile parasite . . . you're hated . . .*

GEORGE: *I'll go down to the brokers' after my lunch . . .*

FRANK: *Everybody loathes you, you slimy idiot . . .*

GEORGE: *No . . . go before the sandwich and finish your lunch peacefully . . .*

FRANK: *I even hear you letch the salesmen's wives, you dirty whoremonger.*

GEORGE: *Haven't visited Shirley for a while . . .*

FRANK: *I'm gonna tell you now . . .*

GEORGE: *Straight after work . . . I'll book an appointment . . .*

FRANK: *Right . . . now let it out . . .* Y'know, George . . .

GEORGE: So, you were er . . . saying, Frank . . .

FRANK: Listen, George . . .

DONNA: (Enters with MOTHER-IN-LAW) *Don't say it, Frank . . . We've got the health insurance to pay this month . . . for all four of us . . . plus the car needs fixing and the roof leaks . . . Don't throw away our first Christmas holiday to Miami . . . You promised me . . . And mother needs back treatment . . .*

FRANK: *Shit to that.*

DONNA: *Don't think just of yourself . . . don't . . . swallow a little pride . . .*

FRANK: *I'm poisoned on swallowing too much pride . . .*

DONNA: *Ignore him.*

FRANK: *But I'm not a man if I keep up this game . . .*

DONNA: *You were a man last night.*

FRANK: *Yeah . . . I was . . . wasn't I? . . .*

HAL: (Enters.) *That's because of me . . .*

FRANK: *Get out . . .*

HAL: *You liked me then . . .*

DONNA: *What does he mean, Frank? . . .*

FRANK: *Nothing . . . nothing . . .*

MOTHER-IN-LAW: *Tell him, the vstinkiner momsa, and he'll have more respect . . . Don't be a worm all your life . . . In front of your mother-in-law you should be a warrior . . . and what would your mother think, God rest her soul? . . .*

FRANK: *What do you care about my mother? . . . Did you see her when she was dying in the hospital? . . .*

MOTHER-IN-LAW: *Ah! now it comes out! Frank, dollink, I was ill myself with gallstones, God forbid it should happen to you! . . . But still from my sickbed I got up and made borscht for your mother, the Russian kind . . . Didn't I, Donna, didn't I? . . . God rest her soul . . . that borscht kept her going . . .*

FRANK: *Stop it, all of you . . . Shut up . . . Go 'way . . . I'll do what I want to do . . . I'll tell him for once in my life I'm gonna stand up for myself . . . You know what, George? . . .*

GEORGE: *Yeah . . . tell me about it, old boy . . .*

DONNA: (Voice over) *Frank, don't do it . . . The microwave . . . the second TV in Jennifer's bedroom . . . the VCR . . . the weekend at the Golden Nugget three nights for the price of two . . . the*

cuisinart . . . *the four-wheel drive . . . the computer for Josh . . .*
FRANK: I remember the book now . . .
GEORGE: Oh, yeah . . . *Shirley or Susan? . . .* What?
FRANK: 'How to Increase your Earning Power' . . .
GEORGE: Good for you . . . Frank . . .
 (Blackout.)

SCENE 2

FRANK: (In the style of a nightclub comic) *Like it must be paradise to
 be without a kvetch . . . a place where you kvell . . . Enough of
 that . . . I had it right up to here . . . like a drum beating the same
 rhythm in your head . . . boom boom boom . . . Say, I was in a bar,
 and there was an Englishman, an Irishman and a Jew . . . Oh,
 you've heard that one . . . oh . . .*
 (Chorus of HAL, DONNA, GEORGE and MOTHER-IN-LAW
 improvise supportive commentary on FRANK's next
 speech.)
 That's a nice stereo . . .
CHORUS: *Ooohh—*
FRANK: *Yeah, that's a beaut . . . amplifier and speakers with a receiver
 and turntable . . . a tape deck with Dolby too . . .*
CHORUS: (Awe) *Ooohh—*
FRANK: *Yeah, you need that and a switch for metal or chrome . . .
 What the hell's that?*
CHORUS: *I dunno—*
FRANK: *God, look at those switches . . . You need to go to night school
 just to learn how to use the fucking thing . . .*
CHORUS: *Hahahaha . . .*
FRANK: *It's a beaut . . . silver and black . . .*
CHORUS: *Tsssss . . .*
FRANK: *It's like a spaceship . . . in the living room it would look great
 . . . yeah . . .*
CHORUS: *Yeah . . .*
FRANK: *I'd get some opera . . . $600 . . .*
 (Whistle from CHORUS.)

It's not cheap . . . but it's state of the art . . . nah . . .

CHORUS: *Nah . . .*

FRANK: *Our stereo's OK . . . but the sound must be like a dream . . .*
Dolby stereo with room for four speakers . . .
(Big gasp from CHORUS.)
Then I'd wire two in the kitchen . . .

CHORUS: *Yeah . . . yeah . . .*

FRANK: *But then I'd need to get the builders in . . . shit!*

CHORUS: *Shit!*

FRANK: *Those bastards would charge a fortune . . .*

CHORUS: *Bastards!*

FRANK: *Maybe I'd do it myself . . . Why not? . . .*

CHORUS: *Why not?*

FRANK: *But then I'd have to pull up the floorboards . . .*

CHORUS: *Uh-oh . . .*

FRANK: *And drill a hole . . . I'd have to buy a drill . . . nah . . .*

CHORUS: *Nah . . .*

FRANK: *Who needs it? . . . I do! . . . $600 . . . I can put it on Visa . . .*

CHORUS: *Yeah . . .*

FRANK: *My stereo's OK . . . My stereo's old . . . nah . . .*

CHORUS: *Nah . . .*

FRANK: *Yeah! . . .*

CHORUS: *Yeah . . .*

FRANK: *I'd like a bit of luxury . . . but it's crazy . . . look at it . . .*

CHORUS: *Oooohh . . .*

FRANK: *Man's genius in electronics . . .*

CHORUS: *Wow . . .*

FRANK: *Maybe I'll put it in the kitchen . . . We eat and spend time in there . . .*

CHORUS: *Eh . . .*

FRANK: *And wire the speakers in the living room.*

CHORUS: *Ayyy . . .*

FRANK: *No, make it a showpiece in the living room . . .*

CHORUS: *Showpiece, showpiece!*

FRANK: *I wonder if I could use a drill . . . then I'd have to pull up the carpet . . .*

CHORUS: *Uh-oh . . .*

FRANK: *She'd go crazy . . . it's fitted . . . wall to wall . . . Nah!* . . .

CHORUS: *Nah, nah* . . .

> (FRANK, HAL and MOTHER-IN-LAW exit, mumbling. DONNA and GEORGE are left on stage.)

GEORGE: So, you want to grab a bite to eat? . . .

DONNA: Sure . . . uh-hunh . . . I guess so . . .

GEORGE: How does Italian sound? . . .

DONNA: I love Italian . . .

> (FRANK, HAL and MOTHER-IN-LAW cross the stage mumbling as DONNA and GEORGE sit.)

GEORGE: *I'm nervous . . . I didn't sell much last week . . . Business is down and silver slumped . . . I think I've got a lump in my guts . . . Is it a growth? . . . My wife's leaving me for a shvartzer who used to wait tables . . . I'm free again but . . . a salesman's wife . . .*

> (HAL enters as a waiter.)

HAL: Buona sera . . . two for dinner? . . . *Thanks for coming in a half-hour before we close . . . assholes* . . . Can I take your order? . . .

GEORGE: We're not quite ready . . .

HAL: Something to drink? . . .

GEORGE: Oh, I dunno . . . Do you want something, honey? . . .

DONNA: Oh, I dunno . . .

HAL: Some wine perhaps . . . red or white? . . .

GEORGE: Which would you like, honey? . . .

DONNA: Oh, I don't care . . . whichever you want . . .

GEORGE: Red . . . do you like red? . . .

DONNA: Red's fine . . .

GEORGE: You want the white, don't you? . . .

HAL: *Make up your minds, you ignorant creeping turds* . . .

DONNA: Whichever you want . . . white is fine . . .

GEORGE: You want the red, don't you? . . . Two glasses of red . . .

DONNA: *I hate red wine* . . .

HAL: Coming right up . . . *I hope it rots your liver . . . I hope you choke on it . . . I hope your kidneys turn to mush* . . . Uno momento . . .

DONNA: Sorry to hear about your wife . . .

GEORGE: I should worry . . . Listen, maybe it's a blessing . . .

DONNA: *He's OK . . . he's quite nice . . . but I don't want to be a stopgap . . . I'm impressing him . . . but don't go to bed on the first time out . . .*

GEORGE: Y'know, Donna . . . I think we just got too used to each other . . . *'Cause she liked a big black dick up her, the filthy slut . . . a huge shvartzer . . . and God forbid even . . . no . . . I can't even look at it in my thoughts . . . yeah, go on . . . see it . . . just think about it for a moment . . . no . . . look at it and then it will go away . . . face it . . . draw a picture . . . yaaaaaaaaaaa!!! . . .* So we decided to have a trial separation.

DONNA: Yeah, my husband . . . well, we fight a lot . . . *Oh dear, maybe I shouldn't have said that . . . He'll think I'm difficult . . .*

GEORGE: Oh yeah . . . fight, fight . . . yeah . . . ha ha! . . . *That's all I need . . . a trouble maker.*

(Chorus of the Fearful appear against the wall in identity parade.)

HAL: *I'm afraid . . . I fear . . . I'm lonely . . . I want . . . I need . . . I must . . . I hunger . . . I feel . . . I desire . . . friends . . . yeah . . . I need friends . . . I won't tell you this because this is embarrassing but I am going out of my mind with loneliness . . .*

FRANK: *I'm afraid . . . I fear . . . I was on the seventeenth floor today and a window was open . . . and there was nothing but space between me and the deck and I kept seeing myself flying through . . . like in the movies . . .*

DONNA: *I'm afraid . . . What will happen? He doesn't love me . . . He leaves me alone . . . I'm getting old . . . I must be loved . . . I'm neglected and shrivelled from it . . .*

GEORGE: *I'm afraid . . . I can't pay alimony . . . My taxes are awful . . .*

HAL: *I'm desperate . . . I can't breathe . . . I am not popular . . . I have few friends . . . few . . . but I am not liked . . . not popular . . . get nervous . . . not funny . . . not handsome . . . not suave . . . ugly . . . plain . . . ordinary . . . simple . . .*

GEORGE: *And I can't keep it up . . . I couldn't get it up there last night . . . So what? . . . So what? . . . I didn't feel right . . . I couldn't get it stiff!! I couldn't say this to anyone . . . I couldn't speak these thoughts even to my shrink . . . I daren't even think it to myself . . .*

but I'm afraid of not having a stiff prick . . .

FRANK: *I saw myself sail through space and hit the deck . . . like a hand was pulling me out or beckoning me . . . a soft invisible hand gathered me up and I was flying . . . What a thrill . . . a five-second thrill . . . That's a good one . . .*

DONNA: *I want to escape . . . I'll find a room but I'm afraid . . . I'll be lonely . . . I'll sit there . . . I'm not so attractive any more . . . I've only one tit . . . Who will desire me now? . . . How can I be alone and undesired? . . . I'm bored . . . so bored . . . I hate . . . The day starts and I hate the light threatening me with another empty day . . .*

HAL: *But I die in company . . . I have to think out the lines before I say them . . . It doesn't gush out like a spring . . . like a torrent . . . but within I have a waterfall . . . a giant explosion could come gushing out . . . but then an iron door clamps shuts on it . . .*

GEORGE: *I can't say this to anyone . . . So I pulled this hooker . . . this shiksa . . . and I started but my will collapsed in my dick . . . My soul and my will is in my dick and it collapsed and so my spirits collapsed if the dick is the barometer of my will . . .*

DONNA: *I'll have an operation . . . I hear they can make one now . . . It's simple . . . Yeah, but costs an arm and a leg just to get a pair of decent tits . . . Yeah, but supposing it fails . . . or looks worse . . . Oh, I don't know . . .*

FRANK: *Stood there with an empty order book and the window beckoning . . . So this is the life . . . to shlepp my guts up and down and lick ass to keep the shreik at home and for what?*

HAL: *So I escape to my room and sit and sit . . . I'm sorry for myself . . . See yourself growing fat in the mirror . . . stare . . . smoke a cigarette . . .*

DONNA: *I'm afraid . . . I fear . . . I want . . . I need . . . I ache . . . I hunger . . . I cry . . . I sicken . . .*

FRANK: *So the window was a ticket . . . like a cheque that I can cash . . . splattered out on the sidewalk and the crowd . . . circling and feasting on the mess . . . as my skull lay cracked open like an egg . . . So I looked out at all the space I would soon occupy but I was afraid . . .*

GEORGE: *And so I'm afraid . . . each new woman inspires the greatest*

terror . . . that I'll shrink because I lack . . . or feel I lack . . . some
kind of power . . . Maybe I'm a fruit . . . no . . . God forbid . . .
(Blackout and return to restaurant.)
You're sure he doesn't know? . . .

DONNA: No! . . . he doesn't even suspect . . .

GEORGE: Donna, I love you!

DONNA: No, no, don't say that . . .

GEORGE: I have to tell you . . . I have to . . .

DONNA: No, don't George . . . I can't do this . . .

GEORGE: You love me too . . . you know you do . . . don't you? . . .

DONNA: But he comes to you for orders . . .

GEORGE: So . . . I buy his shmutters even when I don't want them
. . . to help you, Donna . . . Donna, come on let's go to bed . . .
Hopefully she'll say no but then at least she'll know how much I
care . . . To tell you the truth I don't feel like it . . . I'm off it . . .
but a cuddle I'd like and maybe cook me a meal . . . Sick of having
to deliver on demand . . .

DONNA: I can't, George . . .

GEORGE: *That's a relief . . .* Awww! Come on . . .

DONNA: Don't ask me again . . .

GEORGE: You know I'll never stop . . . *Phew, what a relief . . .*

DONNA: And after . . . huh . . . after you've got what you want? . . .

GEORGE: That's what you think of me . . . I respect you, Donna
. . . as a woman . . . What . . . you think at my age I'm looking
for one-night stands? . . . You know I love you . . . from the
minute I saw you at the annual Christmas party with your
husband . . . I fell . . . what can I say? . . . You're a desirable
woman, Donna, but I respect your wishes . . . *So I don't have*
to fuck and I come across as a horny guy . . . brilliant!!

DONNA: *I'm afraid that when he sleeps with me . . . I've got only one tit*
. . . That's a lot to handle . . . Especially if you are not in love . . .
He'll be put off . . . What if he really loves me? . . . So what's a
little breast? . . . a piece of tissue with a piece of cork on the end . . .
So men act like nirvana lies in a perfect-shaped pendulous breast
. . . fat . . . juicy . . . like a great hanging fruit . . . like a melon
. . . ready to burst and wobbling under a thin shirt with nipples like
armour-plated bullets . . . a whole fat breast hanging in his hand

*like he was weighing an avocado . . . I mustn't get myself into this
state . . . It's silly . . . But he holds each breast and examines me
. . . his eyes narrowing and closing in like a little satellite landing
on the moon . . . scanning the terrain for the best landing site . . .
His mouth's closing in now . . . and the exhaust blast brings up
little goose pimples on the terrain . . . Now he accelerates forward
. . . The moon very slowly turns on a gentle pivot . . . as if by
gravitational pull and his jaw . . . rough . . . two days' growth . . .
opens wide, a dark inferno where a massive snake lolls wet and
expectant . . . His lips, like crimson curtains, pull back . . . And
the moon . . . all white and glowing in its fullest state as the mouth
opens and the snake darts out . . . and . . . with the tip of that
snake-like tongue lifts the cork and gently places it in his warm
mouth . . . where it gets hot and hard inside his teeth and he chews
and bites gently . . . now harder . . . now harder still and then
slowly . . . inch by inch . . . gently . . . gradually . . . sucks it all
back swollen into his mouth again and he looks like he is blowing
up a big balloon and then he lets it whoosh out once more . . . And
then the whole process is repeated . . . Yeah, it would be nice.*
(Blackout.)

FRANK: I'm home, honey . . . What are you doing on the table? . . .

DONNA: Ohh! I thought you were coming home late . . . It's not
ready . . .

FRANK: Listen, who cares? . . . Give me a beer, honey . . . *That
dream I had the other night . . . about Hal, you know . . . That's
bad . . . I mean that must be there in my subconscious . . . I never
knew I had any of that in me . . . It's disgusting what filth I have
up there in my brain . . .*

DONNA: There's no beer in the fridge . . . We don't often keep
beer . . . You never want it normally . . .

FRANK: What do you mean 'normally'? Many times I have brought
home a six-pack . . .

DONNA: Yeah, but you used it weeks ago . . .

FRANK: So you can't say we don't keep it . . .

DONNA: Not normally . . . since when are you a beer-drinking
man? . . .

FRANK: Since when! Since when! Do I have to be an alcoholic to drink beer?

DONNA: We got wine . . . wine we got . . .

FRANK: What wine we got?

DONNA: The wine we use for Pesach . . .

FRANK: I'll go out and get a beer.

DONNA: Frank?

FRANK: Huhn?

DONNA: Oh, Frank . . .

FRANK: Wad!!

DONNA: Why are you drinking?

FRANK: I dunno . . . *'Cause I'm afraid of being a fairy . . . 'cause I have dreams of Hal* . . . I just felt like one . . .

DONNA: It's not like you . . . Is something wrong?

FRANK: Nah, I'm just fed up . . .

DONNA: With me??

FRANK: Hell, no!

DONNA: With what, then? . . .

FRANK: With the work . . . Tell you the truth I'm sick of hustling to that slimy dress manufacturer . . .

DONNA: Which one? . . .

FRANK: The one we met at the awful Christmas party, who said come up and show me your samples . . . that slimy bastard . . . I'm sick of seeing his face . . . I'm sick to hell of it and sometimes I just want to smash him . . . just want to take my two fists and go pow pow pow pow pow, 'Take that, you smelly greasy farty bag of scum . . . I don't need your money' . . . That's what I need, Donna . . . Oh, Donna . . .

DONNA: He sticks it in me, Frank.

FRANK: Break a chair over his head . . . I hold myself back . . .

DONNA: He pulls my panties off and shoves his cock in . . .

FRANK: How dare he look down on me as some kind of peon . . . He makes money out of me! . . .

DONNA: He doesn't even mind my one tit . . . says it cute . . .

FRANK: He makes big profits out of me . . . Mr Greasy . . .

DONNA: Says he can concentrate better on one tit . . .

FRANK: I'm a man, Donna . . . I'll not be spat upon . . .

DONNA: I'm a woman and need a good screw from time to time.

FRANK: It's not enough to shlepp my guts out from one end of town to another begging to be seen like a leper . . . but I make money for them . . . finding them cheap discounted lines . . .

DONNA: Shut up! Shut up! Shut up! Shut up! Shut up! . . . Shut up!

FRANK: Donna??

DONNA: He sticks it into me . . . the manufacturer . . . I had to tell you . . .

FRANK: Wad!!!? Wayasay!!? Wadya saying? . . . Wad's coming out of your mouth??? Donna, am I hearing you??? Is that you??

DONNA: Yeah . . . listen . . . it's kvetching me and I have to let it out . . . that fat greasy manufacturer . . . the one who bosses you around . . . well, he really likes me and though he's screwing you, metaphorically of course, he's screwing me . . . so we're both being screwed, so put that in your mouth and smoke it . . .

FRANK: Donna . . . I never heard you talk like that.

DONNA: I decided to kick kvetching . . . and suddenly like a dam . . . it all comes tumbling out.

FRANK: You kicked *kvetching*!!!!! How?????

DONNA: By deciding to do what I want and let the guilt go fuck itself . . . you know . . . at that Christmas party for the wholesalers . . . you introduced me and he's been after me ever since but I've been afraid 'cause of my one tit and he's been afraid in case he couldn't make it after his wife walked out . . . So we put our two minuses together and came up with a plus . . . It's OK . . . I told you . . . I let it out . . . I won't kvetch any more . . . I'm sorry, Frank . . . I'm sorry . . . My suitcases are packed . . . and your dirty laundry has been done . . . and there's three pints of milk in the fridge . . .
(DONNA leaves.)

FRANK: *Deciding what I want and let the guilt go fuck itself . . . hmmmmn . . .*
(HAL enters and rings the doorbell.)
Oh, hi, Hal . . . Thanks for coming over . . . Sorry for calling so early . . .

HAL: It's all right . . .

FRANK: Cup of coffee? . . .

HAL: Only if it's made . . .

FRANK: Well, I can make it . . .

HAL: No, no . . .

FRANK: You want instant? . . .

HAL: No, I'm OK . . .

FRANK: You want some raisin toast? . . .

HAL: No . . . thanks . . .

FRANK: A muffin? . . .

HAL: No . . . really . . . I just had breakfast . . .
(Awkward pause.)

FRANK: So you see, Hal . . . she's been betraying me all this
time . . .

HAL: You can't trust them, Frank . . .

FRANK: I didn't know what to do or who to call . . .

HAL: I don't mind . . . I really don't . . . and you should call . . .

FRANK: *What is this? . . . I got a hard-on up to my chin . . . I wish I
could tell him how I felt . . .* That's kind of you, Hal . . .

HAL: Hell, kind . . . I've been alone . . . I know what it's like . . .
*God, he's manly but I'm afraid in case I'm making a huge mistake
. . . Why doesn't he get closer or at least make some signal? . . .
Brush my knee or something? . . . Maybe I'll make a move . . .*

FRANK: You do know what it's like . . . *Suppose I revolt him . . .
Suppose I'm crazy and he runs out screaming . . . No, I must suffer
it . . . These are evil disgusting thoughts but I can't stop thinking
about . . . it . . .*

HAL: What will you do?

FRANK: What will I do? . . . I dunno . . . I'm alone . . . at forty I'm
alone . . . Like gotta do it over again . . . like try to meet girls
again . . . at my age . . . like where do you go? . . . You know
what I'm saying, Hal . . . like I can't go to discos and unless I
meet them at maybe a party . . . Where then? . . . And who
invites me to parties anyway . . . huh? I mean like I'm lonely,
Hal . . . Hal? How do you manage? . . . I mean at my age . . .

HAL: Frank . . . Frank . . .
(HAL puts his hand on FRANK's shoulder.)

85

DONNA: I'm free now I've left him . . .

GEORGE: Great . . . You told him it was me? . . . Oi!

DONNA: Yeah, let it all out – what the hell . . .

(FRANK and HAL in bed.)

FRANK: Hal . . . why don't we set up together? . . .

HAL: Are you sure? . . .

FRANK: May as well . . . only don't spread the word . . . OK?
. . . About us . . . I don't need any more kvetches! Hey, Hal
. . . you know what? . . . I don't feel as if I have one any
more . . .

HAL: Did I help you get rid of it?

FRANK: You sure did . . .

HAL: Kvetches gone now, huh? . . .

FRANK: Oh, yeah . . .

HAL: Y'know, Frank . . . I'll give up my apartment if it's all right
with you . . . It's an expensive dump . . . We can split
expenses . . . Listen, it'll be so much cheaper . . .

FRANK: Listen, we'll save a fortune . . . *We get on fine . . . but
suppose after a while we don't get on so good? . . . I mean it's
possible . . . maybe I should move into his and rent mine out . . .
but I like my house . . . Shit, I've just got my freedom!*

HAL: You want to give it a whirl?

FRANK: Er . . . sure, Hal . . .

HAL: Are you sure? . . . I mean, level with me? . . .

FRANK: Yeah, of course I am . . . Let's give it a whirl . . . Hell, it's
not the end of the world . . . *Oh shiiiit!* . . . G'night, Hal . . . *I
don't want him to give up his place and I don't want to move . . .
What's going on? . . . I should tell him . . . but I don't want him to
take it bad . . . but I suggested it . . .*

HAL: Frank . . . aren't you going to kiss me goodnight??
(Slow fade to black.)

ACAPULCO

CHARACTERS

KAREN, an average white American from New Jersey
STEVE, an English actor, taciturn, moody
VOYO, Yugoslavian-Russian type, volatile, exuberant, powerful
  build
BARMAN, faceless, indifferent, a barman anywhere
WILL, New York actor, wiry, dark, satanic, intense with humour
JOHN, Scot living in Mexico, small, wiry, playful, intense but
  inclining to the philosophic

The play is set in a bar at the Acapulco Plaza Hotel in 1984. It's a
modern and elaborate place where people sit at the bar or at tables
nearby. It's a long bar and should stretch from one end of the
stage to the other. The barman should be almost invisible in his
movements but always there to serve and never standing idly.
The actors form a frieze across the bar, reaching over each other
to make their points, ordering drinks to punctuate the long
speeches, lighting cigarettes, etc. The acting style should be easy
and casual broken up by laughter and the normal behaviour
patterns of people relaxing after work.

AUTHOR'S NOTE

Acapulco rolls off the tip of the tongue and sounds like an exotic Mexican dish; mysterious, hot and desirable. I stayed in a hotel on the beach and watched the toilet paper float in shreds since the hurricane had tossed the resort into a giant sordid milk shake and everything was floating out there. Only the Mexicans swam while the white tourists lay around the hotel pools roasting themselves or getting drunk on tequila in the bar. I was there to act Sylvester Stallone's Nemesis in *Rambo Two*. His mission in the film was to investigate missing POWs. The actors playing the POWs sat in the bar each night and recounted their story of the day. They were small part players with the grand ambitions of life and each event that encompassed their world or touched them was the subject of much analysis. I waited for my moment of triumph in the film but it was not to be. It was a sordid, boring affair with long hours eaten away with ennui watching the endless set-ups being prepared. The director wasn't too fond of me but I did what I could with the role. I started writing down the actual dialogue of the actors who played the POWs and weaving a kind of docu-play. These actors fascinated me and were full of the joys of life, thrilled to work and wondering where to get the best margaritas. This is their story as I heard it. I was a spectator at their banquet.

The play was first performed in Los Angeles at the Odyssey Theatre in 1990. The character of Will was based on Will Rothlein, a New York actor who had fire in his heart and whose tales were spice and arsenic. A special character who was unforgettable was Voyo, a giant Jugoslav who in the film was my powerful 'Golem' assistant. Voyo had a unique philosophy and warm nature that made the stay in Acapulco not only endurable but memorable. To them both much thanks.

Acapulco was first performed on 25 August 1990 at the Odyssey Theatre, Los Angeles, California. The cast was as follows:

KAREN	Chandra Lee
STEVE	John Horn
WILL	Tom Flynn
JOHN	Michael Sollenberger
VOYO	Richard Vidan
BARMAN	Sam Vlahos

Director	Steven Berkoff
Producers	Ron Sossi and Lucy Pollock
Designer	Craig Lathrop

Acapulco was first performed in Britain on 5 August 1992 at the King's Head Theatre, London. The cast was as follows:

STEVE	Steven Berkoff
WILL	Terence Beesley
KAREN	Connie Hyde
BARMAN	Paul Bentall
VOYO	Joe Montana
JOHN	Hilton Mcrae

Director	Steven Berkoff
Designer	Nick Burnell
Lighting	Chris Jaeger

KAREN: Hey, I saw you at breakfast this morning.

STEVE: Sure, I remember you . . . How are you? You're the one with the lovely smile.

WILL: Vino tinto.

KAREN: So have you . . . I thought, 'Hey, that guy's smiling at me . . . ' I'm Karen.

STEVE: Steve.

KAREN: Hi, Steve . . . You're in pretty good shape for an older guy. Do you work out?

STEVE: No. Well sometimes, you know. Not weights . . . a few sit-ups to keep trim . . . Used to play a lot of squash.

KAREN: So you were smiling at me . . .

STEVE: Well, you've got a lovely smile . . .

KAREN: You're a handsome guy . . .

STEVE: (Won) Hey . . . you're sweet . . .

KAREN: (To the barman) Hey, you got any matches?

BARMAN: Matches? Si, señorita. (Lights her cigarette.)

VOYO: Jośe, another beer – cold this time.

BARMAN: Cold beer.

STEVE: Where are you from, Karen?

KAREN: What?

STEVE: Where are you from?

KAREN: New Jersey . . .

STEVE: Ah . . .

KAREN: It takes me forty-five minutes to get to Manhattan.

STEVE: Do you go there a lot? . . . Do you get into town?

KAREN: It's so dirty . . .

STEVE: Yeah . . .

KAREN: It's dirty . . . I don't like to go there too much.

STEVE: See any shows?

KAREN: Yeah . . . I saw *Dream Girls*. They were all black.

STEVE: Was it good? . . . I didn't see it.

KAREN: Oh God, it was great . . .

(Loud laughter from JOHN and VOYO.)

Look (Pulls out ring from handbag), I bought this ring for my mother.

STEVE: Oh, nice . . . Hey, nice . . .

93

KAREN: It cost me a hundred dollars . . . Cute, huh?

STEVE: Oh it is . . . yes . . .

WILL: Luis, vino.

BARMAN: Si, señor.

KAREN: You have a nice smile . . . I thought, 'Hey! That guy's handsome . . . '

JOHN: (To BARMAN) Hey, can we have some olives?

BARMAN: Yeah, sure.

STEVE: Come on . . . I think you have a lovely smile.

KAREN: You got a lady here?

STEVE: Nah . . .

KAREN: You ain't got a lady? A handsome guy like you?

STEVE: No . . . I haven't found anyone . . . not here. No, not really.

KAREN: (Looking around) Hey! Where's my friends gone? . . . They've shot off . . . Maybe they're by the pool . . . Wanna come? . . . Maybe they're by the pool drinking. I'll ring the bar.

STEVE: You go see. I'll wait.

KAREN: You make sure you do.

STEVE: I will.

KAREN: You wanna come? . . . You wanna come drink at the pool?

STEVE: I think the pool bar is closed.

VOYO: (Loudly) But she meant bananas!
      (VOYO and JOHN laugh.)

KAREN: I'm a bit woozy . . . shit! Hey, you're nice! How old are you?

STEVE: What?

KAREN: Nothing.

STEVE: Go on . . . let it out . . . How old am I?

KAREN: What's your last name?

STEVE: Bennet.

KAREN: Mine's Ryton.

STEVE: What do you do, Miss Ryton?

KAREN: I'm a telephone operator . . . It's my birthday next Friday . . . I'm gonna be twenty-two years old. Still a baby,

94

right! How old are you?

STEVE: Forty-five.

KAREN: No! You gotta be kidding . . . You could be my dad!
(Swivels on stool to stage right and knocks WILL.)
Oh shit! I spilt your drink . . . I'm sorry . . .

WILL: It's OK.

STEVE: I am old enough to be your dad . . . Do you like that?
(Touches her hair as JOHN orders drinks.)

JOHN: José, how about a beer?

BARMAN: (Annoyed but playing) What do you mean 'beer'? We
have Dos Equis, Tecate, Corona, Pacifico, Superior and
Budweiser!

JOHN: (Bewildered and embarrassed) Uh . . .

BARMAN: Come on! Come on!

JOHN: I'll have a Corona.

BARMAN: Corona, *oh gracias!*

KAREN: I'll go look for my friends . . . (Exits dancing stage left.)

(Music comes up and there is miscellaneous shouting and
ordering of drinks.)

VOYO: (To STEVE as music fades – he has been listening
nearby at the bar) How can you talk to that idiot?

STEVE: She's an idiot . . .

VOYO: How can you talk to that piece of . . .

STEVE: I don't know . . . just another vagina attached to a life-
support system . . .

VOYO: (Laughing) That's very funny . . . She's an idiot . . . Just
because she's a woman!

STEVE: I wouldn't waste my time listening to a man who was such
an idiot, but I waste my time listening to garbage . . .

VOYO: She's stupid . . . José, get me a *cold* beer – this not cold!

BARMAN: OK – cold beer.

VOYO: Just a typical American who's on vacation and drunk . . .
She makes me sick!

STEVE: Yeah, I know . . . We prostitute ourselves for a few
minutes of transcendental bliss!

VOYO: It's terrible, believe me . . . what we do.

STEVE: What do you want to do tonight?

VOYO: I don't know . . . I'll go for a walk, maybe pick something up . . .

STEVE: OK. I'll maybe join you later. Where are you going?

VOYO: Going! Where's to go in this fucking town? Only fucking place to go is fucking disco. So I go to disco. You want to come?

STEVE: I'll join you later.

VOYO: OK.

    (Stands and goes to stage left of JOHN.)

    John, you want to go to disco?

JOHN: No, I think I'll stay here.

VOYO: OK, fuck it, I go by myself pick up nice chiquita . . .

    (Exits stage left.)

    (Music comes up as VOYO leaves and KAREN enters dancing from stage left. She dances to WILL and pulls his hat off, teasing him and dancing downstage left. WILL gets off his stool and follows her, and then KAREN throws the hat back to him. Music is still loud as the dialogue begins.)

KAREN: (Shouting over music) Hey, where'd your friend go?

STEVE: (Shouting too) He went to meet someone.

KAREN: He didn't say much.

STEVE: He's Russian . . . He doesn't understand English . . .

KAREN: He's Russian! Hey, what's he do?

STEVE: He works with me – we're together in this picture . . .

    José, could you please turn the music down!

JOHN: (As the music comes down) José, come on!

KAREN: Do you know Stallone?

STEVE: Yeah . . . I have to work with him.

KAREN: He's got a real beautiful wife . . .

STEVE: Did you read that in a magazine?

KAREN: No . . . somebody told me . . . or I read it . . .

WILL: John, what's the call tomorrow?

JOHN: Eight a.m.

KAREN: So you play a Russian?

STEVE: Yeah . . .

KAREN: Do a Russian accent for me . . .

STEVE: (Hesitates, then in a Russian accent) I am pleased to meet you . . .

KAREN: (Laughing) Hey, that's good . . . That's very convincing . . . Can I sip your margarita? Just a sip?

STEVE: Sure.

KAREN: (To BARMAN) Straw please!

(BARMAN gives KAREN a straw, and she drains the drink loudly.)

I ran in the sea today . . . I got my shorts all wet . . . I went shopping and bought this ring . . . and bought these shorts . . . I'm ready for a jungle trek . . . Ha! Ha! Ooh, look! I've got sand all over my legs and feet . . .

STEVE: You should take a bath . . .

KAREN: Is that an invitation?

STEVE: (Hesitating and unenthusiastic) Yeah . . .

KAREN: Oh! I've got sand everywhere . . .

(Blackout.)

(Music comes up with blackout, and when lights come back on the music comes down and STEVE and KAREN have changed positions slightly.)

STEVE: Sorry . . .

KAREN: It was nice.

STEVE: You sure?

KAREN: Yeah, really it was great . . . You felt just . . .

STEVE: OK!

KAREN: Come on . . . I've had a good time . . . Where are my cigarettes? Shit! Where's my handbag! I left my handbag here in the bar before!

STEVE: It'll still be here . . .

KAREN: Shit! I left everything in it. My driver's licence, social security, my boyfriend's picture . . . shit!

STEVE: I didn't see you with it before!

KAREN: Shit! I had everything in it . . .

STEVE: You took my arm as we left . . . You didn't have a bag . . .

KAREN: 'Cause I left it in the bar . . .

STEVE: I didn't see one . . . I mean, they'll find it if it's here . . .

The Mexicans are honest. They'll give it in . . .

KAREN: Oh shit! . . . You got to be kidding!

STEVE: (Still worried) Was it OK? . . .

KAREN: (Dull) Yeah, it was great . . . (To BARMAN.) Hey did you find a bag in here? It was about a half-hour ago . . . forty minutes tops.

BARMAN: Sorry, señorita . . . there's nothing here.

KAREN: Not now! But maybe someone handed it over . . .

BARMAN: No, sorry.

KAREN: (Furious) Then take my room number – take my room number, or I'll have your ass. *Pronto rapido!*

BARMAN: I'm sorry, señorita . . . There's no bag here!

KAREN: These guys are crazy, I swear . . . Where's the manager? I left my fucking bag here half an hour . . . maybe forty minutes tops . . . Now please take my number and call the police! . . . Maybe somebody took it there. I had everything in there!

STEVE: How much did you have in it?

KAREN: There was no money in it . . . it was personal shit you can't replace! Oh shit! What a fucking night!

STEVE: Sorry about that . . .

KAREN: Yeah . . . if you hadn't smiled at me, I wouldn't have lost my bag. I had pictures and my fucking driver's licence . . . My sister's gonna kill me!

BARMAN: If somebody hands it in . . . I will call you . . .

KAREN: Yeah, OK. Thanks . . . you'd better!

STEVE: Look, I feel responsible . . .

KAREN: Yeah, if you hadn't smiled at me I would still have my bag! (Exits downstage right.)
(Blackout.)

(Music comes up during blackout, and WILL goes to stand downstage right. Music comes down as he starts to talk.)

WILL: I just came in the bar . . . I was walking past . . . I thought, 'Shall I go in or not?' . . . And you're here. (Laughs and points to STEVE.) This is great! I didn't work today. I didn't know what to do . . . I didn't feel like going to the beach at

La Questa. I just didn't feel like it . . . I felt out of it . . . like
I didn't deserve it . . . I would have loved it . . . I mean, I
love it down there. But, I dunno, I just hung around this
awful beach – just walked up and down – and then I went
downtown for a coffee. I felt desperate – like out of it. You
went to La Questa? (Points at STEVE.) Was it Beautiful
there? Did you see those sunsets? You just sit there and can
meditate for hours. Stare at those great breakers rolling in.
No tourists. No americans down there. Just peace.

STEVE: José, may I have just a little more tequila?

WILL: Yeah, I'll have a vino tinto, *Roga*. You went down there,
eh? I nearly went. I got up . . . looked at the day, but felt I
didn't deserve it. I felt out of it, so I walked around and had a
coffee . . . and was walking back when I thought, 'Why not
try the bar?' . . . And you're here! Man, this is great!

STEVE: José, just a soupçon . . .

WILL: You know that chick you were speaking to? She's a cock-
teaser. I saw her in the pool yesterday, and she smiled and
came on strong like she was in to me, you know? She lightly
touched my thigh as she spoke . . . in the pool . . . I just
dived in and, as I surfaced, there she was . . . You know, I
haven't been out with a woman in three weeks.

JOHN: Welcome to the club, pal!

WILL: Like . . . this is Acapulco. You know what I'm saying? Not
even been out with one . . . I had a hard on and I wanted to
put it somewhere and then I saw her talking to the other guys
like I was just a piece of furniture . . . I came out of my hotel
this morning . . . you know . . . to get a coffee . . . and that
stunt guy was walking into the coffee-shop with four chicks!

JOHN: No shit? Get outta here!

WILL: Four! I couldn't believe it . . . Four of them. God, you
know your mind plays tricks. Fantasies of having the
four . . .

BARMAN: (To WILL) More nuts. (Puts a bowl of nuts on to the
bar.)

WILL: Thanks . . . one at a time . . . So I followed him into the
coffee-shop and listened at a discreet distance . . . and what a

piece of shit I heard . . . I immediately went off them. Somehow you know when you hear the stark reality of their minds. I felt repulsed. I couldn't go near them, so I felt down. I was walking past and I thought, 'Why not come in here?' . . . And like magic . . .

JOHN: Steve, can I get a light?

STEVE: Sure.

(Lights JOHN's cigarette.)

JOHN: Thanks.

WILL: You know, Steve, you're the only person that I can relate to in the whole fucking film . . .

STEVE: Is that right?

WILL: The others! That guy playing the sergeant . . . fuck him . . . And that fucking stand-in! I walked past her trailer one morning and she looked nice. You know . . . kind of pretty. So I said, 'Hey, you're looking real pretty today.' And do you know what she said? 'Oh, gimme a break!' I was just being friendly . . . She thinks because I'm playing a POW that I'm scum . . .

JOHN: You're scum because you think you're scum. Because you were hired in Mexico not Hollywood and paid in pesos not dollars.

WILL: You look like scum! . . . locked up in the wooden cage . . .
(JOHN coughs.)
You should stop smoking, man . . . like some kind of animals . . . You know this is such a goyische picture . . . there's not a Jew in the whole company except me . . . and of course you (To STEVE.) But we're not like Jews . . . not like those Jews that worry all the time and are accountants . . . We're tough . . . I'm a tough Brooklyn Jew and they know it . . . you know . . . they can't mess around with me. You are tough too. You came off the streets, right?

STEVE: José, just a tad more . . .

WILL: Stallone's tough, but underneath, you know, Stallone's a very vulnerable guy. He's an Italian. The Jews and the Italians get on. What did you do today? (To STEVE.) . . . Luis, can I get a little more vino?

STEVE: I've not been to the john in the whole of Mexico . . . I wait and hold it until I get back to the hotel . . . It stinks here . . . everything stinks . . . So I went out to La Questa and saw the sunset . . . The clouds moved slowly . . . bloody . . . at the edges . . . like a knife had stabbed the big belly of a cloud . . . and it was slowly going pink and then red . . . I walked back in the dark . . . There were huge craters in the road from the hurricane, so I walked a bit and the sky was like shrieking and the clouds were now bolting home looking ragged and torn . . . There's a lagoon on one side and the sea on the other, and the sea was all rough and the lagoon was like a sheet of glass . . . I walked, and there was junk everywhere . . . mounds of old rotting coconuts and fruit that had been left to the pigs . . . and the lizards were flicking in and out as I passed by . . . I heard them scuffling away as they felt my footsteps . . .

JOHN: José, do you have any Scotch?

BARMAN: Sure . . .

JOHN: No, I mean real Scotch . . .

BARMAN: Johny Walker?

JOHN: OK.

STEVE: I came to the end of the road – there was like a jungle on one side, with tall palms and some dirty old huts and a few tables where you could eat, and some kids were swimming around in the sunset . . .

WILL: Oh the sunsets are beautiful . . .

STEVE: There's a café there called Steve's Place . . .

JOHN: I know it . . .

STEVE: You can sit there and drink and watch the sunset . . . The kitchen's thick with flies, it's all open, dogs and cats sniffing around, and somebody's always eating something indescribable, but the fish was fucking great! Under a palm umbrella I had the red snapper . . . it was laid out on the plate like an offering . . . surrounded by sliced tomatoes and onions and under a napkin were hot tortillas made out of flour . . . Or are they made from corn?

JOHN: Sometimes they're made from corn too . . .

STEVE: So as I sat and watched the sea tearing itself into little pieces against the sand, I prised a piece of fish off with my fork – it pulled away easily . . . beautifully cooked – and wrapped it in the hot tortilla, perched a tomato on it, some onions and folded it. Then I added some salsa – you know, that hot sauce that goes straight for your arsehole, burns a road right through you . . .

JOHN: (To WILL) You hungry?

WILL: Yeah. (Then to BARMAN.) Is the restaurant open?

BARMAN: No, it's too late. Try the grill.

STEVE: So I sat and shooed away the flies and excavated the fish until I came to the head . . . don't like to get near anything that has a fucking face on it . . . But two little kids came and asked for the head like it was a luxury for them . . . They snapped it off the spine of the fish and chewed into it, eyes and all. Boy, they were so happy. They were laughing and chewing the head since it tasted good to them, and they were looking at me and laughing as if I'd been stupid and thrown away a great treat.

JOHN: Oh, that's the best part for the Mexicans . . .

STEVE: Then the kids left and a dog chewed the bones and he left and then columns of ants finished off the rest . . . The sun was by this time slowly sinking into the sea . . . like the weight of it was too much. It sank like a bloated belly . . . bulging even more as it sank, then scorched the sea up and plunged down deep.

JOHN: Do you want to do the grill, then?

WILL: No, I hate that fucking place . . .

STEVE: So I paid and left and walked a bit. The cafés were all lit up, their kitchens all open and frying and cooking and chopping tops off coconuts and this guy had this really fucking sharp machete and he sliced the top off coconuts like he was taking off a skull – and I drank it. It tasted sweet and strange. Then I caught a cab and came back. You're right, though (To WILL) – the sunset was gorgeous. Yes . . . like a multicoloured tropical flower, or like you took a huge sword and stabbed the sea and it spewed blood everywhere with drips hanging off the clouds.

WILL: Sounds like you had a good day . . .
(Blackout.)

STEVE: José – *Porquito mas, por favor*.
(Music comes up with lights. KAREN enters stage left and crosses to downstage centre.)

KAREN: (To BARMAN.) Have you found my bag yet?

BARMAN: We have your number, señorita . . . When we find it, we will call you.
(KAREN exits downstage right. There is loud talking and then a freeze.)

JOHN: (Shouting.) Of course I'm in a cage, that's right – but I'm working . . . I'm earning . . . So what I've no lines? But at least I'm near to something going on . . . (To BARMAN.) Jose, give me another Corona . . .

WILL: Make that two.

JOHN: Listen, my friend . . . we POWs are very important people, and we must sit in that cage all day and concentrate . . .

WILL: You can say what you like . . . we're still the scum . . .
(BARMAN gives him a beer.)
I wanted a Corona . . .

BARMAN: No Corona. He had the last Corona (Points to JOHN.)

WILL: . . . the background – $500 per week and a 'per diem'. So think what you like . . . if it makes you feel better, but I know the truth . . . we're the peons cast in Mexico 'cause it's cheaper to pay us in pesos than fly actors from Hollywood. That's the fucking truth!

JOHN: That's in your mind . . .

WILL: Get out of here!

JOHN: You're the outcast because it's in your mind to be an outcast . . . 'I've no lines. I'm a POW and a piece of shit.' . . . Well, that's in your head . . . I'm important in this movie . . . The director saw a lot of people for these parts in Mexico City and said, 'You're it! You're working on Rambo.' Hey, Will, they're not going to use bums as POWs that Stallone's risking his life to save, right? . . . I'm working, and proud to be in it.

STEVE: José, cigarettes please.

BARMAN: What kind of cigarettes you want?

STEVE: What kind do you have?

BARMAN: We have Lucky, Camel, Marlboro. What kind you want?

STEVE: I'll have Marlboro.

BARMAN: Hard pack or soft?

STEVE: Hard.

BARMAN: Red or white?

STEVE: White.

BARMAN: Regular or hundreds?

STEVE: Regular.

BARMAN: (Looking) Sorry (Slaps his forehead), We're out! Here have hundreds.

(BARMAN lights a cigarette for STEVE.)

WILL: You know the scene where the tarantula walked over my leg? . . . Just took a slow walk, and the director says, 'What's in your mind now?' What's in my fucking mind! Nothing. I'm nearly dead, locked up for ten years in a cage . . . What's in my fucking mind? 'Nothing.' I felt nothing, I told him . . . He said, 'Keep your eyes open and hold your hands like this.' (Puts his hands up, palms facing upstage centre.) What the fuck does that mean? Like this . . . and keep my eyes open. And then they put the spider there . . .

JOHN: He can't direct, anyone can see that!

WILL: That's for sure . . . So we do the shot . . . (To BARMAN) Can I get a clean ashtray here? . . . So we do the shot and the spider walks over me. He just walks and walks, and when he came to my flesh . . . he stopped, like he knew there was something different. He crawled down the cloth and felt safe, but when it came to my flesh . . . it felt warm . . . He didn't know how to handle it . . . He kinda lifted his leg up like he was stepping on hot coals . . .

JOHN: There are too many directors on this movie . . .

WILL: I know . . . So he said, 'Cut,' and came screaming over . . .

'What was in your mind?' he said. I said, 'Nothing.' I mean, I was dead. 'You ruined the bloody shot . . . you moved your thumb!' I moved my thumb . . . What does this mean, I moved my thumb? . . . I'm lying there doing what I was told . . . I'm holding my fingers like he said, and I moved my thumb . . . He's screaming at me . . . 'What are you doing? . . . This is Panavision!' I ruined his shot . . .

JOHN: That's 'cause you're an outcast – he senses you don't care.

WILL: But I care . . . I do . . . I care desperately . . . I'm an actor . . . I've got one line . . . 'He's dead now.' So what? That's OK, I'm working . . . I'm not an outcast . . . Nah, it's the people . . . the people here that make you feel like that . . .

JOHN: Oh, that's shit! You do that . . . You've got to think of yourself as God . . .

WILL: Oh sure!

JOHN: That's what you have to do. You're as good as anyone – you don't think enough of yourself . . . I told Stallone . . . I went up to him . . . I said, 'You look like a man with a problem.' He said, 'You're right, John!' I said, 'Look at yourself! What you're making here is a Tarzan movie . . . that's all.' I told him . . . he lacks culture.

WILL: You said that to him?

JOHN: You were there . . . Weren't you there when I said that?

WILL: I was sitting near, but I didn't hear what you were saying . . . I wasn't straining my ears.

JOHN: I said to him . . . 'You're searching for something else, but you're surrounded by all these bums . . . these heavies . . . all this muscle . . . But inside there's a man trying to get out.'

WILL: You said that to him?

JOHN: No . . . I didn't exactly say that . . . Thanks . . . What I said was, 'You're looking for something. You lack culture.' I did say that. He said, 'You're right, John.' He said, 'You're my man in Mexico.' . . . And that heavy punk that's always around him, wiping his ass for him, said, 'Leave him alone.' I said, 'Listen, I can speak to whom I like. This is a free society.'

WILL: Maybe he asked his man to tell you because he didn't like to tell you himself. Maybe he was sick of punks like coming up and giving him advice.

JOHN: Oh that's bullshit! He loved it . . . He's starving for a bit of human contact . . . The whole place is filled with ass-lickers! I mean, he was glad for someone to come up to him and talk to him straight. I told him . . . I said, 'You need to get back on the track.' But he's surrounded by these toadies. He can't see . . . Like that guy making the documentary. He doesn't know his tit from his asshole. I said, 'What are you shooting?' And he said, 'I don't know yet.' 'Don't know.' I know more about fucking Mexico than he'll ever know . . . I live here and he's making a documentary about filming in Mexico and he hasn't got a *clue!*

STEVE: Yes, but he's making the doc and you're in a bloody cage. (WILL laughs.)

JOHN: What's that supposed to mean?

STEVE: I mean the man's got a budget of maybe half a million to make a thirty-minute doc, direct it . . . travel to Mexico first class . . . have meetings with the producers . . . have the ear of Stallone . . . And where are you? You're sitting in a cage. You're sitting in a cage as fucking background for the film . . . So who listens or cares about what you think? (WILL laughs hysterically.)

JOHN: Yes, but that's only for now, my friend . . . This movie is a matter of convenience, and it suits my purpose . . . I have an office in Mexico and I make Mexican documentaries . . .

STEVE: So what the fuck are you doing in a cage? (WILL and STEVE laugh.)

JOHN: All right, go ahead and laugh! Things are quiet at the moment, but let me assure you, my friend, at six p.m. I am out of that cage and I am making some very useful contacts. I won't always be working in a cage!

STEVE: You will! You'll always be in a cage like he'll always be an outcast! (Points at WILL.)

WILL: (Sotto voce, turning away) Fuck you!

JOHN: But as I said, this is expedient and I have already suggested an idea for Stallone . . .

WILL: Why don't you let him speak? You might learn something!

JOHN: I know we're in cages now. We're all in cages – you're in a cage of your own making . . . Stallone's in a cage . . . Look at him, buried in muscle and a victim of the very thing he succeeded in.

WILL: Let the man speak. He was telling us something . . . Go on, you were saying something, Steve . . . Maybe we can learn something here!

STEVE: What I mean is . . . you live all the time just for the present

JOHN: (Raising bottle) Yes, live in the present for tomorrow will take care of itself . . . Live in the now . . . Enjoy your life.

STEVE: Yes, but somehow in the present we make preparations for the future . . . we build houses for the future . . .
(BARMAN offers him a drink.)
We put a brick down and then another . . . But you want what you can make now . . . like a nice juicy steak, get smashed and fuck your head off . . . because you can do it and finish it in one night . . .

JOHN: Sounds great!

STEVE: You only want what you can do now, and so tomorrow you will face the same possibilities . . . (To BARMAN.) José, not quite so much salt for next time . . . You want excitement and buzz, get pissed and shout . . . maybe go to the disco all night and then find a convenient receptacle for your excess semen.

JOHN: If I'm lucky!

STEVE: I mean, that's all you talk about . . . well, *all right*, not all you talk about, but it takes up a lot of your time . . .
Eventually your dick becomes your salvation . . .

JOHN: Absolutely!

STEVE: Then sleep . . . get up . . . rub your eyes, eat, jump in the studio car . . . what a great night I had last night . . . and then get back in your cage all content. It's natural.

JOHN: So what's wrong with that?

STEVE: It's natural because it's the one thing you can do that has the total world in it. You're like a dirty little animal that lives for the now . . .

JOHN: (Laughing) That's me, sweetheart!

STEVE: That's good, you say. But you carry no concept for the future.

JOHN: Live in the now, mister!

STEVE: (To BARMAN) José, would you kindly whip up another of these chaps please?

JOHN: While you're at it, do you have some milk?

BARMAN: No milk, only Pepto-Bismol.

STEVE: I mean, it's good . . . you rub the magic lamp and the genie appears . . .

WILL: My genie hasn't appeared much lately.

STEVE: And it takes away the emptiness, and then you're back in the cage.

JOHN: Listen, my friend, my life is full . . . It's not empty . . . it's packed every day.

WILL: Let him finish!

(BARMAN gives STEVE a margarita.)

STEVE: There's rather too much salt in this.

BARMAN: Sorry.

STEVE: It's a good life and it feels rich, but there's no pain . . .

JOHN: Who needs it!

STEVE: It's pain that makes you think. You know, a bit of pain makes you aware of other things than the shit you spew out . . .

JOHN: Thank you, professor!

STEVE: (Angry) Pain makes you think of life. What it means. Your appetite makes you feel, and that needs immediate satisfying. Pain makes you think of how to stop the pain . . .

WILL: (To BARMAN) Can I get a shot?

STEVE: That's why you're in a cage . . . You see, the man making the documentary woke up one morning feeling pain . . . He had to express his life on this planet . . . What could he do to express his voice? It gave him pain, made him reclusive, antisocial, pensive, introverted . . . He went to shrinks . . . It was a pain he had to solve, so he thought, planned, observed and analysed . . . became aware, and made telephone calls to important men in the industry. Now these men, who have little time for fools, cocked an ear and invited him to sit in

offices where secretaries are seldom idle and fax machines are
continuously spewing out faxes. They ate lunch, discussed
formulas and budgets, then over the Caesar salad they reached
agreements, and called each other by their Christian names
and left a 20 per cent tip! And lo and behold funds were set
flowing into this project . . . And then one day he flew Western
Airlines, first class, to Acapulco with a TV crew and started
shooting in the jungle of Mexico, a documentary about
Stallone . . . And in the background, in a dirty cage, which
stays mainly out of focus, are five POWs . . . or should I say
OOWAs?

JOHN: OOWAs?

STEVE: Out of work fucking actors, ducky!

WILL: You and me, pal!

STEVE: And in a coffee break, one of these grimy, one-notch-over-
a-crowd artistes comes up and says, 'What line are you taking
in this?' And the chap, not wishing to get involved in the
mêlée or rabble that makes up a movie set, says, 'I'm not sure
yet.' . . . Then the monkey in the case, released for its night of
monkey chat and leaping about, squeals with delight. 'He
doesn't know!', when in fact the man didn't wish to talk to a
monkey!

WILL: You see . . . I told you you'd learn something! You're a
monkey! (Laughs loudly.)

JOHN: (Laughing sarcastically, gets off stool and stands facing
WILL) Aagh! Come on, man – let's go to the disco . . .

WILL: Hey . . . we're just teasing you . . .

JOHN: (Stands downstage left, facing STEVE) You know, Steve,
maybe you can't live in the now! . . . When did you last get
smashed? . . . You know, I've never seen you laugh . . . except
tonight at my expense. This is the first time I've seen him
laugh since I've been here.

(Music comes up and VOYO enters stage left to left of JOHN.)

VOYO: Hello, guys! (All say hello cheerfully for a few seconds.) I
walked up and down . . . nothing!

(VOYO starts to armwrestle JOHN) Aaargh! (Loses wrestle,
others cheer.)

I need a woman . . . Tonight I must fuck! . . . Nice little
chiquita . . . lovely! Maybe nice Mexican woman . . . Not go
with prostitute . . .

JOHN: Yeah?

VOYO: (TO BARMAN) Give me margarita . . . Yesterday with
prostitute . . . She was nice . . . she made me bargain fifty
dollars OK, but all night long beautiful . . . Come on, guys –
let's go eat something, my friend, something nice and hot
. . . like enchiladas with chilli sauce . . . Good for you . . .
Then nice girl . . . This one here in the lobby, I fuck her
already . . . Nice . . . very nice, all night long prick like horse
. . . But it was not the best time of the month . . .

WILL: Oh you're disgusting!

VOYO: Aaah! The sheets . . .
(There are miscellaneous jeers of 'Disgusting' etc.)
The chambermaid had to clean up . . . Oh my god! Still,
they're used to it – it's their job . . .

WILL: (Jousting) Oh come on!

VOYO: Come on, guys let's go get something to eat and then to
disco.
(Music comes up and STEVE, WILL, JOHN and VOYO mime
getting ready, dancing, combing hair. They dance and
strut off stage left.)
(Blackout.)

(Next night. Lights come up and WILL enters stage left with
STEVE to downstage left, talking.)

WILL: So I went to the disco and didn't score with anything . . .
It's been over four weeks and I haven't even been out with a
girl . . . I mean just to sit in a restaurant and talk, you know.
Just talk. That would be good . . . Rap a bit . . . sound off
. . . have a little drink . . . Civilized . . . Not like Voyo – 'I
must have fuck . . . Me have cock like horse prick!' The
disco was poison. It's the worst place in the world with that
jerk Mexicano pop shit. So I left. I couldn't take any more.
You had to shout in that dump. I mean, its the lowest
common denominator of human intelligence and I'm

supposed to find life there . . . So I just walked down the
street . . . It was hot like it always is . . . That hot air that
wraps itself around you . . . and you can't sleep . . . And so I
walked and this woman came up to me and she asked . . . you
know . . . she asked if I wanted to go with her. I said, 'How
much?' And she said 5,000 pesos. That's about twenty-five
dollars . . . What the fuck, I was dying for a woman. I mean,
I could have stuck it in a tree . . . You know, I was desperate
for a good fuck . . . You guys know how it is . . . huh? I get
pretty intense, you notice . . . So OK, she was British . . .
one of his countrymen. (Points to STEVE.) Yeah, some
hooker from England, making a living in Acapulco. She was
a fucking mess, right, but she was OK. Ain't that funny? . . .
Who do I meet in Acapulco but some English girl walking
down a hot street at three in the morning. She had a tooth
missing here. (Points.) So she came back. But it was a
terrible fuck . . . She was terrible, but I enjoyed it. She just
lay there like she was dead, so I ploughed into her. I wanted
a real dirty fuck and I just got on with it. It didn't matter any
more . . . but what a slag . . . What a disgusting British
hooker in Acapulco with a fucking front tooth missing! And
so I fucked her and she just lay there . . . and like I was in
a way glad for her to be there . . . just to have the company.
She passed out . . . and I was going up the wall . . . I couldn't
sleep . . . It was hot, and I got this slag was sleeping in my
nice clean bed. But I had to get up at six a.m. to go to work
. . . It was a work day for me . . . I said, 'Come on, get up . . .
Get out of here . . . I gotta work.' She was out to the world
. . . So I took her by the ears. I said, 'Look, you gotta get the
fuck outa here! . . .

STEVE: No! . . . By the ears?

WILL: Yeah . . . I swear it was the only thing I could get hold of
that was showing above the sheets . . . I got hold of her ears
. . . I said, 'I got to work!' So she got up and left with me,
and we split up in the foyer so no one would see us together
. . . But downstairs I see her queuing for extra work! She was
trying to get on the movie!

STEVE: You have to be careful . . .

WILL: Yeah . . . She was really a slag . . . So I went to the doctor on the set . . . (TO BARMAN.) Can I get a vino here, Luis? (To STEVE.) What are you drinking?

STEVE: Margarita.

WILL: I said, 'Gimme a shot' . . . He said, 'Wait. Give it a couple of days . . . and see . . . Don't panic.'

STEVE: Be careful, you might get herpes . . .

WILL: I had it, it's psychological! It's a piece of shit! . . . I had it and worried myself sick . . . I went to the doctors . . . You know how you know? You get these little blisters on your Dick, and the next day it becomes a sore and it hurts when you fuck. Everybody makes a big deal over it like you got the plague. Everybody worries so much they keep bringing it back. They're always in stress . . . But I beat it. I was strong . . . I looked at that herpes, I said, 'Fuck you!', and it went away. It never once came back. Yeah . . . Oh, once it did come back after three months – same thing. But I said to myself, 'I'm gonna fuck no matter what.' And it went away . . . When I worried it came back, but when I said, 'I'll fuck with it or without it' it disappeared . . . And my woman who I was living with at the time . . . not once did she catch it, Steve, I swear to God!

(VOYO enters stage left with JOHN following.)

VOYO: Hello guys . . . Oh my God! Last night I didn't sleep . . .

WILL: What happened?

VOYO: Drinks for everyone. (There is miscellaneous ordering.) Small one . . . little chiquita in the green top . . . she came back and stayed all night . . . I fuck like horse . . . huge horse prick . . . and do everything. (Mimes with tongue.) Oh my God! Beautiful! It's beautiful! It's what you need . . . be free and enjoy . . . Good food and drink and nice lady, that's life! You think Stallone can do that? Sure he'd like . . . go to disco . . . find nice chiquita. But he can't, he's trapped with those musclemen . . . But they are weak . . . not really strong at all . . . just puffed up with steroids . . . unnatural . . . I am natural . . . real strength . . .

WILL: Yeah . . .

VOYO: Strength . . .

JOHN: Right . . .

VOYO: I have real strength . . .

JOHN: Yeah, we know!

VOYO: When I was little, I would run up mountains in Yugoslavia
. . . I lifted huge barrels in my work . . . My legs are like
tree-trunks . . . Not from gym with weight and faggoty pop
music for homosexuals who want to look beautiful . . .
Weights not give you real strength . . . In fight, I kill these
bodybuilders . . . or karate experts. In street, they are
nothing . . . I say to stunt men . . . 'Hit me. Go on, hit me.'
But they dare not. 'Punch me in the stomach.' . . . But they
frightened . . . I kill them . . . they know that!

JOHN: I'm just exhausted . . . I didn't sleep a wink last night . . .
Fucked all night long – those chicks from the boutique.

VOYO: I fuck the little one in green . . . You know, she sweet. All
night long, prick like horse . . .
(Mime. WILL and JOHN join in for a while. There is
laughing.)
Steve, what you do?

STEVE: I walked down the street . . . It was a hundred degrees out
there . . . It must have been . . .

JOHN: It was fucking hot . . . I know that . . . .

STEVE: The sea was brown from the hurricane . . . like it was full
of shit and mud from the sewage overflow . . . Nobody swam
in it . . . except me . . . Mexicans and their families . . . All
the kids threw themselves into the sea . . . The mothers went
in with their dresses on . . . The tourists stayed inside the
hotel pool and ordered big fruity cocktails and rubbed
themselves with oil. They kept stroking themselves, first one
and then the partner, and you could tell by the way they
applied the oil how much they valued their flesh.

WILL: Vino.

STEVE: Outside it was hotter than hell, but I walked for a while,
like thinking what to do . . . and I passed a mother and child,
like it was familiar . . . the outstretched arm, the baby in the

other arm, sleeping or just half listless . . . And then the
others . . . all the outstretched arms down the street . . . like
branches . . . outstretched . . . And the gesture . . . putting
their fingers to their mouth . . .

JOHN: Don't let them fool you, my friend . . . This is their way of
life. To beg is not dishonourable to them . . . They feed off
the tourists . . .

STEVE: So I sat and had a coffee and saw eyes everywhere . . .
dark eyes following and watching me eat . . . And then
they'd come up . . . like dogs begging for something to eat,
or selling a little plate with a picture on it. So I bought a little
plate and then another came up and then another . . . They
came with their large brown eyes and outstretched hands . . .
begging, cajoling, wheedling . . . trying to sell me chewing-
gum . . .

VOYO: José, cold beer!

STEVE: They had these little boxes of chiclets . . . They tried to
sell me a piece, and the box was already looking old and
broken . . . And the mother would be waiting in the distance
. . . like she was pimping off the only thing she had – the eyes
of her children . . . 'Cause the tourists couldn't resist . . .
They're too much like dolls, maybe three or four years old
. . . little brown dolls. There was this smell everywhere – as I
walked I could smell it – like the sewers had broken down.
And nobody walked except the Mexicans, and the shit smell
grew stronger . . . like the whole town was built on a great
cake of shit and was on the breaking point. And then it was
too hot, so I sat for a while and more kids came by, like
moths around a flame. And the cats were so thin . . . they
looked like Hollywood starlets . . .

JOHN: I'm going for a piss. (Exits stage left.)

STEVE: There were little stalls selling dead bits of fish that you
daren't eat, like the slimy bits of offal that you would prefer
not to think about . . . they were cooked and chopped up
with onions and rolled into tortillas . . . Some shelled things
that looked like sea lice – little sluglike things. So this man
was selling corn on the cob. He was sitting on a little wooden

box with his cobs – maybe a couple of dozen – sat there all
night, facing the street, the exhaust pipes from the buses
belching all over him, and he waited and waited . . . And this
was his life for ever.

JOHN: (Entering stage left) You're romanticizing. He enjoys his
life. He has his friends and community . . . Don't project
your Western lifestyle on him. He's happy.

STEVE: That was his life. And I walked past and saw the wooden
box, and he had laid it out to be attractive . . . He laid out the
corns like they were gold, and in the corner of the box was a
sauce for the corn. And they were sixty pesos . . . that's
thirty cents. And if he sold them all he'd make three dollars
fifty. But he would have to sit there for maybe seven hours.
That's fifty cents per hour, and then he would have to be
fucking lucky!

JOHN: It's probably pin money for him. He's got a job somewhere
during the day, my friend. It's probably a way of making a
few pesos . . . He's happy like that. He's happier than
you . . .

STEVE: Is this the fruit of Christian civilization? So that an Indian
can stand outside the Acapulco Plaza Hotel . . . all day long
. . . in the heat . . . just in the hope that a bored tourist
might, might with that greed that all tourists have, that
desire to consume, might buy something from him . . . That
thing being an elephant badly carved out of onyx . . .

JOHN: José, can I get some pretzels?

BARMAN: Nuts . . .

STEVE: But he won't sell it, because there are hundreds and
hundreds outside these charnel houses like the Acapulco
Plaza Hotel . . . So when he wakes up in the morning his
hope and future lie in that little elephant.

JOHN: Oh come on . . . You're talking history . . . *La quanta, por
favor* . . . I'll get it . . . How much?

BARMAN: (Totals up bill in Spanish) That's twelve dollars, thank
you my friend.
(There is general discussion of 'I'll get it' etc., and then
JOHN pays. They all freeze.)

JOHN: It was the last day . . . At last we were getting out of the cage. We'd been in there for four weeks, and we were being rescued. Heyyy! Well, ten years according to the script . . . So Stallone comes over and springs us . . . 'Come on,' he said . . . 'Come on out of there.' So we dash out . . . But we haven't been out of the cage in ten years . . .

WILL: No, fifteen . . . He said fifteen!

JOHN: Fifteen years we'd been in that cage . . . maybe fifteen years and you'd stumble out . . . right? You'd fall out, you'd crawl out . . . But we had to dash out and run! . . . Run! We'd crawl, we'd be all feeble and frightened – 'Hey, what's going on?' . . . all confused. Maybe we'd even try to go back to the cage . . . You know . . . it's been fifteen fucking years, man. One guy would run back . . . yeah, to the cage . . . Maybe that's his home . . . the cage is what he *knew! At least he knew there he was safe!* But no, we'd dash out like we were rushing to get dinner at the Acapulco Plaza.

WILL: I saw the explosion . . . They were blowing up the camp . . . We were being saved . . . It was amazing!

JOHN: But the first assistant . . . the Englishman . . . said, 'Come out of the cage like you were leaving a Glasgow pub on a Saturday night . . . ' That was perfect . . . that was the image we needed!

WILL: The blast of the explosion was deafening . . . We were being saved . . . What would we do in that situation? . . . The director said, 'Do something . . . You're being saved . . . You're happy . . . You're crazy . . . You're getting out!' I tell you it was great – we were working at last.

JOHN: Not just background . . . Not just scenography . . .

WILL: No! We were actors . . . We had to do something . . . I hugged the prisoners . . . I hugged and kissed them . . . There were tears in my eyes . . . I was screaming . . . I put my hands through the bars like this (Mimes putting hand through.) . . . I put my fist through and shook it at the bastards. It felt great! I was happy . . . I was hugging and crying. And then that idiot . . .

(JOHN mimes idiot.)

. . . That other idiot in the cage had to copy me. He put his fist through the bars and did the same as me, the fucking moron . . .

(JOHN mimes moron.)

The fire was everywhere, the blaze was amazing . . . You felt it going through you, and the cameras were on us the whole time . . . You *had* to do something . . . And then Stallone came to get us out . . .

JOHN: 'Come on out of there!' He came up . . . big machine-gun . . . like a great phallus! . . .

WILL: He looked at me . . . For a moment he looked me right in the eye . . . There he was . . . sweatband round his forehead . . . muscles and veins bulging out . . . gripping a huge black machine-gun, an M-60, like a god . . . He looked like the angel of death . . . Sweat pouring out . . . muscles all flexed for action . . . this M-60 like a huge cock . . . (Shoots into audience with gun.) You're right, he looked me in the eye like he knew me, like he actually felt I was all right, and he said, 'Come on, come on . . . Move it . . . Let's go!' And he put his hand on my shoulder . . . and it felt good! . . . Like he was acknowledging what I had done . . . Maybe he touched the other prisoners as they came out – I didn't see – but he touched me, and it felt like a god was touching me, and it felt great! . . . You see, 'cause I was locked up in that stinking cage for fifteen years. I was in that shit and filth, and along comes this guy – hair flying and built like he was carved out of rock – and takes me away from all that . . . And we did the shot again and again and again, and he touched me on the shoulder each time – like it wasn't just an accident the first time . . . as if we had some sort of unspoken communication . . . I worked . . . It felt great . . . I'm high now . . . I'm high from it! . . . It's good to work . . . Luis, can I get a vino tinto?

VOYO: Great! I like to act . . . I want to act the big parts . . . Spartacus, Odysseus, Zorba . . . strong men. There's no strong men anymore. They are puffed up in expensive gyms in Hollywood. That Schwarzenegger, he is nothing . . . If I went to him and say, 'Fight,' he would turn away! . . . There used to be strong men . . . Anthony Quinn . . .

JOHN and WILL: Oh yeah!

VOYO: John Wayne – like a piece of mountain . . . Marlon Brando
. . . You believed them . . . Now they are nothing . . . In this
film I must pretend to be weak . . . How can Stallone kill me?
. . . How? . . . I kill him . . . I am much stronger than he . . .

JOHN: It's supposed to be acting . . .

VOYO: Yeah, I know . . . But the audience has got to believe . . .
He cannot beat me with fist . . . If he hit me on head with
hammer I just stand there . . . It must look real . . . People
aren't stupid . . . Wad you think – the American people all
stupid idiots? . . . They laugh . . . He goes, 'Boom! Boom!'
and I supposed to collapse? . . . They laugh . . . No, he must
use trick . . . like Odysseus . . . He use brains and escape
under sheep . . . So Stallone must use trick 'cause he cannot
beat me with fist . . . It's stupid . . . I'm like giant!

JOHN: Kirk Douglas . . .

VOYO: Right, Kirk Douglas!

JOHN: They could act!

VOYO: Oh my friend!

JOHN: Rod Steiger. (Does impersonation.) When he comes on
the set, the whole place lights up . . . He just comes on . . .
First take perfect . . . Two takes and that's enough . . . He
says, 'That's enough!'

JOHN: *Napoleon* . . .

WILL: *The Illustrated Man* . . .

JOHN: *Across the Bridge* . . . Shot that in Mexico.

WILL: God, he's a great actor!

JOHN: *The Pawnbroker* . . .

WILL: The scene in the cab . . . *On the Waterfront!*
(All three break out into a Marlon Brando impersonation –
WILL, then VOYO, then JOHN.)
'Charlie . . . I could have been somebody . . . I coulda had
class!' Great acting . . . You know what I'm saying . . . I'd
love to act – I mean act on the stage . . . I'm dying to act . . .
There's nothing like it . . . I love it . . . I'd work for nothing
. . . Naturally I gotta earn a living . . . but we start with

nothing. Schmucks *only* work for money, a warrior works for life! He'll work for nothing if it touches him on the soul . . . Pay the rent . . . that's all I ask.

VOYO: Spartacus, Odysseus, Zorba, Dostoyevsky!

JOHN: Dostoyevsky? . . . Oh come on, let's eat!

(ALL exit stage left, naming Mexican foods as if they were great actors.)

(Blackout.)

STEVE: I woke up . . . it was still dark . . . Like I was waking with the beat of others thousands of miles away, I lay in thought and was not here . . . I haven't been here since I've been here. I've been here only in the body, but my mind has been trapped elsewhere. It's been in a cold, dreary country . . . like it was pulled back into the fog . . . I awoke in the sun . . . I was like Frankenstein's monster . . . all there except for something missing . . . Like a soul that couldn't catch up with the body as the body flew through space . . . the wrench pulled it away like you pull the skin away from a fruit. I was there except in soul, so I watched the souls of others – I watched and observed them from my body . . . like I was secretly stealing bits of them to make up one of my own . . . I watched their passions and frustrations . . . their needs and joys so easily spilling out. I watched them and heard them, but I was in a block of ice . . . Their breath warmed me and made cracks in it sometimes . . . I awoke and it was dark, the dawn was just edging the darkness away and the sea was pounding against the shore . . . I heard the beating of my heart . . . I lay alone in a large bed without a soul to comfort me . . . I awoke like I was keeping time with another land. The bed was large, and there were drinks in the fridge which were replenished daily . . . The fishing nets were out and it was still dark . . . He was thrilled to be sitting in a cage . . . so excited . . . Stallone touched me! The day oozed slowly on to Acapulco Beach . . . Scuba diving or a one-day trip around the city . . . The stretch of beach was lined with huge hotels like ancient temples where you came to make your sacrificial

offerings . . . They lay around the pool like white slugs . . .
At four p.m. is volleyball in the pool . . .
(Music rises with lights, and VOYO , WILL and JOHN enter
stage left, music low as JOHN starts to talk.)

JOHN: I know the Mexicans . . . they can't be bought . . . They'll
give you anything and they'll take your money, but they
can't be bought . . . They'll say, 'Fuck off, gringo!' They
want respect. That's important to a Mexican . . . There are
lots of Mexicans in this movie and you notice they're all good
workers. But they must have respect. This film's costing
twenty-eight million dollars. That's the budget – twenty-
eight. It's no secret . . . I even read it in the *Acapulco News*.
And do you know what Sly's getting? Six million, or even
eight . . .

WILL: No . . . He's getting maybe four up-front.

JOHN: All right, so he's only getting four million. So he must have
made millions already . . .

WILL: Maybe another ten million from the 'Rocky' movies . . .

JOHN: All that money . . . But he invests it and makes more
money, and that creates labour, doesn't it! I'm doing all
right, do you want to know how much I'm getting? I'm
making $500 a week plus my per diem.
(STEVE laughs.)
And I'm saving money! I'm actually saving. Listen, it's like a
fortune that has no meaning. If it's three million it might as
well be four . . . And it's cheap to shoot in Mexico, so you
can save another few million . . . They get nothing here since
inflation . . . You know how much a labourer gets? My
friend, do you know? . . . To build one of those
condominiums? . . . Five dollars per day. He'll be happy to
shift cement for five dollars per day . . . 'cause that's all he
gets paid . . . So you can buy places cheap here. That's why
all those fucking yuppies pour into Mexico . . .
(They stop to eye an invisible woman crossing downstage
left to right. Catcalls – 'Hey, look at that!', 'Sling some over
here!', 'Hey, sweetheart!', 'Hey, I want you to have my
children!' etc.)

You can buy an apartment overlooking the sea you'll get for $20,000 or a palace for 40,000 and a couple of peons as staff . . . They'll do it for nothing. They come with the apartment to clean up . . . do your cooking . . . They're happy to do it!

STEVE: Like slaves . . . Better the master they know . . .

JOHN: No! It's in your mind they're slaves . . . They want to work for you . . . They're proud . . . They want to show you how good they can be . . . They don't *need* like you or the Western gringo – don't project your needs on to them . . . They're happy to show you their skills . . .

WILL: Yeah . . . Like that party on Sunday . . . Steve, we went to this party, given by those rich Mexicans, where all they wanted really were just a few actors from the set for decoration . . . And the slaves were skulking around the kitchen while the self-important slugs made small chat 'round the pool . . . Yeah, while the monkeys made their idiot chat and talked money and the biggest pile of bullshit I've ever heard . . . the Mexicans are sitting in the shadows preparing the food . . .

JOHN: They are happy, my friend . . . They are happier cooking in the kitchen and taking pride in the food than making small chat with the idiots outside . . . You're right . . .

WILL: I was there . . . These people talked shit from beginning to end . . . I couldn't hear it any more! . . . I felt sick . . . Then they had a game of throwing each other in the pool. Ha! Ha! Ha! . . . Luis, another vino . . . Why is it that so many people with money act like assholes?

STEVE: I know a few without money who do too!

WILL: And their faces were so ugly . . . Tell me, why are the very rich so very ugly? . . . The Indian peons are so beautiful, slim and agile . . .

JOHN: Don't be so fucking romantic!

WILL: If I had a choice of what to be. . . A rich and ugly white, or a poor and beautiful Indian . . . I know what I should be . . . 'Cause you can always get rich – or *maybe* you can – but if you are a fat, ugly, self-centred, greasy white bastard, it's very difficult to be beautiful. Hey, Luis, help me out here . . .

BARMAN: Thank you very much. It goes back to Cortés, the great
Spanish conqueror, who surrounded Mexico and starved
them out and then burned it to the ground . . . Montezuma,
the Aztec king, waited in his palace listening to the
messengers tell him news of the strange white men who were
half-horse and half-man. And they had never seen a horse
before . . . What do you think of that? They must be gods,
they thought. So Cortés marches in and stole the gold and the
treasures of the Aztecas and then he destroyed Mexico, which
was the most beautiful city in the world . . . But he gave them
Christianity . . . He raped the Indian women, but he gave
them Christianity . . . You cannot conquer any other way. If
you leave a people with their religion you will leave them with
a spark that will one day become a raging fire . . . and the
priests told them about Christ and that Christ was a man and
Mary his mother and God his father and the Aztecas were
confused by these three gods when Cortés said there was only
one, *un asshole grandiose*. Then they were told about eating
Christ on a biscuit and drinking his blood, and the Aztecas
said, 'We too eat the flesh of our enemies.' But they were
punished by the Spaniards for doing such terrible things . . .
Then they were confused by worshipping two sticks and three
gods. But in time . . . Now there is poverty and disease where
before there was none. The Aztecas had built highways, and
along these highways there were toilets – no shit, believe it or
not! There were toilets, and the waste was used as fertilizer
and so everything had a value . . . But then the Spanish
brought little glass beads and exchanged them for gold by
tricking the Indians into believing they were precious stones.
But the gold was not enough . . . Spain wanted to own the
whole goddam place, and so cut down the Indian . . . The
Indians wandered around confused. They had lost their city
and their gods and were offered instead two sticks to worship,
since they could not yet understand the new gods.
Convenient, no? . . . But out of the ashes of the past, a new
temple arose to celebrate the recreation of Mexico . . . the
Acapulco Plaza Hotel! What do you think about that?

(Shouting and clapping from WILL and JOHN.
KAREN enters stage left.)

KAREN: (To BARMAN) Have you found my fucking bag yet?

BARMAN: Oh si, señorita. Didn't they call you?

KAREN: No. Hand it over then!

BARMAN: It's at the front desk . . .

KAREN: Everything had better be in it!

BARMAN: Everything was in it – your licence, your pictures, your condoms . . .

KAREN: Fuck you! (Exits downstage right.)

BARMAN: Come on, guys – *está mañana*. I got to close the bar, gentlemen.

(GUYS all pay up – JOHN first, STEVE last.)

STEVE: (Crossing stage left, to left of JOHN) So you finish next week?

JOHN: Yeah, I think so . . . We're out of the cage now . . . We're doing the chopper scene.

STEVE: That's a relief, eh?

JOHN: You can't imagine what it's like . . . five of us in a cage . . .

STEVE: So you're free . . .

JOHN: Yeaahhh . . .

STEVE: What you gonna do?

JOHN: I'll head back for Mexico City . . . I've got this office there I was telling you about, and there's been a lot of work coming in . . . You know I make commercials . . . Sure, for Mexican TV, but since the peso was devalued it caught us all with our pants down.

STEVE: (To WILL) What about you?

WILL: I dunno. Maybe I'll go back to Mexico City . . . It was always good for me . . . I had this instinct to come . . . I can always escape to Mexico. I got married here, you know . . . We stayed at this amazing place near Oaxaca on the beach . . . Nothing – just nothing . . . Only the Indians, and you could hear the animals at night . . . When I need to escape I always come here . . . It's real . . . You know what I mean? If you ever want to look me up, I live in a small hotel in the Pink Zone. It's called Hotel Angelo . . . Five dollars a night

123

 . . . But I'm thinking of going to Paris to see Polanski . . .

STEVE: How will you do that?

WILL: Just go up to him . . . He's a man . . . he knows . . . Just
 say, 'I want to work for you . . .'

VOYO: (Getting up) OK guys, goodnight . . . I got big scene with
 chopper tomorrow.
 (ALL say 'Goodnight.' VOYO exits stage left.)

WILL: '. . . I've come 6,000 miles . . . I'd be a good pirate . . .'
 He's doing a movie on pirates . . .

JOHN: (Rising) Hey, I'm gonna split too . . . Goodnight, guys.
 (ALL say 'Goodnight.' JOHN exits stage left.)

WILL: He needs someone like me . . . 'Use me, Roman!' I'll find
 him . . . Shit! I won't go to a casting director, I'll find *him*. I
 hear he's a good guy . . . I'd be good in his film, in the galleys
 . . . Hey, don't you think I'd be a good pirate?

STEVE: Sure, why not? (Exits stage left.)

HARRY'S CHRISTMAS

Harry's Christmas was first performed at the Donmar Warehouse Theatre, London, in December 1985. The cast was as follows:

HARRY	Steven Berkoff
Director	Steven Berkoff
Set and Design	Manny Fagenblum

AUTHOR'S NOTE

There are many people for whom Christmas comes attended by the terrors of isolation, loneliness and enforced camaraderie. For the sociable it is a time for the mad scramble to organize as many encounters as possible lest we drop points in the stakes of popularity. With the innate laziness which has become part of the British heritage Christmas now seems to go on endlessly, engulfing New Year and more monstrous clambering on to the wagon of joyless mirth.

Christmas was never a festival I would particularly look forward to and those without families, separated, bereaved or just congenitally introverted find the spotlight of Christmas exposes a false sense of worth or an exaggerated sense of worthlessness as the meagre cards are counted. Harry is one of those whom the buffets of the world has left stranded on a barren shore and he is dealing with it for the last time. But it is an amalgam of many of us.

I played this play at the Donmar Theatre in 1985/6 and no play I have done received so many responses from people who found in Harry's dilemma and, may I say agony, echoes in their own lives.

The play is a monologue spoken by HARRY.

Time: Christmas. Place: A room
HARRY *is counting his Christmas cards.*

Four, five, six. That's all. That's the lot . . . but there's some
from last year . . . let's see. (*Looks through last year's.*) I could
maybe add a couple . . . No you shouldn't do that . . . that's silly
. . . to make it look better . . . who cares? But it looks a bit thin.
YOU WORRIED WHAT PEOPLE MIGHT THINK? Yeaah! PEOPLE
WHO MIGHT DROP IN, MIGHT THINK, POOR HARRY, NOT VERY
POPULAR? Something like that yeah. LOOK AT THE SIX CARDS
AND PITY YOU? Maybe, yeah maybe. THINK, WHAT HAS HIS
LIFE BEEN – TO HAVE SO FEW CARDS? Maybe yeah. WHO AND
WHAT DOES HE MEAN TO THE WORLD? Christmas tells you . . .
that you have sweet FA. Christmas says that's your standing in
the world . . . you score six miserable Christmas cards . . .
Christmas to make you feel like you don't exist . . . Christmas is
like an avalanche coming . . . you want to run away, but you've
nowhere to hide . . . I hate it . . . Nah! It's not so bad . . . that's
average for the season. But if I don't get more than six I'll definitely
add two from last year . . . maybe three. Ha ha, maybe I put up all
last year's, nah, the last five years' and have a bonanza. Ha! Ha!
Gee you're popular Harry! Why save them? They're nice though,
some of them. They remind me. It's piece of memory. (*Looks at
cards.*) Mum and Dad, brother and aunty . . . one from work and
two from . . . friends. Those two . . . not seen them for years . . .
but every year they send a card and I send one back . . . so they
know I'm still alive . . . and the message is always the same: "Give
us a ring sometime." But I don't, because they don't want to hear
from me . . . not really . . . but it's nice to rub the old memories
up bit and then they get a card back . . . but not before. I wait and
if they miss a year then so will I. But they only missed one in the
last ten years. I had moved so it got misdirected or lost or is still
seeking me out . . . four days to go. I might get four more . . .
That's all I need, four more to make it ten. That would be
acceptable . . . that's a reasonable bottom line because three are
from your family and don't count, so six more would be very good
but even two would be tolerable . . . But one more . . . or none

. . . that's impossible. No, ten would give me a real stake in the world and as Santa comes and delivers all the goodies just a couple more down my chimney. What are stinking cards anyway . . . a desperate message of "I love you; please love me" and hang up all your stupid cards on a line in the lounge . . . prove how you are loved . . . I don't care . . . I don't send cards unless I get them . . . I don't want to get cards from people who would never dream of sending me a card but for the fact they received mine, so I get an obliged card . . . so that doesn't count. I want cards from people who want to send me a card. Not obliged but I send a card back if my old friend sends me one. Yes. But I don't feel obliged. Maybe I should send loads. Like putting out lots of lines and getting a bite . . . maybe just flood the world with cards for every human being who touched me . . . or I touched . . . all the ones of the past . . . the history of my being . . . then they would send me one and then we'd continue by picking up the threads . . . that dropped . . . like a light bulb with the threads broken . . . the tiny filament . . . so no current pours through . . . so a card would be attempting to light up the filament and make the connection. And if they reply then it lights up. Too late now. Only four days to Christmas. I used to get more . . . in the past. I had cards . . . sometimes a dozen . . . once I got twenty . . . yes. That was a record year. I was working in an office and everyone felt they should send each other cards. So it was a freak year but then it dropped back to twelve and then ten then six or seven and so decreasing year by year. Then, if my parents died I could only guarantee myself four . . . even three. That's not so good . . . I'll put a few more out for now. (*Puts four old ones out.*) WHY DID YOU DO THAT? DOES IT MAKE YOU FEEL BETTER? Yes. IN CASE ANYONE COMES TO VISIT? Yes, they'll see . . . HOW POPULAR YOU ARE? Not even popular but normal . . . at least normal . . . like everyone . . . not . . . LONELY, UNPOPULAR, UNLIKED, UNDESIRABLE, UNBEFRIENDED, UNKNOWN, UNCARED FOR, UNINTERESTING . . . UNBEING . . . No, I don't care . . . if I sent more cards I'd get some more . . . I don't care . . . THEN WHY PUT UP LAST YEAR'S? Ashamed for them. WHO IS THEM? YOUR LANDLADY, YOUR ONE FRIEND, A VISITOR, A CHANCE CALLER?

NOBODY CALLS YOU BY CHANCE. Somebody may. I'm expecting someone . . . what the hell . . . does it matter? (*Takes cards away.*) How stupid, how foul . . . (*Puts them back.*) But they look cheerful. I don't care . . . better make sure there isn't last year's date on them. (*Studies card.*) "Give us a ring sometime." Hmmn . . . I didn't ring the whole year . . . I thought about it . . . maybe I should . . . maybe they'd even ask me over . . . Nah! They make their plans weeks ago . . . those kind of people prepare for Christmas like you prepare for war . . . or as a kind of obstacle course . . . I don't care . . . so what's Christmas . . . another day . . . where the non-beings get counted . . . you could vanish among the mob the rest of the year . . . but now the mob gathers its forces and flees and you're exposed . . . naked . . . with your cards . . . not enough to cover your nakedness . . . why join the mob . . . preparations . . . and stand in a queue in supermarkets dragging home some dead poisoned bird . . . Nah! Christ was born so I could count my cards . . . he came to earth to make me lonely as a piece of shit that didn't go down when the loo was flushed. Still, it might be nice . . . sitting round a table and getting a bit pissed with the kids leaping around and watching TV films . . . Nah . . . I could watch it at Mum's. I'm sick of going to Mum's at Christmas . . . sick of it . . . she's old and falls asleep in front of the telly so I end up watching it alone . . . and then I go home in the evening and end up watching more of it. Wonder if I should ring them . . . just say . . . I'm ringing 'cause you said, "Give us a ring sometime" . . . so here's the time . . . "Happy Christmas" . . . that's all . . . don't say, "What you doing?" or they'll think I'm begging to be invited . . . no just "Wishing you a happy Christmas" . . . they'll say, "Come over and have a Christmas Eve drink" . . . no doubt they'll be having friends over. I wonder . . . (*Stares at the phone a long time.*) DO IT . . . DOES IT KILL YOU TO MAKE A CALL . . . EXTEND A HAND . . . MAYBE THEY'RE LONELY TOO . . . MAYBE THEY NEED FRIENDS, SO LIFT UP AND DIAL. THAT'S WHY THEY SEND YOU A CARD . . . THEY LIKE YOU . . . YOU USED TO DO EVENING CLASSES TOGETHER BEFORE THEY GOT MARRIED . . . THEY'D BE PLEASED . . . YOU USED TO MAKE THEM LAUGH . . .

REMEMBER THE STORY THAT YOU TOLD ABOUT APPLYING FOR A JOB AS A SECURITY GUARD . . . YOU COULDN'T GET THE BUTTONS IN THE UNIFORM AND SO YOU DIDN'T EVEN START . . . YOU COULDN'T COPE WITH THE BUTTONS . . . REMEMBER HOW THEY LAUGHED . . . GO ON . . . DIAL IT. No! No! Don't ring in desperation . . . ring out of pleasure . . . they'll hear it in my voice . . . desperation . . . it will put them off. SO WHAT . . . PUT THEM OFF . . . YOU DON'T GET ANYTHING BY BEING AFRAID . . . EXCEPT PEACE IN YOUR LONELINESS IN FRONT OF THE TV . . . THE GIFTS FOR THE FEARFUL, YOU FRIGHTENED LITTLE WORM. Yes, a worm . . . frightened . . . they're together . . . and if they say, "Yes, come over" . . . a single man . . . nearly 40 and still sees him mum . . . had a woman once . . . as a matter of fact I had quite a few . . . years ago . . . she still writes. (*Looks at the other card.*) "I hope you are well" . . . Clara – Clara was nice . . . lasted six months . . . pretty good . . . but she didn't send a card this year . . . not yet . . . but left her address on top so I sent a card instead . . . wish I had contacted her . . . maybe she's lonely . . . maybe she never found anyone . . . but a year without a word. STILL YOU COULD PHONE HER AND SAY, "MERRY CHRISTMAS, CLARA, COME OVER FOR A DRINK." Yes . . . JUST A DRINK WOULDN'T HARM AND CHEW OVER THE OLD CUD . . . SHE MIGHT LIKE THAT. She might indeed . . . Christmas Eve, come over and split a bottle of wine . . . NO, MAKE IT CHAMPAGNE. Champagne . . . yes . . . why not! Hey, that's good . . . I'll do that. YES, DO IT NOW WHILE THE SPIRIT IS UP . . . YOU JUST IGNITED A LITTLE SPARK THERE. Keep it aflame . . . don't dampen it with doubts or fears . . . like she might have a boyfriend or even a husband. DON'T . . . YOU'RE DAMPING IT RIGHT NOW . . . YOU'RE PUTTING OUT THE SPARK. No . . . No, do it now . . . just ring up . . . to hell with the consequences . . . WHAT CONSEQUENCES . . . WHAT ARE YOU TALKING ABOUT . . . YOU'RE ONLY ASKING HER OVER FOR A FEW DRINKS . . . WHAT CONSEQUENCES? Like she thinks in two years I haven't found anyone . . . or she thinks I'm still trying to get her back or she'd be confused since it's been two years, she'll think I'm desperate . . . to ring after such a long time . . . "Why the hell is he ringing now . . . he's lonely and can't find anyone else." NO! YOU'RE THINKING THAT . . . SHE'LL MORE THAN LIKELY THINK, "OH, HOW NICE TO HEAR FROM YOU AFTER ALL THIS TIME . . . HEY, WHAT A SURPRISE . . . SURE THAT WILL BE NICE . . . A LITTLE DRINK AND TALK OVER OLD TIMES." NO MORE THAN THAT. Even if she does have a husband she'll still think, "That's nice" . . . people like to see old friends . . . you're right . . . you're right . . . the spark's coming back . . . I'll do it now! Right now. Clara . . . Oh, she was nice. A drink. THAT'S RIGHT, DO IT NOW. But what if she has a husband and says, "Can I bring him?" FACE THAT BRIDGE WHEN YOU CROSS IT. Sure . . . bring him, it's still company . . . it's still living . . . and talking and not watching TV. THAT'S RIGHT, SO PICK UP THE PHONE. But . . . WHAT NOW, YOU FOOL? STOP DIGGING UP THAT CESSPIT OF DOUBT. IT'S A BOTTOMLESS HOLE . . . YOU COULD DIG THERE FOR EVER – SO LEAVE IT BURIED. Yes, but it has to be worked out . . . come for a drink . . . but then she'll expect others to be there. If it's the two of us or even the three it'll be odd . . . if I say a drink there should be two or three others there or it's a bit personal. SO WHAT? YOU WERE ONCE CLOSE FRIENDS . . . LOVERS . . . SHE KNOWS YOU. But if there's no one else she'll know it's because I'm lonely . . . or want to get her back or she'll be uncomfortable . . . now if I could get two or even one other then it was a Christmas drink . . . otherwise it's a bit depressing just the two of us on Christmas Eve. YOU'RE DIGGING A HOLE FOR THAT SPARK AND BURYING IT DEEPER AND DEEPER INTO THE EARTH . . . GIVE THE SPARK SOME AIR AND WATCH IT CATCH ALIGHT. OK . . . I know . . . but I have to work it out . . . maybe ask the couple who said ring . . . and her . . . then if both come it's like a little party . . . . . . or leave it . . . I'm confused. I'll ring the couple, then if they say, "Yes we'll be delighted to come" I'll ring her . . . it's difficult with women . . . they always think you want something out of them. WHAT? FRIENDSHIP, COMPANY, WARMTH, DIALOGUE . . . ? SO WHAT'S DREADFUL ABOUT THAT? HOW BAD THAT IS! That's not so bad . . . I could ask her . . . just take the consequences of my action . . . whatever happens . . . ring now. YES, RING NOW. FORGET MAKING A

STRUCTURE OF HAVING THE OTHERS OVER . . . YOU JUST WANT
A FRIEND TO SHARE A FEW DRINKS WITH . . . MAYBE GET A BIT
PISSED . . . MAYBE SHE'S ALONE AND DYING TO SEE SOMEONE
. . . HOW DO YOU KNOW UNLESS YOU MAKE THE EFFORT AND
BE BRAVE? Be brave, that's it . . . I'll ring now . . . then if she says
yes I'll call the others . . . if they can't come . . . that's it . . . OK.
She's here anyway . . . good . . . (*Stops and looks at the cards.*) Oh,
I'd better take her last year's card down . . . I'll put some other
cards up . . . say two or three more . . . now that looks much
better . . . I smoke a fag first . . . Now. (*Picks up the phone and
stares at it; starts slowly to dial.*) I hope she's away . . . or not in . . .
but I'll be brave . . . be brave. (*Dials – it rings for some time . . .
keeps ringing – puts the phone down.*) Phew! She's not in . . . that's
OK. I did it! I'll ring later on. Maybe she's moved . . . so what
now . . . I'll ring the other people . . . but if they say yes . . . then I
won't be able to have a quiet drink with her . . . but that's not
what I wanted . . . I want others around to defuse the situation.
WHAT SITUATION? YOU LIKED HER ONCE. DEFUSE WHAT? WHY
ARE YOU DOING ALL THIS FOR HER? DO IT FOR YOURSELF . . .
INVITE THE COUPLE BECAUSE YOU WANT TO NOT BECAUSE TO
HER. That's right! I'll ring them and if they come that will be
good. Now they did say, even this year, "Why don't you ring us
sometime?" They were nice . . . we had some nice times. (*Dials.*)
Oh God, it's ringing . . . Oh God . . . what shall I say . . . it's still
ringing . . . Hello! Jack? Hello, Jack, it's me . . . Harry! You
know, from the institute . . . Harry Glebe . . . You sent me a card
. . . Oh, Barbara sent it! That's nice . . . well, it said . . . both . . .
of . . . Oh, she sent all of them . . . Ha! Ha! . . . that's nice . . .
that's really nice . . . yes, Glebe . . . sure, don't apologize! I knew
you'd remember . . . Oh yes, the kids shouting in your ear and
you couldn't . . . sure I'll hold on . . . Oh, I'm sorry . . . you're in
the middle of a kids' party . . . No, just to ring and wish you a
really great Christmas . . . Is Barbara . . . ? Busy in the kitchen
. . . uh huh . . . Hey! How many kids you got? . . . Wow! three
now . . . sure I can hear them . . . Oh, I'm fine . . . yeah . . . sure
I'll give you and Barb a call sometime . . . when you're not so
busy . . . Ha ha . . . Yeah, in the new year. (*Sudden*) Sure . . . Oh,

what are you doing for the new year? . . . Lovely . . . Is it hot
there now? Wow! I must try that sometime . . . no, never been
. . . no, it's OK, Barb doesn't have to call back . . . you said ring
sometime so here it is . . . Ha ha ! Sure, thanks and to you too . . .
have a good one . . . a nice Christmas . . . you got the whole family
staying . . . my God, yeah . . . sorry? . . . I can't hear . . . the
baby's crying . . . what? Oh, I remember Michael . . . he was just
born . . . three now . . . my god . . . yeah. He wants to talk on the
phone . . . he likes that, yeah . . . sure, put him on. SHIT, WHAT
AM I DOING HERE? LET ME GET OUT OF . . . Hallooo, Michael
. . . this is Harreeee . . . you having a lovely Christmas . . . aren't
you a big boy now . . . a big boy . . . big, I said . . . big! What?
What? Oh, you wanna bikey . . . oh ho your dad will give you one
. . . you're a big fella now . . . fella . . . oh, never mind . . .
CHRIST AND SHIT!! Whadya wan for Christmas? A bikey, oh yes,
of course . . . a red one . . . now Mike, if you pray to Santa and say
I'll be a good boy . . . Gooood! (*Aside*) For God's sake! Oh, I'm
sorry, Jack, I thought he was still on the line . . . sure, you're
busy . . . yeah, you too . . . yeah, sure, will do . . . bye. SHIT!
SHIT! SHIT! SHIT!

Lights fade to black, then come straight up again.

Three days to go and no cards today. Who cares? Do I . . . no
more work . . . for a week . . . so it starts . . . one, two, three,
four, five, six . . . still six. I'll put these others out in case she
comes . . . Clara . . . what about thinking of someone else? Still,
there's time. No one rang . . . yet . . . inviting me . . . anywhere
. . . still they all go to families . . . yeah . . . they don't enjoy it too
much . . . better off here . . . really . . . watch a few movies and
get pissed in front of the telly. Ha ha! See Mum . . . she needs
cheering up . . . lots to do really . . . three days . . . Friday
Saturday Sunday and then D-Day . . . I don't want to be alone
again . . . not again, not like last year! I can't stand it . . . it
mustn't happen! . . . I won't let it fucking happen . . . No! No!
No! No! No! No! No! THEN DO SOMETHING ABOUT IT . . . RING
YOUR FRIENDS . . . RING ANYONE YOU KNOW. MOUNT AN

ATTACK ON LONELINESS . . . KILL IT . . . DESTROY IT . . . YOU
HAVE TO MOUNT A MILITARY OPERATION . . . NO ONE WILL
RING YOU. Why? . . . Why do I know that no one will call . . .
why am I certain in every cell of my body that no one will come
here . . . phone here . . . because . . . because . . . WHAT?
ANALYSE WHY NO ONE WILL CALL YOU. Because they go off to
. . . NO, THAT'S NOT THE REASON. ANALYSE FOR YOURSELF
WHY NO ONE WILL PHONE. (*Cuts off suddenly as phone actually
rings, snatches it up.*) Hallo!? Oh . . . hallo, Ma . . . yeah . . . fine
. . . I haven't rung? Oh, it's week already, yeah . . . fine . . . how's
everything? (*Pause.*) Then you should lie down . . . I know,
you're sick of lying down, then try walking gently around . . . go
to the park . . . yeah, it is a bit cold still . . . still the days are
getting longer now . . . yeah . . . what's the doctor say? Just to
take it easy . . . that's why you have to do, yeah, so watch the TV,
put your feet up . . . You're sick of the TV? Well, so am I, Ma.
I'm sick of it, too . . . yeah, I am really sick to death of it! . . . You
watch more than me!? Then you must be even more sick of it than
I am . . . ha ha! So discover something else to do and you'll make
a fortune . . . sure, I'm coming round . . . yeah . . . No! I'm not
being forced . . . I want to . . . yeah I will . . . no, I don't feel
obliged . . . I know I'm free . . . don't talk like that . . . I come
because *I want to I said!!* . . . Sorry . . . didn't mean to shout,
don't get upset . . . (*Pause.*) Ma . . . Ma . . . ? You still there?
OK. You got all you need? I'll bring something anyway . . . what
do you need . . . no, don't go out shopping . . . I'll bring it . . . it's
not a chore. No . . . I'm not putting myself out . . . don't go out,
you're supposed to be in bed. For God's sake, I'll get the bloody
stuff . . . no, I'm not upset . . . cheese with the holes? That's all?
You got the rest . . . OK, then . . . maybe Christmas day . . . yeah
. . . Oh, nothing frantic, maybe some friends over Christmas Eve
for a drink . . . you know . . . colleagues . . . No, you wouldn't
know them, Ma . . . How's who?? I haven't seen her for five
years, Ma! Oh, for God's sake . . . so lie down and I'll bring some
stuff . . . yeah, the cheese with the holes . . . and some new green
cucumber . . . yeah, not if it's soggy . . . OK . . . Benny Hill's on
. . . OK. Watch it . . . OK.

Ma . . . look after . . . No, I don't need anything . . . the cat's fine. Ta da, Ma. SHIT SHIT SHIT SHIT SHIT.

Lights fade to black, then come straight up again.

Two days . . . I don't want to analyse anything . . . why should I? BECAUSE YOU'LL FIND THE ROOT OF IT . . . THEN YOU CAN TEAR IT OUT LIKE A VERRUCA . . . YOU HAVE TO MAKE AN EFFORT. Sometimes my whole body feels like one giant verruca . . . it starts in my foot and grows larger, then there's more to cut out and then it reaches my leg and then it takes over all of me and then there's more verruca than me . . . so the only way is to cut the whole thing out . . . and that's me . . . get rid of that. DON'T BE STUPID . . . GET IT NOW . . . LOOK FOR IT AND PULL IT OUT. Yeah . . . if I could find it. OK . . . I'll try Clara again. (*Dials – it rings and rings.*) She's away or working . . . maybe . . . I could call (*consults address book*) Annie again. She was nice . . . yeah . . . we had some nice times together . . . but I don't know . . . YOU HAVE TO . . . YOU MUST OR YOU WILL DIG A DEEPER PIT FOR YOURSELF. OK. I'll try . . . maybe I should also try some men friends. But it's not the same . . . they're both with their women or family . . . or don't want to be bothered. WHY NOT INVITE PAUL ROUND OR AL? I could . . . I could but I don't feel right about it. WHY? THEY MIGHT BE PLEASED TO HAVE A CALL . . . HAVE THEM ROUND CHRISTMAS EVE, THEN THAT WILL BREAK THE ICE . . . SO MUM WON'T BE SUCH A CHORE. You have to make an effort . . . an attack on loneliness . . . but Christmas they all have arrangements. Wives . . . girlfriends . . . YOU DON'T KNOW FOR SURE . . . MAYBE THEY'RE LIKE YOU . . . WAITING FOR A CALL . . . MAYBE YOU'LL BE DOING THEM A FAVOUR . . . CALL NOW! I don't want to call anyone . . . I'll read or go to a movie . . . have a meal somewhere . . . time will fly . . . why should I have to think of suiciding bits of my life . . . time should be precious to me . . . it should be like gold . . . more than gold . . . and I want to piss it away . . . my life is a . . . stink . . . that nobody wants to get near. ANALYSE IT. No No! I don't want to analyse anything. PHONE SOMEONE. No! I'm sick of begging for a handout. FRIENDS. I don't even like Paul and Al that much and even if they were free . . . what for . . . to stand in the pub and tell jokes . . . why, I'm sick of that . . . I'm lonely . . . I'm desperately sodden and need someone to hold . . . that's all I want to do for God's sake. Hold someone . . . what's to analyse, it's flesh and blood . . . some warmth . . . just to hold hands and go for a meal. What did I do . . . I don't care normally . . . I cope . . . but now I feel as if the whole world was in some kind of conspiracy against me. They're all holding each other . . . all grabbing on and holding and kissing and climbing all over each other and having friends round for drinks and answering the door and kids shouting and making dinners and chatting but where am I in all this? DID YOU MAKE THE EFFORT? DID YOU TRY? Yes . . . yes, of course I tried . . . I went out with them . . . I made them happy sometimes . . . we went to bed and sometimes it was OK . . . but it always ends . . . it comes and goes like musical chairs and Christmas is like standing as the music stops . . . and you're without a chair not for a few seconds but for days . . . Everybody is at a feast from which you are excluded . . . (*Long pause, takes a cigarette out and dials a number.*) Hell . . . can I speak to Annie? . . . Hi, Annie, it's me. Harry! Yeah . . . good . . . great . . . What are you doing with yourself these days? Uh huh . . . uh . . . huh . . . uh huh . . . no . . . no . . . I haven't found anyone to match you! Ha! Ha! Ha! Have you ah found . . . oh good . . . that's good, sure, it's good to . . . how long . . . you've been living together that long . . . and he's OK? Yeah, great . . . Oh, I dunno . . . looking at our old photos and I thought what the hell . . . let's see how the old girl is . . . you know. I know it was difficult sometimes . . . yeah, but there were some good times . . . yes there were . . . Oh, come on, Annie . . . everybody fights . . . but we had some nice times . . . you don't remember . . . you focus . . . what about the days we went to Bournemouth . . . and we didn't fight . . . not all the time . . . so . . . I should see someone about what . . . I'm OK! I don't need help, damn it! Well, not that kind . . . I didn't depend on you . . . you were my ally. Sure, friends . . . I got loads of friends . . . don't lecture me for God's sake . . . you see, you're making me angry again . . . so I won't ring . . . shit, I won't . . . why did I . . . ? To invite you over for a Christmas drink, you pig. (*Phone clicks off*.) DON'T GET INVOLVED . . . YOU SHOULD HAVE JUST SAID . . . COME ROUND FOR A DRINK. Should I? Who gives a shit? Now who else . . . ? (*Hears noise*.) The postman just dropped by . . . hold on there . . . (*Goes to door*.) HO HO! What's this . . . another card . . . Wa hoo! Who's a popular boy today . . . now . . . who is this from? (*Opens it slowly*.) "Happy Christmas, just to remind you that your subscription is due at . . ." Shit! Still, it makes seven . . . that's better . . . it looks a bit healthier . . . I wonder if Clara is back now . . . WHY RING ANYONE . . . WHY BOTHER . . . PUT IT DOWN TO EXPERIENCE AND GO AWAY NEXT TIME . . . JUST LIVE AND BREATHE FOR NOW. GO OUT, WATCH TV, SEE YOUR MOTHER, DO THE SHOPPING, GET CAT FOOD, SMOKE A CIGARETTE, GET PISSED, GO TO SLEEP, GET UP, MAKE A CUP OF TEA, SMOKE A CIGARETTE, GO FOR A WALK, BUY SOME GROCERIES, COOK A MEAL, HAVE A DRINK, SMOKE A CIGARETTE, WATCH TV, GET PISSED, HAVE A WANK, SMOKE A CIGARETTE, GO TO SLEEP, GET UP, WALK ABOUT, GET DRESSED, GO OUT, COME BACK, GO OUT, COME BACK, GO TO SLEEP, WAKE UP, SLEEP, WAKE, SMOKE, EAT, WATCH, DIE, SHIT SHIT SHIT SHIT SHIT SHIT SHIT.

Blackout. Lights come up again.

One day to go . . . no more cards today . . . still seven is nothing to be ashamed of . . . maybe Clara's in today . . . she'll see me I'm sure . . . Clara! . . . been drinking too much . . . got black on my lips . . . look at me . . . forty, not bad-looking . . . not fantastic . . . sure, there'll be lots of women who would like to have a friend over Christmas . . . think of all the thousands, the tens of thousands of lonely women everywhere and I don't bloody know where they are . . . wish there was a signal you could use . . . "Look at me, I'm lonely" . . . I'm not bad . . . I've got arms and legs and a heart . . . I've got all the equipment to do it with . . . I've got a voice to say things . . . like . . . "You're really nice . . . I love you . . . I want to be with you . . . come on" . . . I've got all this body . . . all this shape . . . occupying space . . . and no one to give it to . . . all my hands and fingers and lips . . . all my arms and legs and thighs and mind . . . it's all here. (*Makes a shape with his arms as if holding a woman round the waist.*) This space to let . . . loneliness is like a disease or smell . . . when you give off a whiff it puts people off. Why did I get like this . . . tomorrow is Christmas . . . Christ's day . . . he came to give us love and everybody goes away and gives it to someone else . . . he came to say, "Share your love. Give it . . . take it . . . don't withhold . . . suffer everything" . . . what is it . . . "Suffer the little children to come unto me" . . . I'm one of them . . . I'm a child of his . . . so where's my crumpet for Christmas . . . who cares about crumpet . . . it's not about that . . . it's about something else. WHAT ELSE, WHAT IS THE ELSE? ANALYSE THAT. ANALYSE IT AND YOU'RE NEAR TO SOLVING IT. Solving what – what is there to solve? THE PAIN THAT BLOCKS OUT THE FEELING. What pain . . . it's all pain . . . pain came from somewhere, get rid of the pain and feeling floods back . . . like taking a thorn out . . . YES, THAT'S RIGHT, GET RID OF THE PAIN AND YOU'LL FEEL . . . ANALYSE IT. What? I don't know what there is to analyse . . . I'm lonely, that's all . . . how can I analyse that? BUT WHY? WHAT'S THE REASON? I don't know . . . who knows? It's bad luck. NO SUCH THING . . . YOU DON'T KNOW, THEN ASK YOURSELF . . . BEG IT OF YOURSELF AND YOU'LL DRAW OUT THE PAIN WITH THE BEGGING. Beg what?! Maybe I'm not interesting enough. TO WHO? TO YOU? WHAT ABOUT THE OTHERS – WHO ARE YOU TO JUDGE YOURSELF? They judge me! WHO ARE THEY? Them (*points to cards*) those cards are my judge, six miserable fucking cards . . . they are my witnesses with one from the Insurance Company reminding me . . . and the ones that aren't there . . . YOU DIDN'T PLAN . . . YOU DIDN'T TAKE TIME OR THINK OF OTHERS . . . YOU WERE INVOLVED WITH YOUR OWN PAIN AND IGNORED THE WORLD . . . YOU LOVED YOUR OWN LITTLE AGONY. I did? I sweat for it . . . I plead . . . I ask . . . I phone up . . . ONLY FROM PAIN . . . NOT FROM PLEASURE . . . IN DESPERATION AT THE END. So what should I do if not now . . . wait until I'm happy enough to crack a few jokes . . . what now

. . . wait for the pain to go and sit in an empty room studying my pain with the TV on . . . ? I'd rather die . . . yes, die . . . that's better than this. DEATH IS THE FINAL SOLUTION OF TAKING YOUR PAIN TO YOURSELF AND HUGGING IT TO DEATH . . . DEATH IS YOUR PAIN TAKEN TO THE END . . . GET RID OF IT SLOWLY . . . A BIT AT A TIME . . . How?! How?! I'm lonely and miserable . . . How do you get rid of that? Eh! Tell me that! ANALYSE IT . . . WHY AND HOW . . . AND THEN IT WILL DISAPPEAR. Bollocks! It stays with me like a lump on my face or a growth . . . in the morning when I get up, the night when I sleep . . . my ache grows bigger and bigger . . . I'm starving for friends and love I ache and hunger . . . SO WHAT DOES THE STARVING MAN DO TO GET RID OF THE PAIN? Yeah . . . he eats . . . where, show me where? Give me a clue, for God's sake . . . I'll try anything . . . just show me . . . please God tell me how? (*The phone rings . . . He is startled and rushes to the phone; waits for it to ring a couple more times and picks it up.*) Hallo . . . ? (*Trying to sound calm and relaxed*) Hallo? Who is this? No, this is Harry. Yes! Oh, you have the wrong . . . no, wait . . . who did you want? Terry? You don't mean Harry, do you? No, definitely Terry. Wait . . . er, just a minute. Did he live here? Oh, it's a different . . . no. That's OK . . . no, no trouble . . . er sometimes it could sound the same . . . Harry . . . Terry . . . yeah . . . er . . . what's your name . . . it makes no difference . . . it's just that you sound like someone I . . . sure, that's OK . . . have a nice Christmas . . . er, what are you doing . . . (*Phone cuts off.*) Wrong number. Strange . . . (*Stares at the phone a long time, picks it up and dials.*) No . . . maybe she'll be in, it's late for Christmas . . . I'll meet her in a pub . . . that's better than nothing . . . Hallo, is Clara there? Harry . . . she's not . . . oh, out shopping . . . . . . OK . . . no message . . . oh wait, say that Harry called, will you . . . yeah, Harry and to ring him . . . me . . . if she feels like a Christmas drink . . . yeah, would you tell her that, please . . . sure, she knows my number . . . bye . . . So that's OK . . . it makes it easier if she doesn't ring . . . so that's it . . . yeah, that's easier . . . she'll ring me if she wants to. That's good . . . feel better. Analyse my pain . . . fah! I analyse a broken leg . . . it's broken. BUT WHY?

Oh shuddup! Shuddup! Shuddup! Shut the voice up . . . it's broken because it's broken . . . there's no why . . . it's done to you. NO, YOU DO IT TO YOURSELF. Jesus Christ help me . . . SHIT SHIT SHIT SHIT.

Lights fade to black and then come up again.

Merry Christmas . . . no more cards . . . sod'em . . . who cares . . . do I shit and piss on the lot of you . . . (*Puts radio on: carols, etc., maybe a sermon.*) It's only a day like any other . . . across the length and breadth of Merry England the rosy faces beam . . . greedy little fingers tear off the ribbons gazing in awe at the wrong size shmutters they are forced to wear and granny will sit in front of the flickering idiot box farting quietly away as she dies slowly in a haze of chintz and lecithin chocolates. Doorbells will ring and boring evil relatives will descend grasping in their hands bottles of cheap plonk and more ghastly toys for their stupid kids to scare the cat with. Nah! Who cares . . . I didn't plan it right . . . Next year I'll arrange something in advance . . . but not too far . . . maybe a couple of weeks . . . just get myself together a bit more . . . yeah . . . ring a few faces and not leave it to the last second . . . Clara could have rung even if she couldn't see me . . . she might have called . . . so what to do . . . listen to them all . . . shrieking about nothing, sweating over their stupid turkey . . . still it might have been nice to sit with a few faces and talk . . . I need to talk . . . desperately . . . need to say a few things and tell somebody something but their pain stays there like a lump and I can't even do that . . . maybe that's why I am alone . . . maybe I made it happen this way because I couldn't bear it . . . to sit there and answer their stupid questions . . . "When you gonna get hitched up Harry?" "What are you doing with yourself?" "How's your life?" I have a nail through my head that gives me a constant pain . . . could be through my hands . . . I feel pinned . . . nailed up to my own cross . . . my own guilt . . . so that's why I am alone . . . I have analysed it . . . my own guilt for my own life. BUT WHERE DOES THE GUILT COME FROM? Who cares? I was given a life and I didn't use it properly . . . I was given a garden and I neglected it and I can't let anyone in the gate because I am ashamed of how mouldy and overgrown the garden is . . . weedy dishevelled dung heap . . . so that's the answer . . . how it came to me! SO SUDDENLY LIKE A REVELATION . . . HOW DID IT HAPPEN THIS GUILT? Happen? It happened . . . I neglected the garden . . . I like that . . . I am a garden of delights and there was one tree I cultivated until it was bare and I ate off this one bloody tree but neglected all the rest and the fruit of the tree yielded less and less fruit and smaller and smaller because I didn't heed the rest or weed the garden and so the roots became choked . . . oh shit, what am . . . what am I saying . . . Ma . . . phone Ma . . . I can't sit there again . . . watching the bleary eye that's wasting me away . . . I can't . . . I'd rather sit here alone. (*Phones Ma*.) Ma! Happy Christmas . . . yeah . . . listen, Ma . . . I'm a bit tied up . . . yeah, people poppin' round . . . a party, etc. . . . . so I thought I'd pop over for Boxing Day . . . are you sure . . . you'll be OK? Sure? I can come if . . . no . . . no . . . I know I'm old enough to please myself . . . but I don't want you to be lonely . . . You're happy just to have a rest? Yeah, put your feet up and watch? Oh good . . . yeah, you'll be OK . . . sure, I know, Ma . . . I love you too . . . Haven't I said that before . . . 'course I have . . . maybe it's because I know you know. I know you love me, Ma . . . 'course I'll do what makes me happy . . . you're OK? Good . . . yeah, tomorrow . . . see you then . . . yeah, the cat's fine, he loved the pilchards . . . you have a nice Christmas too, Ma, ta da . . . Maybe I'll sleep through the day . . . turn the box on and nod off in front of Clark Gable. (*Goes to the box and takes out some pills*.) One, two, three, no, maybe four, that's enough. (*Swallows pills*.) Now I shall sit down and wait . . . doesn't take too long . . . just have a nod and then it's all over . . . Christmas is gone . . . housewives' pill, they call it. How about a drop to wash it down with? (*Does so*.) Hey, that felt pretty good . . . hey, I'm having a nice time here on my lonesome . . . it ain't bad. WHAT'S NOT BAD – KILLING TIME BECAUSE YOU CAN'T FACE YOURSELF . . . KILLING A BIT OF YOURSELF SO AS NOT TO FEEL? I feel OK, so what . . . it is killing a bit of yourself at a time . . . it's true . . . I'm burning up the garden . . . or drowning it out . . . THE WEEDS

WILL SURVIVE AND CHOKE YOU UNLESS YOU TEAR THEM OUT
. . . CLEAN IT UP . . . START AGAIN. With what? Where do I
start . . . go out in the street . . . walk . . . run . . . do something
. . . what? Anything . . . get out of that room . . . don't just sit and
rot . . . don't look at that thing . . . it's a death-ray machine . . . it
pours evil rays into your head . . . maybe that's what's wrong . . .
I'll get out . . . where? I'll go to Clara's . . . bust into their cosy
Christmas dinner, say, "Here I am, folks . . . Merry Christmas!"
See their faces, what can they do, chuck me out . . . No . . . they'll
say, "Come in, Harry, what a pleasant surprise . . . have a drink,
old boy." I will. I'll say, "Happy Christmas . . . I'm alone, you
wouldn't want to enjoy your turkey without me?" . . . do I dare, I
wonder . . . it's better than dying alone here . . . what's the worst
that could happen . . . they won't shoot me . . . I'll take a few
more of these things . . . it's beginning not to make any difference
. . . then I'll do it . . . Ha ha ha! WHAT AN ACHIEVEMENT . . .
THE SUM TOTAL OF YOUR COURAGE . . . TO KNOCK ON A DOOR.
Yeah, that's my achievement . . . to knock on a door . . . to build
up the courage to do what anyone in the world does normally I
need a mountain of courage to do . . . so what . . . who cares . . . I
must do something! I'll ring first, yes! I'll just ring and say,
"Clara, I'm coming over for a drink" . . . and she'll say, "Good,
Harry, just come over" . . . it's Christ's birthday for God's sake.
Didn't he die for us? Aren't we supposed on this day to give . . .
yeah . . . I'll just ring and say Merry Christmas and nothing else
. . . she'll say, "How are you spending it?" . . . and I'll say "*Alone,
you pig . . . alone and bleeding to death on the cross of my own guilt*"
and she'll say, "Come and have a sherry." (*Refers to pills.*) The
feeling isn't getting into me . . . (*Takes more pills.*) One, two,
three, four . . . five . . . six . . . more . . . it's too much . . . but
what the hell . . . how many is that? Ten or twelve . . . oh well, it's
Christmas . . . you can indulge . . . I'll ring. (*Goes to the phone,
picks it up . . . starts trembling, looks at it and tries to dial, does so and
clicks it off before it starts ringing, tries it again and again; it clicks
off.*) For Christ's sake, it's only a call . . . wouldn't you be glad if
someone called you? On Christmas Day . . . just say, "Have a nice
Christmas, Clara" . . . No! "Merry Christmas, Clara!" No. "Guess

who this is, Clara . . . hey . . . have a great Christmas . . . yeah,
I'm taking it easy . . . sure, I'll drop in . . . just for a few
minutes!" Shit . . . the pills're making me woozy. YOU'RE
KILLING YOURSELF SLOWLY INCH BY INCH SLOWLY BLEEDING
TO DEATH. STOP IT . . . STOP IT NOW . . . GO FOR A WALK . . .
SEE THE SKY . . . VISIT YOUR MOTHER . . . GO TO BED. SHOUT
. . . SCREAM OR RUN . . . GET OUT OF THIS ROOM. Get off the
cross kid . . . but I like it here . . . there's a good view . . . I'm
above the crowd . . . (*Takes more pills.*) One . . . two . . . three . . .
four . . . five . . . . . . si-ix . . . No, that's enough . . . put me asleep
for the day then no more . . . awake tomorrow and see Mum . . .
Christmas over . . . I feel really good . . . hey, that's better . . . no
more pain . . . then that's what it's like . . . then it's good . . . no
more now . . . WHY NOT TAKE THE LOT AND BE RID OF IT
ALTOGETHER? THEN NO MORE CHRISTMAS . . . WHY GO
THROUGH THIS NEXT YEAR AND THE YEAR AFTER AND EACH
DAY AND EACH MINUTUE . . . DON'T DIE IN BITS . . . DO IT
NOW . . . Then I'll ascend . . . THAT'S RIGHT . . . DON'T
ANALYSE ANY MORE . . . DON'T QUESTION THE PAIN . . . IT'S
THERE . . . YOU'RE RIGHT, YOU'RE BLEEDING TO DEATH
SLOWLY . . . SO HASTEN IT. Nah. Nah! that's defeatist . . . but
I'll maybe just get a taste . . . one . . . two . . . three . . . four . . .
five . . . six . . . and a couple more . . . (*Swallows.*) Be daring . . .
go on . . . don't stop at the edge . . . jump – Nah . . . I'm a coward
. . . NO, YOU'RE NOT . . . YOU'RE BRAVE NOW . . . IT'S EASY AND
IT'S PAINLESS WHEN YOU JUMP . . . YOU'LL SLEEP. Like
forever . . . it's tempting . . . Ha ha . . . Shit, it feels nice . . . who
will feed the cat? YOU LEAVE A NOTE . . . THE NEIGHBOURS
WON'T LET IT STARVE. I can't . . . what about Ma . . . she'll be
alone . . . she'll fret. SHE WON'T . . . SHE'LL UNDERSTAND . . .
YOU HAVE TO LIVE YOUR OWN LIFE . . . That's right . . . OK
. . . I feel good now . . . OK . . . I don't know how many that is
. . . maybe these will do . . . only ten left . . . OK . . . I'm tired
but the view is good . . . I can see the crowd running about . . .
but I'm still . . . and the wind is licking my face . . . and the sun's
warm . . . Clara's there! She's watching . . . and smiling . . . she's
proud . . . I loved Clara . . . Boy, this is some trip . . . I see colours

. . . Hey, Clara's taking me down . . . I come off easily . . . like peeled off . . . and float down . . . (*Drowsier and deeper as the drug takes effect*) We're together now and walking along a beach! Come, Clara, let's have a run . . . she tilts her head . . . her hair falls down like a waterfall . . . she's smiling at me . . . what you giggling at . . . big blue eyes . . . laughing . . . it's starting to rain we'll snuggle up in the car . . . Hey, that's good . . . we're going to the mountains . . . (*Miming*) we'll wrap up in the cold bedroom and hold on tightly to each other . . . hold on tight, Harry, I'm cold . . . sure . . . sure. There's no heat in this room . . . so hang on . . . we're taking off . . . into the night . . . Ha! Ha! Here we go . . . you asleep yet, Clara? No? We'll have breakfast in bed . . . and . . . then . . . we'll have a walk . . . in the mountains and be breathless and cold . . . we'll sing to keep warm the songs we half remember . . . you start . . . shh . . . go to sleep now . . . we've got a big day tomorrow . . . hold on tight hold me . . . I fancy kippers and masses of toast and pints of tea . . . do you mind if I have a smoke in bed . . . "I love you, Harry" . . . "I love you too, Clara" . . . "How much?" "Bucketsful" . . . it's really getting cold and the nights are drawing in . . . (*The lights are fading and tightening, leaving only his face.*) It's cold but we're OK . . . "Don't fall asleep with your cigarette, Harry" . . . "I'll put it out . . . good night" . . . we're floating into an endless night . . . we're going upwards . . . taking off . . . hold on to me . . . always . . . hold on . . . don't let go . . . you're slipping . . . away, Clara . . . you have to hold on . . . don't go . . . don't . . . it's cold . . . it's dark . . . where . . . are . . . you? I'm alone.

HARRY *is dead*.

BRIGHTON BEACH SCUMBAGS

AUTHOR'S NOTE

I was walking along the Brighton promenade one weekend afternoon when I heard a rather corpulent lady screeching at a couple of heads that peeked over the deckchairs facing the sea, 'WHAT D'YA WANT ON YOUR BLEEDIN' HUMBURGERS?' . . . It was the primitive battle-cry of Dagenham or Romford, it curdled the air with its reek of deep loathing, frustration and hatred. The sea draws all to its comforting hypnotic rolling surf and to the memories of childhood and innocence and a belief that all will be well at the bland soothing coast with its aura of freedom from toil and possibility of fun. The contrast and disappointment creates a kind of dumb fury that things are not always what you hope they will be.

So these two couples embark on Brighton beach with their dreams of the past competing with the reality of the present. They are British archetypes representing a programmed beast that at heart is still innocent in its beliefs but has been corroded by the deadening effects of a rotten sub-culture, cheap tabloids, easy racism and slobbering consumerism. It is the other side of Brighton. They express a terrible kind of loathing for all that does not fit within the simple guidelines that they believe are the route to contentment. Yet they have humour and defend themselves within their shells of self-delusion. We might call them yobs and laugh at their Neanderthal struggles with existence, but within there is an awful sadness as they try to claw happiness out of their day.

CHARACTERS

DINAH
DEREK
DOREEN
DAVE
TOM
TED

Brighton Beach Scumbags was first performed at the Sallis Benney Theatre, Brighton, on 23 October 1991. The cast was as follows:

DOREEN   Tessa Burbridge
DEREK   Jimmy Flint
DAVE   Steve North
DINA   Belinda Blanchard
TOM   Jason Merrells
TED   Ralf Higgins

Director   George Dillon
Designer Andrew Kay

*The set. A few deckchairs face upstage as if facing the sea. Puffy pale
clouds are painted on a lyrical blue sky, and the sea is azure blue with
a ship sitting on the horizon. A pier juts out on the back-drop on a
diagonal. There are railings just before the beach. Sounds of gulls and
waves. All is summer and surf. A fat woman leans against the railings
facing audience.*

  *Fat woman is screaming at the men in the deckchairs whose heads
we see. In the other chair is the friend* DOREEN. *The men are* DEREK
and DAVE.

DINAH: (*screaming*) What d'ya want on your bloody hamburger,
    eh!? What do you sodden well want? (*silence from chairs.*)
    You want me to get your bleedin hamburgers . . . so . . .
    cheeseburger?!! Or what. Sod ya, ya stupid bastard!
    (*Silence from the two men and one woman who look up but are
    unwilling to confront the storm. She wanders off.*)

DEREK: Bleeding hot! It's really bleeding 'ot . . . so she gets in a
    tantrum . . .

DOREEN: Nah, she's awright . . . take no fucking notice . . . nah,
    she's lovely . . . she is . . . she's awright . . .

DAVE: She'll be OK . . . throw her in the water, cool it down and
    she'll be laughin . . . 'tsot for her . . . get her to splash abaht a
    bit . . .

DEREK: She won't get in the fuckin water . . . no fuckin way . . .
    she's self-conscious of the way she looks . . . of the way her
    fat wobbles . . . its'er flamin fault . . . she won't stop
    noshing.

DOREEN: 'Snot her fault. It's glands . . . don't be so unfair Derek
    . . . I swear Sandra's mum suffers with glands, eats like a
    sparrow and swells up . . .

DEREK: Sandra's mum?

DOREEN: You know, she's in those renovated council blocks
    opposite the sewage works where those Pakis live . . . The
    council flogged them mostly to Pakis, mind you they 'ad the
    dosh, anyway Sandra's mum got thick ankles from glands
    cause she retains water . . . 'snot her fault Derek, you know
    that, so the heat gets to her . . . she retains fluid . . .

DEREK: Yeah, she swelled up when she 'ad Tony, when she had

Tony she didn't 'alf swell up . . . I swear I thought she was
having quins, fuck me she ballooned right up . . .

DOREEN: Water . . . like Sandra's mum . . . she retains the
water . . .

DEREK: She got so fucking big . . . I tell you, I mean like a
747 . . .

DOREEN: Fluid . . . after pregnancy the works get all mucked up,
like they don't restore themselves . . .

DEREK: So she's fuckin ratty when the sun's hot! Like she says,
let's fuck off down to Brighton . . . I mean she loves
Brighton, you know the Lanes and the Pavilion and all
that . . .

DOREEN: The Pavillon's beautiful, it's supposed to be copied
from the Taj Mahal.

DAVE: Who told ja that . . . you donarf come out wiv em . . . fuck
me, she just made that up Del . . .

DOREEN: Don't be an ignorant bastard all your life, Dave, I know
it's based on the Taj Mahal 'cause I read it didn't I . . . some
prince went to India and fancied it so much he built it
'ere . . .

DAVE: First time I heard that, that is, I never knew that . . . and I
been coming here for yonks, I know it's 'istoric, I know
that . . .

DEREK: Your misses aint got no fuckin flies on her! Ay? She
fuckin knows somefing.

DOREEN: He finks that if his nibs aint copped it, then it don't
exist, dontcha doll?

DEREK: We used to come down on the train, it was a quid return
from Victoria, fuckin great, Dinah made sandwiches and tea
but we used to scoff the fuckin lot before we got here . . .
soon as we got in the fuckin train we'd get 'ungry like . . .
you know like the fuckin train got us in the picnic mood . . .
we'd scoff the lot . . . great it was . . . now it's a fuckin
tenner return . . . so we come down on the A23, through
Croydon and Streatham.

DAVE: M25's triffic. You get on the fucking A2 to Devon . . . nah
Dover (I'm a cunt) then hook off on to the M25 . . . piss off

down there until you see the M23. Hit that and stay on the cunt until you hit Brighton . . . it's all fuckin motorway Derek, you're mad staying on the A23.

DEREK: Fuck me, Dave, we waited for you in the pub . . . we were waiting for you for over half an hour, didn' we, you went miles out, you have to loop out east towards Dover then make a return, you put twenty mile on the journey!

DAVE: Nah, nah, you're wrong Derek, it's better 'cause you avoid the build-up on the A23 and on Satday you can't fuckin move and getting through Streatham and Brixton is bloody murder . . .

DOREEN: It's Bangla bloody Desh down there on Saturday . . .

DAVE: Nah, that's Brick Lane in the East End, that's Bangladesh, that's Little India, nah Brixton's little fucking Jamaica . . .

DOREEN: How can they eat those green bananas?

DAVE: So if you go that route, sure yeah if you get up at the crack like, but not on a fuckin weekend, you'd bleedin boil your rear-end gaskets! You must have left at the crack to get'ere before us.

DEREK: Not really, we sailed through the Oval, and slid down through Streatham, and dived through Brixton like a dose of salts, yeah we got a bit hung up in Croydon with the roadworks and they 'ad millions of red cones out . . . there were a lot of fucking poofs in the pub. Don't remember that . . . no, not years ago when we came down on the train . . . no fuckin way . . .

DAVE: There's a lot about now, don't do up your fuckin shoelace in Brighton, hahahahahahahaha.

DEREK: I mean, maybe you'd see 'em sitting in a fuckin corner . . . quiet like, you know, a touch of fuckin mascara, but bothering no one.

DOREEN: Live and let live, that's what I say, anyway it's their hormones, they got female hormones and think they're birds, can't help it, it's nature's way if you got female hormones you fancy fellas.

DEREK: Nah, they don't all have hormones, some become pooftas, like they're corrupted . . .

DOREEN: Nah, it's 'ormones, honest, a scientist did a test and said it was too many female 'ormones . . .

DEREK: They say once you've ad it up the kyber, if you'll pardon my expression, you'll be 'ooked for life . . . that's why they try to get 'em young, get in their cherry and then you're done for . . .

DOREEN: Sandra's mum washed and cleaned for two pooftas who got a sandwich shop in Dalston and she says they're the nicest couple you could hope to meet, clean and keep a beautiful flat and are wonderful cooks . . . she says they're ever so funny!

DEREK: I don't say they're all bad, do I?

DAVE: He didn't say nuffin bad Doreen . . . 'e ain't prejudice, I mean they can't 'elp it . . .

DEREK: Nah, fuck all that prejudice, nah I got nuffin against them 'cause they leave more crumpet for us, right!! I mean that can't be bad can it . . .

DAVE: Fuckin nice one Derek . . .

DEREK: Fuckin good yeah, tsawright for the pussy stakes as long as those turd bandits keep their shit diggers to themselves . . .

DAVE: There's gold between them thar hills, hahahahahahahaha!

DOREEN: Do you mind, there's a lady here!

DEREK: Well you know what I mean.

DOREEN: You're definitely out of order talking like that, no respect . . .

DEREK: Well all I'm saying is don't get near me that's all I'm saying . . .

DOREEN: You don't think they're such sex maniacs that they'd want to get too near you do ya, I mean they got standards like anyone else . . . I mean they're not that desperate . . .

DEREK: They'd stick it in anything, they can't 'elp it, they'd stick it in a fucking tree . . .

DAVE: Dee, you're definitely out of order so leave it out will ya . . .

DEREK: Look, all I'm saying is . . . fuck me, I'm only havin a giggle, that the pub me and Dinah went to for years and I fuckin mean years, where they had wines by the bottle that they'd get out and dust, not just red or fuckin white . . .

DAVE: Or sweet or dry . . .

DEREK: Yeah well that same pub used to be a fuckin great wine
bar wiv a wine list as long as yer arm and sometimes a pianist
ticklin a joanna, not some poxy sod going down on a fuckin
mike but a real instrumentalist . . .

DAVE: You're outa order Derek . . .

DEREK: Well you know what I mean . . .

DAVE: I know watcha mean . . . fings have changed . . .

DEREK: You know, you'd sit outside wiv half a bottle or a bottle
and there'd always be a few old biddies having a tipple of
sherry, yeah it was a fuckin sherry house . . .

DOREEN: Oh I like those places, they 'ad a real atmosphere didn't
they?

DEREK: Yeah, fuckin great wooden barrels up there on the
shelves, great fuckers they were, great fat old barrels . . .

DAVE: Like Dinah . . . Oooops!

DEREK: Here . . . who's out of order . . . eh!

DAVE: Sorree, you're right, I took a diafuckingbollockal
liberty . . .

DEREK: You did, so don't 'out of order' me.

DOREEN: That was out of order Dave . . .

DEREK: Thank you!

DOREEN: No, I mean that was definitely out of order.

DAVE: Jokin' weren't I . . . Dave knows I wouldn't pull a stroke,
Dave knows that . . .

DEREK: She can't help it Dave. (*Maudlin*) You're lucky. I mean
you take your luck for granted, you don't wanna extract the
urine from those who can't help it . . .

DOREEN: It's fluid retention . . .

DAVE: Awright I'll go and get another six Special Brews for that
OK? It's down to me anyways, another six fuckin
specials . . .

DEREK: No need, you got the last six . . .

DAVE: No no, I was out of order, I was.

DEREK: Anyway that wine bar's full of ginger beers now, packed
full of them . . .

DOREEN: They gotta go somewhere.

DEREK: Nah, as I said, I'm not prejudice, I'm not, I swear, you know that Dor. We got some Pakis down our street, sweet as a nut, little corner fuckin shop that they bought off some saucepan lids.* Open day and night. You run out of fags, you run in there . . .

DAVE: Fags you can buy in the pub.

DEREK: Awright . . . milk, butter, bread, awright, fucking tea, *News of the World*, bacon, err . . .

DOREEN: We got a Paki round our way, get anything, tomatoes, eggs, frozen TV dinners.

DAVE: They *are* good . . .

DOREEN: (*Continuing*) Chicken chop suey, frozen of course, beans, Heinz vegetable salad, Dave likes that . . .

DAVE: (*Sheepish*) I do, I must confess I don't half go a bundle on Heinz vegetable salad . . .

DOREEN: He loves it, can't get enough, we 'ave to ask them to order more tins, he don't half get fru em . . . so we 'ave to ask the Paks to order some in case they run out . . .

DEREK: Dinah won't have the *News of the World* in the house!

DAVE: You're joking!

DEREK: Nah, I swear.

DAVE: The *News of the World*?

DEREK: Yeah, I buy it at the Pakis and have a quiet read in the pub, right and bung it!

DAVE: You're 'aving me on. *News of the World* . . . that's a good read, that's awright . . .

DOREEN: It's very suggestive sometimes . . . a bit candid.

DEREK: That's what Dinah says, I says it tells what 'appens in the world, it's only the truff, swot people get up to, but Dinah say it's 'sexist'.

DAVE: Sod me, what's fuckin sexist? Everyfing sexist nowadays right?

DEREK: Dinah's got involved with some bint at work who turned her on to being feminist, she even taught her that word and

*yids

so she won't have feminist stuff in the house.

DOREEN: You mean sexist, that's what you mean, sexist!

DEREK: yeah that's right . . . yeah, I'm sexist and Dinah's feminist . . . she won't have sexist stuff in the house . . . she'll get over it, like it's a phase she's going through, she shouts at men all the time on the TV . . . drives me fuckin mad . . .

DOREEN: Could be her glands, could be exacerbated by her glands . . .

DAVE: She gotta take a broader outlook Derek . . .

DEREK: She hates the page three girls and the tits, I mean I don't mind, I mean God made woman didn't he so why be ashamed to flaunt a bit of what you got . . .

DAVE: Well, he must have been overworked when he made Dinah!

DEREK: Nah, he was pissed as a newt and said let's have a giggle . . .

DOREEN: You men can be very cruel . . .!

BOTH: Joookin!

DOREEN: You men have no real idea of what Dinah's had to stomach, she's given birth, what you bloody good for?

DEREK: Now don't get stroppy Doreen, I slave my fuckin guts out at Dagenham Car Works to keep her and us, working a fuckin assembly line, while she sits on her fuckin fat arse watching videos which she forgets to return, right and I pay, right one quid a day fine, like she forgets to return *Friday the Thirteenth, Part Five* right, forgot abaht it for five fucking days . . . five quid yeah, five fuckin quid, plus two quid for the hiring . . . and occasionally she pulls out a tit for the kid to have a nosh so don't get your knickers in a twist please . . . I'd swop any fuckin day . . .

DAVE: Give it a rest Del.

DEREK: Dinah must be killing them cows.

DOREEN: When I was a kid we used to go to the library, that was our video then, then we'd sit in and read and if you were late with your book you'd be fined two pence a day, that's all . . .

DAVE: Nah video's triffic, I mean the advances are fucking

unbelievable, I mean years ago it were only the movie stars who would watch home movies like, weren't it, like you'd read abaht some poncy sodden movie star watching movies in his front room while we'd be queueing in the fuckin rain for the one and nines right . . . 'member us kids queueing wiv mum for bleedin yonks and I remember when we missed the first show and stayed in the bloody queue to get in for the next session.

DOREEN: Yeah and you was always firsty, remember, you'd always get firsty and so you'd drink the pissy orange muck and it was always warm weren't it . . . ? We'd be sucking the last drop out and whole cinema sounded like croaking sodden frogs, 'member?

DAVE: Yeah. It was great though, used to snog a lot in them days, in fact it was amazing what you got up to in the dark . . .

DOREEN: Dirty bastard you were I'm sure.

DAVE: Nah, I mean you, Dor, I mean wiv you, did narf get up to some stunts in the dark . . . dontcha remember, eh? You do, you little bugger . . .

DOREEN: Get out of it you, mixing me up wiv someone, don't embarrass me Dave, you bastard . . .

DINAH: (*Returns with the burgers*) Fuckin soddin queue a bleedin mile long . . . oh yeah, nice for you! Wad ya want! I got two cheeseburgers and two plain. So wad ya want? You want the sodden cheeseburgers? Eh?

DEREK: I don't mind . . . do you want cheese Dave?

DAVE: Yeah, whatever comes up Dee . . .

DINAH: FUCKIN OLD LADIES MAKE A DECISION FOR ONCE IN YOUR FUCKIN LIVES. CHEESE OR PLAIN! THEY'RE GETTING COLD!

DEREK: (*Quick*) Cheese!

DAVE: Cheese!

DOREEN: I'll have plain Dinah, that's lovely darlin, I'm sorry you 'ad to queue . . .

DINAH: I was glad to get away from him for twenty minutes . . . it was bliss not to hear his bleedin moans . . .

DEREK: I appreciate your efforts on my behalf but it's luke bleedin warm . . .

DINAH: Next time . . .

DAVE: Mine's OK . . .

DINAH: Next time Derek . . .

DAVE: Mine's still quite hot.

DINAH: Next time Derek you bloody well . . .

DOREEN: Mine's still hot, wanna swop . . .

DEREK: Nah, I like it with the cheese . . . thanks though . . .

DINAH: Next time get your own sodden one!

DEREK: (*Loud*) Relax fuck it, you gotta fucking cheeseburger . . . you didn't fuckin swim the fuckin channel!!!

DOREEN: She queued for half an hour Derek.

DEREK: Ten to fifteen minutes.

DOREEN: Half an hour, she left at two p.m. . . . .

DEREK: Fifteen minutes top . . .

DOREEN: And now it's two-thirty by the clock on the Dolphinarium!

DEREK: We've been rabbiting for five minutes on how fantastic she is! I work five days a week on a conveyor belt, put the sprockets on the rear ends of exhaust pipes, an 'undred a day, I tell no lies and I don't make as much fuss . . . ah bollocks . . . you take my appetite away . . .

DAVE: Mine's delicious Dinah, ta muchly, triffic, gone down a treat, starvin I was.
(*Silence while they all eat and perform the usual, squeezing ketchup out of little sachets, getting it on their fingers and clothes, cursing, dribbling down their cheeks, bits falling out, dusting it off, wiping their faces, borrowing Kleenexes and handkerchiefs.*)

DEREK: So you think the A25's a better route, I mean it's longer.

DAVE: Doreen, tell him . . .

DOREEN: It is Derek, it is . . . it takes a smidgeon longer but it's a lovely drive and you can always stop at the Little Chef.

DEREK: You stop, what for a one and a half hour journey you stop! What, you fink you'll die of hunger!

DAVE: Got to, Doreen's waterworks, won't hold.

DOREEN: Daaaaaaaaaaayve!! Do you mind!

DAVE: 'Snatural . . . you're human ain't ya? Ay? We're not sodden machines . . . tsawright if you wanna splash your boots, who gives a fuck, come on, anyway we stopped and 'ad egg on toast. It weren't 'alf bad, and they got a playground for kids wiv plastic elephants . . .

DINAH: Oh, that's nice!

DEREK: (*To Dinah*) I was telling them about the poofs . . .

DINAH: What sodden poofs?

DEREK: In that wine bar stroke fuckin pub!

DINAH: Horrid!

DEREK: See!

DINAH: Horrid!

DEREK: What'd I tell you.

DINAH: Makes me shudder.

DEREK: See?

DINAH: It makes me go hot and cold.

DEREK: Right! See.

DINAH: I mean, there were so many.

DEREK: See what I mean?

DINAH: All together with moustaches and leather jackets . . .

DEREK: See? I mean, see!

DINAH: They was laughing all the time, like laughing at nuffin.

DEREK: See? They do, they do that. Laughing at nuffin.

DINAH: They were laughing like laughing at fuck all.

DOREEN: Wajamean?

DINAH: Like everything was funny, they kept saying things they thought was funny . . .

DEREK: See . . . we're not prejudice . . . we're not . . . honest, go on Dinah, go on . . .

DINAH: They kept laughing at nothing, like somebody who's dressed different, or they way they 'ad their hair or what they said, laughin all the time . . .

DEREK: Go on, go on, tell 'em . . .

DINAH: We waited 'cause we got there first, which I thought funny cause you said you were taking the M25.

DEREK: (*Sotto voce*) We *were* lucky with the traffic . . .

DAVE: It is faster Dinah, I swear, but we had to stop for muvver nature . . .

DOREEN: 'Snot my fault and give it a rest . . . you wanted to stuff your fat face . . .

DAVE: Tell you the truth the motorway cafe's diabloodybollical, straight up, but she needed a leak . . .

DOREEN: Shut up! Shut up! Shut up! About my bloody bladder . . .

DINAH: Take no notice Doreen, he pissed and he's known as 'tramlines' in our old street.

DAVE: 'Ere what you on about . . .

DINAH: Nuffin, 'cept you were known as tramlines in school (*laughs*).

DAVE: What!!? What she on abaht? (*Nervous.*)

DINAH: I'll save it for a more appropriate occasion . . .

DAVE: Nah, go on now, I can take it . . .

DINAH: Later.

DAVE: Now.

DINAH: Later.

DAVE: I said now.

DINAH: I said later . . .

DAVE: I bloody said now.

DINAH: I fuckin said later, aresehole.

DEREK: Leave it out Dinah, OK, leave it out . . .

DINAH: OK, but my cousin Barry, who works for the Brewery in Whitechapel, says at school you were known as tramlines 'cause you always wore the same knickers. (*Everybody snickers at this while* DAVE *looks mighty sick.*)

DAVE: OK, what a FUCKINDIABOLICALFUCKING-LOADABOLLOCKS. I mean bo. lax. Your fuckin cousin Barry, I don't know no Barry, but I do remember a squint eyes git that would go fuckin running to the headmaster every time I clipped the cunt round the ear called Bennet . . .

DINAH: That's 'im . . .

DAVE: What a fuckin miserable heap a shit he was, his mum fucked darkies in Cable Street, on the game she was . . .

DOREEN: OK leave it out . . . anyway Di what 'appened at the wine bar . . .

DAVE: 'Tramlines', what a lot of old cobblers I swear . . .

DOREEN: What happened at the wine bar with the poofs, you were saying about them laughing.

DINAH: Oh yeah, before you come we had a drink 'cause we always went there you know, always made a bee-line 'cause you could sit outside, when we courted Derek and I would drink there . . . got the train from Victoria, a quid return, a quid, went swimming by Black Rock, by the cliffs, lovely it was . . . it was then . . .

DEREK: Oh it was a treat, definitely a treat, walk to Rotters, Rottingdean, tea and scones, jam and butter and cream.

DINAH: Sat outside, it was a bit Continental, or we had a plate of fish and chips.

DEREK: Yeah, and we swam cause we loved swimmin then until one day we saw that turd swimmin in the water, well I could never get in there again . . . never.

DINAH: Horrid!

DEREK: Never!

DINAH: Just horrid.

DEREK: I did say at the time that it was probably an isolated turd, not a fucking sign like of sewage seepage, probably a one-off turd by some little bastard who couldn't hold it, but I never got in there again.

DINAH: Horrid, it just floated past my ear.

DEREK: Before that we'd love a swim, just let the waves grab you and throw you abaht a bit, love it that, triffic, a wave would pick you up like a dog wiv a bone and bung you down again on the shingle, cor didnarf sting at time but it was handsome, then we'd got for a tandoori in the Lanes, triffic place, did a right handsome prawn vindaloo!

DINAH: (*Drooling*) Ooooooooh!

DEREK: She'd love a fucking prawn vindaloo now wooncha girl . . .

DINAH: (*Overcome*) Hmmmmmmmmmmnnnnnn!

DEREK: You could waste a bleeding biriani and an onion barjee, eh plus a popadom . . .

DINAH: *Chicken Tee Kah*!!!

DEREK: Oh, they made a wicked chicken tikka.

DINAH: Shall we go there after!?

DEREK: We could, we could.

DAVE: I'd like to get my 'ands on that Barry Bennet bastard!

DEREK: So we'd have a good swim, get up your appetite and then bowl into some chink house or have your curry . . . curry's triffic after a swim though . . .

DOREEN: Don't half make you run in the morning . . .

DINAH: They say if you're constipated it's the best fing to eat, better than all those pills, just an hot curry, and you can order extra hot, make your eyes water, I like really hot . . .

DEREK: Or we'd bowl in to see the dolphins . . . they're smarter than most humans I know, it's fuckin brilliant the capers that they get up to.

DOREEN: I fink it's cruel . . .

DEREK: Nah, they're fuckin happy as larks swimmin about, smiling their fuckin head off, doin tricks, I mean some of the stunts they perform are unbelievable, they couldn't do it if they were pissed off could they, I mean they'd sulk . . .

DOREEN: Don't you think they miss their ocean home . . .

DAVE: That burger went down a treat.

DINAH: We could go after to that Indian for old times' sake . . .

DEREK: Yeah after, not yet, just stuffed a cheeseburger down me, let's bowl on the pier . . . play the slot machines and walk to Rottingdean . . .

DINAH: 'Stoo far.

DEREK: Two miles, slow canter . . .

DINAH: 'Stoo far for me fucking legs.

DEREK: We'll walk slow, you'll build up an appetite for your vindaloo . . . we'll stuff ourselves rotten, nan, marsala, onion barjee, walk slow . . .

DINAH: 'Tsmy legs . . .

DOREEN: Leave her Derek, she can't walk properly yet, so leave her, we can take a gentle stroll along the pier and back . . .

DEREK: 'Tsonly a short pier . . .

DOREEN: That's awright, fresh air, small walk, a bit of a natter, you can go in the leisure centre and kill a few Nazis on the video machines, you'd like that . . .

DEREK: Oh yeah ta, I used to like that walk to Rotters under the cliffs, hear the gulls screaming their heads off, watch the sunset, fucking handsome, watch the boats goin . . .

DINAH: (*Cutting in*) I CAN'T, MY FUCKING LEGS HURT!!!

DEREK: (*Shouting back*) I know, I know, I know, I was just saying it was nice . . . I know your fucking legs hurt! I was only saying, that's all . . . sayin!!!

(*Silence. Beer-drinking, smoking, make-up, farting.*)

DOREEN: A lot of black people down there (*Looking towards beach*) . . .

DAVE: So, they like it here, Brighton is the Caribbean of England . . .

DOREEN: I never understand why they lay there like they want to get a tan . . .

DAVE: Dor, you are dozey, they like the heat, they like the sun, I mean they come originally from the jungle don't they, so their memories are still in the sun, like they're drawn to it . . .

DINAH: Look, they're all in families, with the kids and grannie . . . see? They like to be together don't they . . .

DAVE: It's cheaper, they get 'em all in one motor . . .

DINAH: Ah look at the kids, they're ever so cute, aaaah look . . . init lovely wiv its little brown face and those sweet little plaits . . . oooh it intarf nice . . .

DAVE: I'm off for those Special Brews, anyone want anyfing while I'm there . . .

DEREK: Yeah, get us some Silk Cut while you're there, ta. If they ain't got that then Marlbro . . . you want some dough . . . you're awright for the dosh till you get back . . .

DINAH: Oh, I tell you what, I'd kill for some Maltesers, I got such a fancy for 'em right now, suddenly I got a yen . . .

DAVE: Right, Marlboro, Maltesers, Dor, dya want somat?

DOREEN: Maybe I'll have some crisps if you're goin.

DAVE: What kind, vinegar or prawn and onion?

DOREEN: I fink prawn will do Dave, ta . . . So, what 'appened in
the pub?

DINAH: Nah, nuffin really, just noticed how all the old biddies
had gone and they were all blokes. No women and I felt . . .
uncomfortable.

DEREK: See? Tell her! You know there's a nude beach now where
they go with their dicks hanging out, hunting for minors,
and I don't mean the ones who get their noses black . . .

DOREEN: You're joking.

DEREK: Straight up . . . I kid you not, a nude beach for . . .
men . . .

DOREEN: I like nudity . . . I mean, I don't fink there's nothing
wrong with it . . .

DEREK: Not if you're normal, awright, it's the most natural fing
in the world, I mean we're born without knickers I suppose,
right, I go along wiv that, specially if the bird's got a nice
pair of Bristols . . .

DINAH: Oh shut up, gutter mouth.

DEREK: You see . . .

DINAH: You see what?!

DEREK: You don't like exposure, you fink it's rude . . .

DINAH: Not rude, not rude jerkhead, fucking disgusting, 'cause
it's whoring by men to sell their shit newspapers to wankers
like yourself . . . yeah, and while they pretend to be
broadminded and all that bollocks, I'd like to see the editor's
limp dick and beer belly on page three! He's no better than
pimps who put birds on the game . . .

DEREK: Oooh, oooh, sorree, see? Didn't mean to bring it up, as
the actor said to the bishop!

DOREEN: I must say Dinah, I've never thought of it like that
before . . . it makes sense I must say . . .

DINAH: Soft porn!

DEREK: Nah, don't make me laugh, . . . 'snatural . . .

DOREEN: Dinah, so why did you feel threatened in the pub?

DINAH: 'Cause there were so many and I knew they hated
women . . .

DEREK: Not necessarily, I mean they may be turd burglars, but that don't go to follow that they hate women, they just don't want to get near them and when you look around I must say I don't entirely blame them . . .

DINAH: Maybe you got a touch of the 'iron' yourself!

DEREK: You gotta be fucking joking, my old sweetheart, iron hoof*? 'Mazing init, whenever you don't want to swing a leg over, you're accused of being a poof . . .

DOREEN: So what happened in the pub, Derek?

DEREK: We were waiting for you in this pub, right, what they call a gay pub now, so people know and don't go, whereas before everyone went there . . .

DINAH: Yeah, it was for everyone.

DEREK: Like a family pub.

DINAH: Where we courted when we came down years ago . . .

DEREK: So we bowled in, innocent like . . .

DINAH: And it was packed with geezers.

DEREK: Chocoblock.

DINAH: And they stared, they make you feel like *you're* queer, not them . . . Then two blokes kept looking at me . . .

DEREK: They just stared at her . . .

DINAH: They kept turning their heads and looking at me, it was just before you came. I felt good when you turned up 'cause there were more of us . . . Well they stared and then turned back and giggled, like giggled and turned and made sure that you knew they were taking the piss out of you, like they wanted you to know that they didn't want you there, that they hated you . . . and I stared back and they turned away, but they knew that you had caught their look, they knew you'd be clockin what they did, and they giggled their heads off 'cause I'm not a svelte young poof, I'm a woman and I've given birth . . . I can't help my fat, I hate it, Doreen.

DOREEN: It's fluid retention.

DINAH: Doreen I can't help it, I'm fat, I am fat, I admit I'm fat. A fat wobbling lump . . .

DOREEN: It's medical, it'll go . . .

*poof

DINAH: 'Cause I gave birth to Tony.

DEREK: I know darlin, but you do put it away, you do you know . . .

DINAH: I fucking eat less than you, it's just that you're always fuckin watchin me!

DEREK: To encourage you to fuckin diet . . .

DINAH: (*Screaming*) You had the fuckin cheeseburger . . . I had the plain burger . . . you drank six Special Brews, you and Dave . . .

DAVE: (*Returning*) Fuck me, I could hear you down the fuckin marina. Marlboro, Maltesers and onion crisps – didn't have prawn . . . Here wanna go to the Pavilion? . . .

DEREK: Nah, seen it, it's poxy and it costs a bomb . . .

DAVE: Wajawanado?

DEREK: (*Pissed off*) Fuck all.

DAVE: Hey, let's go on the fucking bumper cars!!

DOREEN: Yeah . . . ain't done that for yonks, that'll be great!

DEREK: OK . . . Dinah, do you wanna go on the bumpers?

DINAH: I'm not paranoid Doreen, I'm not. I know I'm fat . . . I *know* it's medical and I know I'm not very attractive but either you take me as I am or . . . fuck off!

DEREK: (*Softly mocking*) I take you as you are, for better or for worse (*holds her round her shoulders*). Come on, you old boot, you know I luv ya, I do, fuck the others on page three . . . it's you I luv . . . I do doll . . . I do . . . I luv ya, so don't get funny fucking ideas 'cause you know that you're my mate . . . gis a Malteser . . .

DINAH: You're pissed!

DEREK: No no, I've had four, maybe five . . . I swear I'm not Brahms, I'm sober as a judge, maybe more sober . . .

DOREEN: He means it Dinah, he does, I know he's not foolin . . . he's not . . .

DEREK: (*Pissed*) 'Cause I mean it and I don't give a monkeys what size you are doll, 'cause there's more to cuddle.

DINAH: (*A little sobbing*) You're pissed!

DEREK: I swear by my eyesight I'm not!

DAVE: Let's go on the bumper cars . . .

DEREK: I mean it.

DINAH: You mean it really?

DAVE: Come on you two . . . let's walk down the front . . .

DEREK: I mean it . . . I could have killed those two in the pub . . .
I wished I smashed a broken bottle in their ugly mugs . . .

DINAH: I'm glad you didn't.

DOREEN: So what happened in the pub, I mean after?

DINAH: I told you, they just stared at my body, they just stared
and giggled, trying to get me to go, to die of shame . . . there
was about twenty of them.

DOREEN: Well, just two of them were nasty, they're not all bad,
just those two, ignore them, ignorance is bliss is what I
say . . .

DEREK: Wanna do some slot machines first?

DAVE: Nah, let's get on the bumpers, bang about a bit, feel like
some exercise . . .

DEREK: OK doll?

DINAH: I'd rather see the dolphins . . . can't we do that?

DAVE: Look Doreen, tell you what, you go with Di to the
Dolphinarium and we'll go to the bumper cars and we'll
meet back here in an hour . . . OK?

DEREK: 'Kay. In an hour here, same place, but don't be two
hours.

DOREEN: One hour give or take ten minutes . . .

DINAH: Goody! I'm dyin to see the dolphins!

DEREK: And don't get up to mischief girls, don't get tempted . . .

DOREEN: Depends if anything tempting comes along, don't it?

DAVE: Awright, see yas back here in an hour, give or take ten
minutes, OK.

DEREK: OK.
DINAH: Tada.
DAVE: See ya.
DOREEN: One hour.

(*They split.*
Chairs are empty, noise of gulls louder, sounds of sea,
two chaps sit on the deckchairs.)

TOM: I'm sodden well knackered.

TED: So am I darling . . . we must have walked for miles . . .

TOM: Listen, I've got to get home, Richard will be furious, I've got to help him with the party.

TED: Don't go yet.

TOM: Doll, I must.

TED: Kiss me, just quickly.

TOM: You're potty.

TED: There's no one watching . . . just a quicky, come on . . .

TOM: Piss off Ted, you want to get us arrested . . .

TED: Don't be so stupid, you don't get arrested for kissing in public . . .

TOM: Want to bet . . .

TED: You've a lovely mouth, I keep wanting to bite it, like a cherry . . .

TOM: I'm exhausted, but I did enjoy it, I love being with you, and sex with you, but I love Richard, love living with him . . .

TED: Who says you have to leave him, just give me a bite of the cherry from time to time . . . look at those lovely black boys on the beach . . .

TOM: They are lovely.

TED: They're so carefree and so happy, that's what so beautiful, they're so at ease.

TOM: I hate Brighton on the weekend, every yob and his sister comes down from Chingford.

TED: Tight miserable bastards and all they want to do is get pissed and fight . . .

TOM: It's horried . . .

TED: Awful.

TOM: It's beautiful out there, just staring at the sea and sky, so calm, like a painting . . .

TED: It is . . .

TOM: And then you look down, yuk, empty beer cans, look, the dirty bastards who sat here couldn't even put their cans in the waste bins.

TED: I know, it's vile, but they don't know any better, they're like dumb beasts. They're sad, it is sad . . .

TED: Horrible, look at this filthy mess, bits of old hamburger and
fag ends, disgusting yobs . . .

TED: They can't help it Tom, that's all they know, you should feel
sorry for them . . .

TOM: Yeah, you mean like that fat woman in the pub who kept
staring at us, with that Rottweiler husband.

TED: I *know* . . . she was obsessed by you . . .

TED: Every time I looked up she was staring at me with her big
cow eyes, like a great fat cow, horrible, she looked like she
wanted to kill me!

TED: They *were* weird, like they didn't like what they saw . . .

TOM: Really! I thought I'd done something to her . . .

TED: Maybe she was worried her husband fancied you more than
her . . .

TOM: Well that wouldn't be too hard to imagine! Oh, he *was*
weird.

TED: I thought they were going to say something and then
another couple of freaks turned up and joined them . . . you
know why they hate us so much?

TOM: Why? Oh do tell, apart from the fact that we smell nicer . . .

TED: They hate us because they're trapped, they're trapped with
each other and we're not . . . not unless we want to be . . .

TOM: Yeah . . . wanna fag . . .
(*Silence, cigs smoked, sea sound grows louder, gulls, sounds of
slot machines, and merry-go-round, bumper cars, etc.*)

TOM: Tom . . . don't look up but I do believe our friends are
coming this way . . .

TOM: What friends.

TED: Your friends from the pub.

TOM: Oooh shit, I do believe they are . . . oh crap . . .

TED: Let's move, it's time to go anyway . . .

TOM: Why? Let them walk past us, we've done nothing. They
won't even notice us . . .

TED: They've stopped, they're talking as if they've seen us . . .

TOM: They're not, don't be so melodramatic, relax, they're not
about to do something . . .

TED: Come Tom let's go, they've left their women and they're walking this way, slowly, they don't know that we've seen them. Tom come on, let's just go . . .

TOM: *Sit down!*

TED: Sod you, I'm off! (*He leaves.*)

TOM: Shithead!

(DEREK *and* DAVE *both stand over him.*)

DEREK: I've seen you before?

TOM: Oh really . . .

DEREK: In the pub, you were in the pub, weren't cha, a couple of hours back . . .

TOM: Well what a coincidence, we use the same pubs don't we?

DEREK: Poofs pub!

TOM: Oh of course, we're all raving queer . . .

DEREK: You think women are funny dontcha, you fink my old lady's a gas?

DAVE: You fink his woman's something to laugh at?

DEREK: We're speaking to you, you want my cock up your arse?

DAVE: Wanna chew my dick?

TOM: (*Getting scared*) I couldn't think of anything nicer. Now why don't you go back to your monsters, they're getting jealous.

DEREK: What you say? My old lady's a monster?

TOM: No, just leave me alone . . . I've done nothing to you . . .

DAVE: You dying with AIDS?

TOM: Of course, now why don't you go away and let me die in peace . . .

DEREK: *You* . . . called my old lady a monster after laughing at her . . . *you* . . . who give people diseases.

DAVE: Diseases! They're fucking killing people . . .

DEREK: You're right, he's a potential killer . . .

DAVE: I think she's shitting herself.

DEREK: You shitting your drawers Sheila?

TOM: Why don't you relax! I've done nothing to you!

DEREK: Very lively ain't she, I fink she's craving a bit of pain . . .

DAVE: You took the piss out of his missus, in the pub . . . I mean that's a bit bold ain't it, 'cause you were wiv all your pooftas . . .

TOM: I didn't do anything, what am I supposed to have done?

DEREK: Laugh, you were laughin, werentcha, have a right laugh, cause my missus suffers from what we might call a generous form, so you were laughin werentcha, right giggle weren't it, eh, you fink yourself so pretty? Eh? So you were pissing yourself laughin, eh, werentcha taking the piss, having a laugh, go on, have some guts, admit it and you can go . . . fair's fair, you took a liberty but apologize and we'll forget it . . . you can piss off, come on don't sulk, we won't 'urtcha, just say, it was a wee bit naughty, sorry guv, I was laughin, I was out of order, that's all, won't do it again, like, laughin at others.

TOM: I never saw you before, I don't know what you're talking about . . .

DEREK: You're telling a nasty fib . . .

TOM: Oh, were you in that pub? What am I supposed to have done? I wasn't laughing at you, I wasn't.
(DEREK *viciously kicks him from the back of the deckchair.*)

TOM: Ooooooooow! LEAVE ME ALONE YOU BASTARDS.
(*Gets up.*) I'LL CALL THE POLICE.
(DEREK *kicks him again.*)

DEREK: (*screaming, as* TOM *goes*) GO ON YOU DISEASED FUCKING FAIRY! YOU DIRTY FILTHY BASTARD. I HOPE YOU FUCKING DIE OF AIDS, ALL OF YOU, YOU ROTTING FAGGOT!

DAVE: (*Impressed*) You really kicked the cunt . . . Fuck me, I heard a bone crack.

DEREK: Well Dave, I nearly lost my foot up there, didn't I . . .

DAVE: Shit Derek, I thought I heard a bone crack . . .

DEREK: Bollocks, I hardly touched him, don't talk cobblers, he just got a light whackin, a bruised arse, he'll be a bit sore there, might affect his love life for a couple of days . . . Hahaha!

DAVE: When you started screaming, they was all watching ya, them niggers looked up, fuck me Derek they looked up like they thought you lost your rag, and their kids looked up . . . half the fucking beach looked up . . . sod me, you weren't half screaming . . .

DEREK: Well I was double choked weren't I?
(DINAH and DOREEN *enters*.)

DINAH: Christ, what a commotion, poor kid had tears in his eyes.

DAVE: He only had a whacking.

DOREEN: You din't harf kick him vicious, he couldn't walk . . . he went white!

DEREK: He was awright! I did it for Dinah, right! He got what was coming his way! So he learned a lesson and that can't be bad! I was mild, some other geezer might have put him in hospital!

DOREEN: Still there's two of you, you could have just given him a ruckin, and warned him not to get stroppy again, but you didn't have to boot him, he could get you for assault . . .

DEREK: Sod all this, I mean I did it for you Dinah didn't I? Give me some credit, I mean where is the fucking age of chivalry, he insulted me 'cause he insulted my woman so I whacked the cunt . . . 'tsall over, finished.

DINAH: Still, he did deserve it, I give Derek that, he only got what he asked for . . .

DEREK: I'm still shaking (*Smiling with amazement*).

DAVE: You are!

DEREK: I got so fucking spare, I wanted to kill him!

DOREEN: Why?

DEREK: Why??

DOREEN: Yes why?

DEREK: Wajamean why?

DOREEN: I mean why . . . like why jawana kill 'im . . . I mean why?

DEREK: Listen Dave, she's asking why? 'Cause he insulted . . .

DOREEN: I know he was out of order and took the piss . . .

DAVE: Don't interfere Dor . . .!

DOREEN: Yeah, so give him a slaggin, or a backhander but he wants to kill him!

DEREK: Well if you want my opinion they're a menace to society, they're fucking evil!

DINAH: Well, they're killing theirselves off mostly, ain't they?

DEREK: Not fucking quick enough, funny though ain't it when

you come down to it. I mean you said something there! I mean, it attacks only the poofs, like nature sussed out it don't *like* it! I mean that's fuckin nature for you, red in tooth and fuckin claw . . .

DAVE: Well don't bend dahn in Brighton . . . Hahahahahaha! Here, who fancies some more Special Brews.

DEREK: I'm still shakin' . . .

DAVE: 'Ere Dor, do us a turn, why don't you and Dinah get the beer this time.

DOREEN: Okaaay! Come wiv Di?

DINAH: Yeah OK.

DAVE: See if you can get cold ones.

DINAH: You won't drink six now!

DEREK: What we don't drink now we'll drink in the car . . . then we'll dive into a tandoori!

DINAH: Lovely . . . I want my prawn vindaloo . . .!
(*They exit.*
Silence, sounds of sea grow louder, the sky darkens a little, gulls screech louder. They light cigs and sit back and inhale deeply. Well and truly satisfied with the course of events.)

DEREK: Been a good day . . . 'tsbeen nice!

DAVE: Yeah, ain't half been bad, weather kept up . . .

DEREK: Bit of a nip now . . . just a touch of parky . . .

DAVE: Nice though, I like it fresh . . .

DEREK: Gets the old appetite goin' . . .

DAVE: You goin' to Italy?

DEREK: If I can scive a week off, I will . . . I'm goin' sick . . .

DAVE: Cor, there'll be a lot goin' sick next week! Fancy England to win the cup?

DEREK: They could, they could, their forward line's triffic, although to be honest it's a touch weak in the centre field but they got some triffic talent and a great fuckin scorer. Trouble is the German bastards are not fuckin bad, we gotta watch out for the huns . . . yeah, the Argies are poxy and the Cameroons are a right fuckin laugh, but they did get in which is more than those dozey fucking Ozzies could do, the Italians are a bunch of fuckin cheating sods but they got one

diabolical good fuckin player, but they foul all the time. I
mean lying, fouling and cheating are the Itis'
characteristics . . .

DAVE: Yeah, you can tell a country by the way they play football I
fink . . .

DEREK: You're right Dave you do, you do . . .

DAVE: (*Looking right offstage*) Hold on.

DEREK: Wot?

DAVE: Hold on, hang abaht . . . I don't fuckin believe it . . . that
little poofta's back again!

DEREK: Wajamean, he's back?

DAVE: Up by the pier, look real slow, by the pancake stand, about
a dozen of 'em . . .

DEREK: Nah, don't piss abaht, they're just queueing for a
pancake . . .

DAVE: They're all looking this way though Derek and chatting,
fuck me, they're moving this way . . .

DEREK: I think you're fucking right, 'ere there's that poofta with
them, he's limpin, the cunt, and he's brought his chinas with
him . . . hold your ground Dave . . .

DAVE: (*About to go*) Don't be stupid, there's too many.

DEREK: But they're poofs! They're not blokes! You don't run
away from poofs!

DAVE: But Del, they're over a dozen handed, it doesn't matter,
let's have it away . . .

DEREK: Bollocks! Fuckin stay, you yellow cunt! Don't shit
yourself, they ain't got no bottle!

DAVE: Let's go Derek!

DEREK: Stay Dave, they got no guts, they've the guts of girls,
they're gutless! We'll waste all of 'em . . .

DAVE: I'll get the law! (*He goes.*)

DEREK: FUCKING COWARD, YOU FUCKING
GUTLESS BASTARD!
(*The sound of the sea grows stronger and the waves are crashing
in, the gulls shriek, the lights go slowly out as we see* DEREK
*looking in fear and resignation. The lights slowly come up and we
see* DEREK *a mass of tangled limbs and blood in his deckchair.*

He slowly moves and we see it's still living. He takes out a fag
and lights it . . .)
DEREK: Bollocks!
(*Lights snap out.*)

DAHLING YOU WERE MARVELLOUS

CHARACTERS

GARRY
SAMANTHA
DICKY TONG
KEITH
LINDA
STEVE
BRICK BERGMAN
SIR MICHAEL WALLY
MAITRE D'
TERRY ADAMS
BILLY TALL
MORRIS WELDER
WOULD-BE PRODUCER
SID
GUESTS
WOMAN FRIEND
PRODUCER
ASSISTANT
PRODUCER'S SECRETARY
HANGERS-ON
FAT PRODUCER
WAITRESS
ACTORS
TART
SLOANE
HACKS
SYCOPHANTS
SISTERS

AUTHOR'S NOTE

I tried to write a TV play set in a watering hole that caters for the theatrical chattering set. I modelled it on Orso's, a popular and very good London restaurant. It follows an evening after a first night at the theatre and it was an attempt to parody those precious dahlings and those utterly self-important creatures whose lives desperately depend on the outside world to give them form and shape, adulation and importance, having very little substance of their own. They float in an ether of seriousness that they believe wafts from their every utterance but they are well-meaning in their theatre babble.

It was very tempting to parody certain figures and the fun is trying to identify who they might be. Their lives are demarcated by the slogans posing as wisdom which they emit and the narcissism which is their philosophy. I have not hesitated to use myself in the rogue's gallery of frauds since one easily slides along the muddy road from time to time and it can be difficult to extricate oneself. We live through the good words of others and hope we will be popular, get good reviews and be recognized for our temporal talents. In the end the world inside is a parody of real life and outside the real world is being destroyed as the riots inspired by the Poll Tax bludgeon their way down the Strand burning cars and looting. Meanwhile the chatter goes on regarding the latest revival of *The Three Sisters*.

*A fashionable cafe . . . crowded . . . clumps of people at various
tables. Animated gestures and talk. Showbiz watering hole.
Unimportant people trying to get a table and pleading unsuccessfully
with the* MAITRE D'. WAITERS *are buzzing around and a small group
of waiters are singing Happy Birthday round a celebrating table. As
we pass round the tables we see another group celebrating a first night.
A dozen or so* GUESTS *are present around the* LEADING ACTOR.
Glasses of all colours festoon the table.

FIRST GUEST: *Hated* the first act but it warmed up in the second.

SECOND GUEST: Like last week's stew you mean? Please! So
    predictable darling . . .

THIRD GUEST: So over the top, you know what I mean?

FOURTH GUEST: Yes, he must have had his mum out there!
    (*Squeals of laughter.*)

FIFTH GUEST: Mind you I had the best sleep I've had in weeks.

SIX: You were lucky, I had to listen to that shit . . .

SEVEN: That love scene! I nearly heaved up . . .

EIGHT: Mind you in all fairness the direction didn't help him.

NINE: Didn't he use to direct traffic!
    (*Squeals of laughter.*)

TEN: Wasn't it exciting when he forgot his lines?!

NINE: Oh! I was cringing with embarrassment.

TEN: Well, it was the most honest he had been all night! (*He now
    turns to the actor who is sitting next to him.*) You were
    marvellous tonight, no I really mean . . . super . . . well
    done!

ACTOR: Thanks, a bit of a sweat but we got through, I must admit
    I was shitting several bricks before the curtain went up!

NINE: I wouldn't have believed it, you looked so calm and
    confident, so in control!

TEN: Icy, like you'd been playing it for a month and that scene
    when you attacked your wife, powerful stuff.

ACTOR: Not O.T.T.?

TEN: You? Over the top, never. You could never be over the top
    Garry, (*sotto voce*) when you enter, the stage comes to life!

ACTOR: Aw come on!

TEN: No really, I mean you have . . . presence!

NINE: You have it or you don't . . .

EIGHT: Cheers Garry and a long, long run!

SEVEN: (*Sotto voce*) How long do you give it?

EIGHT: A month at most.

SEVEN: You're too generous . . . I'll make it a week.

SIX: He was outrageous!

FIVE: Nerves, poor man suffers terribly with first-night
      nerves . . .

FOUR: Well he sprayed the first three rows with spit.

FIVE: Live theatre darling . . .

THREE: Mind you he had a good reception at the curtain . . .

TWO: Sheer bloody relief sweetheart . . . !

ONE: Cheers darling Garry and bloody well done!!

ALL: Terrific, smashing, stunning for a first night, fab, brill . . .

ACTOR: Thank you all . . . a big thanks . . . and a special thanks to
       my director who unfortunately couldn't be with us tonight
       but we wish him luck at Channel Four . . . and to Frank
       Drek who wrote words that actors would die for!

ALL: Here here!

ACTOR: To my leading lady Samantha who I know gave up a
       lucrative mini series to be able to do Frank's play . . .

SAMANTHA: (*Earnest*) Let's face it, that's why I came into the
          business, when do you get a chance to get your mouth
          around something like that . . .

ALL: Ooooooh! You are outrageous Sam . . .
     (*Much giggling at her cheekiness.*)

Linda and Steve's Table

*Camera wanders over to Linda and Steve's table or the waiter
wanders over, who we follow while the chat continues naturally from
the table we have left.*

LINDA: I think you'd be a fabulous Macbeth . . .

STEVE: Yah? I'd love to get my teeth into that. I really would.

LINDA: You'd be super really, you ought to play it!

STEVE: I think I'm ready for it, yah . . .

LINDA: You are you know, you should do it somewhere . . .

STEVE: I'd love to really, I think I'm right for it . . .

LINDA: You are, you'd be terrific, you're the right age . . .

STEVE: And temperament . . . I think I've got the temperament for it . . .

LINDA: You've definitely got that . . . you should have a go . . . you should . . . I think you'd be terrific . . .

STEVE: You think?

LINDA: Definitely!

STEVE: Not too old?

LINDA: No, no, you're just the right age, you've got the . . . maturity . . . he should be . . . mature. He's at the age when he wants . . . *recognition.*

STEVE: So he shouldn't be too young . . .

LINDA: No it's not interesting if he's too young . . .

STEVE: Some boring young fart won't give it . . . maturity!

LINDA: That's why you'd be good.

STEVE: I would?

LINDA: Definitely. I definitely think so, you'd be great, it's a great role for you . . . terribly sexy!

STEVE: Yeah, it is . . . it's got to have balls . . . you know I see him with balls . . . ballzy . . .

LINDA: He must have balls . . . It's terrible when he's played without balls . . .

STEVE: Awful! You know . . . you'd make a splendid Lady Macbeth . . . you would you know . . .

LINDA: Really . . . really . . . why??

STEVE: *You've* got balls!

LINDA: You are sweet . . .

STEVE: No . . . I mean it . . . you know what I mean, you've got more balls than most men in this place.

LINDA: Oh, do you mean it?

STEVE: I do really . . . we should do it together . . .

LINDA: Put all our balls in one basket . . . (*To* WAITER) Two more Margaritas please . . . Look who's come in . . . Isn't it Sir Michael Wally?

(SIR MICHAEL *enters with* TART *and* ACTOR . . . *goes from table to table, people rise and greet him unctiously, spilling their drinks as they rise trying to be effortless.* SIR M. *navigates the room with everybody rising and falling, drinks spilling into the laps of their partners at the tables. Hugs, kisses and masses of 'Darling . . . it was super'.*)

SYCOPHANTS: So moving fab!

Again! I don't know how you do it . . .

Let's have a meeting next week.

You must come over.

Tremendous, Sir Michael, I mean really tremendous.

Simply genius, I was enthralled.

You haven't met my wife . . .

(SIR M. *moves on.*)

WIFE: (*Crushed*) I'm sure he didn't hear you.

SYCOPHANTS: Sir Mike, you bastard, you've done it again.

(*Hugs.*)

Did enjoy it, super brill!

(SIR M. *joins the Producer's table where sits the star actor,* BRICK BERGMAN, *and various* SYCOPHANTS *and* ASSISTANTS.)

PRODUCER: The advance is fabulous! I mean *fab you luss*! and the word on the street is good . . .

ASSISTANT: Lionel Retch of *The Sunday Times* simply adored it . . . mind you he adores your work . . . loves everything you do.

(*Next table, asides.*)

VOICE 1: Especially the blow jobs!

VOICE 2: Don't be so wicked.

PRODUCER: Also, Martin Billious was enthralled, simply enthralled, and he loved you Brick. Thought you 'captured the character'.

BRICK: (*American Movie Actor*)Yeah? . . . Fucking great . . . Hey! I got through it didn't I, Sir Mike, at least shit, I didn't fall on my arse. The lines, the lines, they stayed in my brain . . . !

SIR M.: You did awfully well, simply super brilliant and of course your usually fabulously inventive, and intuitive street-wise self but you must find the light . . . your special spots where you do those marvellous soliloquies. We couldn't see you

Brick and we must see you. . . .

PRODUCER: I saw him, I saw him . . .

SIR M.: Not completely, the punters have paid fifteen quid to sit in a small hot smelly theatre with no air-conditioning in order to see all of you! So find your spots!

BRICK: Yeah, I'm thinking too much about the fucking verse that I miss the fucking lights . . . I must find them, I thought I was in them . . . I swear I could feel the heat!

SIR M.: You were just on the edge of the light Brick and we see the tip of your adorable nose which fortunately is a must when you come to play Cyrano de Bergerac (save a fortune on nose putty) so please I do beg of you, please do not have it snipped off, but we must see the rest of you . . .

BRICK: Tomorrow I'll find the light . . . definitely . . .

SIR M.: I mean they haven't come to see the rest of the boring farts I've cast . . . they're just there to give you the cues and then piss off . . .

Reception

A couple of idiot tarts come in.

MAITRE D': Hello! Long time no see . . . you're looking fabulous! Hey that coat is AMAZING . . . and it suits you so well, the reviews were MARVELLOUS . . . at least the ones I read!! Who cares about the others . . . Of course we've got a table, for you always, but if you could just wait at the bar.
(*A couple of nobodies come in*) Yes? Ooooh I am sorry, no I am sorry we don't have a single table, not a thing, terribly busy, try the cafe next door . . . yes . . . sorreeee . . .
(*A couple of regulars enter.*) Hello! Of course we booked your usual table if you don't mind a short wait, have a drink at the bar, you're looking very well, how was New York . . . Oh I love the energy too, it's so ALIVE, you know, so VIBRANT. Oh I love cities that stay awake, you feel the power soaring through you, I love your jacket, from L.A., of course you can tell, they have that zany laidback but very cute, very sheek, très elegant . . .

Brick's Table

BRICK: What about the fucking verse? I think I got the rhythm better, no?

SIR M.: Yah! No question, the metre was almost perfect. (*Goes into a trance-like state*) You see the metre is the music and the music is the metre . . . once you find the pulse in the line Shakespeare does it for you, like . . . 'Now is the winter of our discontent' (*thumps table*) 'made glorious summer by this sun of York' (*thump*).

BRICK: . . . 'and all the clouds that loured upon our house'
(*The whole table thumps.*)
'in the deep bosom of the ocean buried' . . .
(*Whole table thumps.*)
'now are our brows bound with victorious wreaths'
(*Thumps.*)
Yeah, I'm getting closer . . . I can feel it . . . the metre . . . the music's in the metre and the metre's in the music . . . right!
'Now is the winter of our discontent' (*thumps the table, the glasses jump and spill*).

SIR M.: Yes, yes,
(*People are beginning to stare from the surrounding tables.*)
You've got it . . . (*To* WAITER) Champagne and some mineral water . . . What mineral water do you have?

WAITER: (*Reels off the list*) Badoit, Perrier, Highland Spring, Malvern, Buxton Special . . .

PRODUCER: The advance is building up nicely, we're up on yesterday already . . .

ASSISTANT: I think Frank Bitch adored it . . . he was seen smiling when you did 'A horse, a horse, my kingdom for a horse'.

PRODUCER: That's right, he smiled, I heard that . . .

ASSISTANT: Yeah, he was seen smiling on very good authority, and at the curtain he did not rush out . . .

PRODUCER: No . . . he could have done but he stayed for the *curtain call*! Most unusual.

ASSISTANT: Very unusual, they usually rush out . . . to get their copy in . . .

PRODUCER: He stayed right to the last . . . most uncommon . . .
(*Next table, asides.*)

VOICE 1: He was asleep.

VOICE 2: Don't be so wicked.

BRICK: (*Practising*) 'Made glorious summer by this sun of York'
(*thump, glasses jump*). That OK Sir Mike? . . . It's getting to
me this fucking metre!
(*Next table, asides.*)

VOICE 1: I left my car on a meter this afternoon, it over-ran and
I got bloody towed . . .

VOICE 2: 'Cause you didn't pay attention to the meter!
(*British film actor,* TERRY ADAMS, *enters and goes to Brick's
table.*)

TERRY: Heard it went great . . . congrats . . .

BRICK: Yeah, well you know I got through it Terry . . .

TERRY: That's the main thing, as the actress said to the bishop
. . . I'll be in to see it . . .

BRICK: (*Excited*) Great! But don't tell me when you're in. OK? I
hate to know when anybody's in . . .

PRODUCER: Give it a few weeks . . .

SIR M.: It's true some actors are like that . . . they become
terribly self-aware when they *know* when someone they
know is in . . . it robs them of their character since they
know that *they* know who he is under the make-up and the
audience don't . . . the audience only know the mask . . .
you know Brick, the man beneath the mask . . .

TERRY: I won't breathe a dicky bird.

BRICK: Bless you Terry, you're a sport but will you have dinner
after?

TERRY: But you might be having dinner with someone else that
night . . . mightn't you? And I can't let you know I'm
coming in, less it interferes with your concentration . . .
unless I take pot luck . . .

BRICK: Oh shit shit shit! I know! You let my secretary know
when you're coming in and then she'll make a phoney
dinner engagement . . . OK? So when you're in I won't
know because I'll be having diner with so and so . . . you

arrive and then she says the other dinner is off!

TERRY: Double brill . . . you're terrific . . . (*To* SECRETARY.)
OK, book two tickets for Fri night . . .

BRICK: AAAAAAAAAAH! I heard it! I heard it!
(TERRY *wanders round tables.*)

TART: Oh Terry, you're looking so well, you've lost weight . . .
it suits you.

TERRY: Cambridge Diet darling . . . also don't mix carbs and
protein, that's it, no carbs with protein . . .

Linda and Steve's Table

LINDA: You really would make a fabulous Macbeth . . .

STEVE: You sure? I mean you really think I should do it?

LINDA: Definitely, you've been talking about it for the last
twenty-five years!

STEVE: OK . . . I'll do it . . . but who would direct me?

LINDA: That's a point, direct yourself! Like Keith Bragmuch!

STEVE: But I'm not like Bragmuch, I want guidance, someone to
open me up . . .

LINDA: I wonder who . . . ??

STEVE: I mean that's the nub of it. In fact who will employ me?
I haven't worked in five years except for two voice-overs.

LINDA: (*Jealous*) You get voice-overs? I've been trying to do
voice-overs for years but it's a closed shop . . .

STEVE: Well I know a fabulous agent . . .
(TERRY ADAMS *has now joined his table of four.*)

TERRY: (*To* BILLY TALL) You're looking more scrumptiously
eatable each time I clap my minces on your delectable
form . . .

BILLY: Ah bet you say that to all the crumpet!

FAT PRODUCER: Give us a piece of 'Marlon', Terry . . .

TERRY: (*Ever obliging*) 'I coulda been somebody, you shoulda
looked after me a liddle more . . . we going for the odds on
Wilson . . . it was you Charlie . . . you wuz my brudder . . .
and I wind up with a one way ticket to Palookaville.'

BILLY: Heyyy! That's fabulous . . . Ah think you're so clevah you English actors . . .

FAT PRODUCER: Billy, I think you're pretty good yourself, I
mean you got a standing ovation, right? I mean there you
are, one of the most beautiful women in the universe and
every shmock thinks . . . aah wiv all that beauty you gotta be
as thick as two planks and you get on those boards and knock
them out . . .

BILLY: Aaaah, you're too kind, 'Ah have always depended on the
kindness of strangers'.

FAT PRODUCER: Well darlin' . . . (*dirty aside*) I'm hardly strange
am I?

BILLY: I was quoting from the great master Tennessee Williams,
you fat groping greasy pig, now get your hand off my leg
before I catch your herpes!

TERRY: HAHAHAHAHAHAHAHAHAHAHAHA!

STEVE: I did a voice-over once for cornflakes playing the voice of a
six year old . . . that was my voice . . .

LINDA: I saw that! That was your voice? You were
MARVELLOUS!!

STEVE: (*Little boy's voice*) Mummy give me some more scrunchy
cornflakes (*beats spoon*).

LINDA: Darling that was really fab, you've got the character so
well . . . if I shut my eyes you could be a six-year-old toddler
. . . *how sweet*!

STEVE: 'Mummy can I have some more cornflakes?' (*beats plate
with spoon enthusiastically*.)

Terry's Table

PRODUCER'S SECRETARY: Terry do you have any plans to return
to Hollywood?

TERRY: Funny you should ask me that . . . I was thinking abaht it
but my agent woke up the other day and we're hanging about
to encourage him to *stay* awake . . . it's all quite exciting and
he's amazed at the changes in the industry since he's been
asleep. Apparently he said there's a film being made here in
England next year . . .

PRODUCER'S SECRETARY: What!! A film made here, in
England!!
(*Whole restaurant has stopped eating, silent, ears on stalks.*)
You're joking.

TERRY: No it's a fact. I bet you didn't know that did you. They're
going to make a film here . . . there might even . . . be . . .
two!
(*Noise returns to room, much gossiping and murmurs.*)

FAT PRODUCER: So you're still with the Living Dead Agency, in
case we need you?

TERRY: Of course, been with them since I was a super superstar,
but when I was just a superstar I was with Skunk and Thief.

FAT PRODUCER: Whatever happened to them?

TERRY: They do mostly animal acts and rock singers . . .

PRODUCER'S SECRETARY: So you want to return to Hollywood
. . . ooh, we'll be so happy!

TERRY: Dunno really, but I do like the lifestyle and the sun . . . I
mean here it's always pissing down . . . mind you, you've got
less chance of being shot dead. Do you know there were 6000
murders with hand guns in America in one year, while here
there was eight!! Bet you didn't know that did you?

FAT PRODUCER: They're a violent people, what can I say, but the
size of the sandwiches is remarkable *and* you get a second
cup of coffee for free! So it's swings and roundabouts . . . and
they love you in Hollywood . . . you get feedback.

TERRY: Not so sure, I've been taken off the 'A' list at parties!

FAT PRODUCER: You've got to be kidding me . . . !

BILLY: Oh no, that's terrible! Why should they do that to you.
You're never an empty seat at the dinner table . . . you
always give so much! Terry . . . why?? I can't believe that
. . . that's awful . . . I'm going to ring my agent and find out!
That's really awful . . . off the 'A' list . . . I'm going to
cry . . .

FAT PRODUCER: Terry Terry, why didn't you tell me this
before . . .

TERRY: I didn't want to tell anyone, just the missus and me . . .
the thing is I can take it . . . know what I mean . . . I've gone

through worse things in life . . . I was brought up in the East
End . . . My dad was a bus conductor on the 38 bus. It was a
bad route until you got to Piccadilly. Have you ever been on
a number 19 bus from Walthamstow on a Saturday night,
Billy?

BILLY: (*Thinks for moment*) No, Terry, I don't think so . . .

TERRY: Then don't, it's seriously unfunny . . .

FAT PRODUCER: (*Serious*) There's a film there Terry, there is the
making of a film. Quick somebody give me a napkin, I
wanna write down the synposis, maybe we'll get some
development money from Hemdale . . . but who can play
Terry?! That's the thing, who could play you????

TERRY: Me??

FAT PRODUCER: No, no, not this one, you're not right for the
part, but I'll think about it . . .

PRODUCER'S SECRETARY: What about Brick Bergman, he's
here, you could mention it Terry, he likes you, you like him,
you like each other. He respects your work, you respect his,
you respect each other's, he's had ten tonies, four oscars, two
monties, and never made a penny for his backers but he's
respected and . . . and . . . he's on the 'A' list for parties . . .

TERRY: On the 'A' list, hmmmmmnn . . .

Brick's Table

BRICK: (*Getting pissed*) So you think I did OK. I mean really. I
mean level with me . . . I mean I can take it, you know that
. . . I mean you can say 'Brick, Brick, you acted tonight like a
brick . . . I can take it . . . whad, you think I can't take it,
well I can take it . . . Look, last year I earned ten million
dollars for one movie. Man that movie stunk and lost more
money than your gross national product . . . So what I'm
saying is I'm here to learn . . . right . . . so get that sword fish
out of your mouth and speak . . .

SIR M.: (*Struggling and mumbling*) I can't, it's stuck in my throat!
(BRICK *slaps him on the back and a bone shoots out of his mouth
like an arrow and impales itself in the wall, if not in a* WAITER.)

Aaah, that's better. You were saying, Brick?

(BRICK *repeats last speech 'I mean I can take it . . .' at five times the speed to get it over with.*)

SIR M.: Ah . . . no . . . you did extraordinarily well, there's a certain rhythm, a textured sound that you got . . .

(*Whole table sycophantically listens to the 'guru'.*)

You see Shakespeare sounded more like you in his time than like me today . . .

BRICK: (*astounded*) Wad! Like me . . . you gotta be kidding!

SIR M.: No, in fact the Pilgrim Fathers brought to America the southern English twang which you preserved so your rhythms and accent are closer to Bill Shakespeare than mine. I mean my accent sounds like someone straining over the loo . . . Yah!? (*demonstrates*) you see . . . uuugh! Such strain, well that's years of public school and repression . . .

BRICK: Hey, that's good to know that old Bill spoke like me. How about that! Mind you Sir Michael, I really love that British accent . . . that straining at the loo effect . . . I wish I could get it . . .

SIR M.: Well it's not difficult . . . Imagine you're on the loo, right?

BRICK: (*Adjusts his bum on the chair as if he was on the loo*) OK, I'm on the loo.

SIR M.: Now try a line in the play, any line and at the same time you're straining a stool.

PRODUCER'S SECRETARY: Oh Sir Michael, not now please, people are watching him . . .

BRICK: It's OK . . . I wanna learn . . . who cares who's watching . . . tonight I had a thousand people watching me at the Fleabox Theatre, so should I care if a few down and outs, who collectively make less in a year than I do in a week, are watching . . .

TART: Brick, preserve your dignity . . .

BRICK: OK, when you pay for it I'll preserve . . . they don't keep me! Right? That's what my Ma said to me . . . 'Don't be shy, are they keeping you?' She said that . . . I'd come home after traipsing round the town . . . looking for work, anything! I'd do anything . . . I'd go for an audition with a stain on my hat and a shine on my shoes and be rejected . . . But Ma would wait up with a plate of borscht and a pumpernickel bagel . . . that's what kept me going . . . so I should care if they are watching me. Who are they? Huh! You tell me who are they? (*Table breaks into spontaneous applause which* BRICK *shyly receives.*)

PRODUCER'S SECRETARY: I adore borscht . . . How did your mother make it?

BRICK: She'd cook the beets in water to which she'd add the yolk of two eggs . . . not cream! But eggs . . . with cream, that's the European way, where do you think they'd get double cream in the back streets of Kiev? But chickens they had . . . chicken everybody kept in the front room . . . laying eggs on the armchair . . . OK, Sir Michael, I'm sitting on the throne . . . not Richard the Third's throne . . . ha ha ha . . .

MORRIS WELDER, English Producer's table

WELDER: We're packed each night, we're grossing 110% but he won't play more than three months, so we only get our money back . . .

WOULD-BE PRODUCER: Oh dear, oh dear, that's too bad, I have a wonderful play I'd like you to . . .

WELDER: Mind you I love stars! I can't help it, but so do the public, the public love to see a star on the stage . . . you think the public want to see Doreen Sludge do *Mother Courage* again with a shmutter on her head and holes in her stockings . . . nah, they want stars . . . (*confident*) I want Marlon Brando to play Lear!

WOULD-BE PRODUCER: Oh, oh that's fabulous, what a unique fabulous idea, that's brill! Marlon!!! Oh that's brill . . .

ACTOR: (*At same table, as Brando*) 'I coulda had class, but you sent me on a one-way ticket to Palookaville . . . not my night? . . . You wuz my brudder . . . you shoulda looked after me a little more.'

WOULD-BE PRODUCER: Oh that's really superb, really, no really, no really, no really, seriously though . . .

ACTOR: (*continuing*) 'That's right, I'll make him an offer he can't refuse' . . .

WOULD-BE PRODUCER: Ha ha, you know Mr Welder, I have a play that would be . . .

WELDER: (*Cuts him off*) He's good, the kid's good . . . I'm flying to New York tomorrow. I want Greta Garbo back on stage.

WOULD-BE PRODUCER: But she's dead, she died last year . . .

WELDER: She's dead?? . . . you sure it's not just another PR job . . . You can never tell, film rentals will try anything to increase sales . . .

WOULD-BE PRODUCER: No, she's definitely and very sadly . . .

WELDER: Well, we'll try Anthony Quinn, Robert De Niro and Al Pacino . . . gimme the phone . . .

WOULD-BE PRODUCER: (*Impressed*) No time like the present . . . (*hands him the mobile phone.*)

WELDER: (*Punches out number*) But first Marlon!

ACTOR: (*Brando*) 'How come you don't come round for coffee . . . '

WELDER: Ooh! Marlon? Is that you? Or are you impersonating yourself. How do I know it's you? Yes, it certainly sounds like you . . . Give me a clue so that I know it's you . . . (*aside to table*) You see he doesn't want to talk to the press so all his staff are employed to impersonate him . . .

TABLE: AAAAAH!

WELDER: Now Marlon to make sure it *is* you, what were you doing in a stretch limo with your trousers half-way down, with a blonde bimbo called Marina . . . on the way to the airport in June 1979? . . . Yes! Yes! It is you! How *are* you? Now listen Marlon I have a fabulous idea for you . . .

Brick's Table

BRICK: (*Straining*) 'Now is the winter of our discontent' (TABLE *thumps for him.*)
'Made glorious summer by this sun of York.'
(*Thump.*)

SIR M.: That's better . . . the accent's coming! It's really coming!

BRICK: God it's hard at first but it's beautiful, I love it . . . I can feel it . . . Wow!

TART: Be careful you don't have an accident!!

(BRICK *looks at her in disgust*.)

Linda and Steve's Table

STEVE: You don't think I'm too . . . how shall I say it . . . too mercurial for Macbeth, I mean I love the role, I do, but I think I'm more Iago-ish or Mercutio-ish.

LINDA: You'd be a fabulous Iago . . . yes, you have that quicksilver mind. You'd make a very funny Mercutio. HAHAHAHAHA.

STEVE: You think?

LINDA: Yah, very funny, very witty, but I'd love to see your Macbeth.

STEVE: You don't think I'm too mature for it . . .

LINDA: No, he should be mature . . . ready for the big one . . . and you've got the balls . . .

STEVE: Sometimes Linda, I wonder where my balls are . . .

LINDA: I suppose they're where they usually are . . . in the top drawer next to your dentures . . . HAHAHAHAHAHA!

STEVE: You're wicked Linda, you should know how 'artists' struggle with decisions . . .

LINDA: Don't be so silly, I'm teasing you . . . Of course you've got balls, you've got the biggest pair of balls in this room!

STEVE: What about Brick Bergman?

LINDA: What about him?

STEVE: He's a ballzy actor . . .

LINDA: But you have a different type of balls, all he is is balls but you have sensitive balls . . .

STEVE: Ahh, you're just saying that . . .

LINDA: I'm dying for a drink . . .

STEVE: Sir Michael's totally without balls.

LINDA: Not totally but small balls . . .

STEVE: And Terry Adams?

LINDA: Medium-size balls, no, I will say I have seen him be convincing. Where's my bloody drink? . . .

TV Hacks' and Media Pimps' Table

HACK 1: So what you up to you old farter?? (*To* WAITRESS.) Another Chablis . . . no make it Sancerre.

HACK 2: Channel Four.
(*A buzz down the table, 'Channel Four, on Channel Four, Four, Channel Four'.*)
I'm doing a film for Channel Four.

TABLE: Channel Four.
He works all the time for Channel Four.
Really *the* Channel Four?
I had a commission for Channel Four.
Channel Four promised me a commission.
Why don't you try Channel Four?
Who's at Four now?

HACK 2: It examines the role of Russian housewives engaging in prostitution in their lunch breaks . . .

HACK 1: That sounds *fasc*inating, did you submit it to Channel Four?

HACK 2: Oh no, Channel Four commissioned me!

HACK 1: Channel Four commissioned *you*! How fabulous. Good budget?

HACK 2: Enough, not grand, stick to House Red
HAHAHAHA! Use stock newsreel, talking heads, prepared a treatment, they loved it, went upstairs, got the OK.

TABLE: Who do you know at Channel Four?
At Channel Four? Channel Four?
I used to know the secretary of the Commissioning Editor.
Channel Four once asked me to do a thirty-minute chat show but the buggers shelved it.
What was it about?
Culture in Nineties Britain.
Sounds fab, why shelve it?

Couldn't get enough material.

A VOICE: I nearly had my play on Channel Four, Channel Four
saw it at the King's Head in part of their lunchtime Festival of
Plays and simply adored it but some wanker at the top of
Channel Four vetoes it, a jealous bastard who was afraid of its
dynamic social implications.

VOICES: Channel Four
Channel Four
Channel Four
Channel Four
Channel Four

Two Left-wing Fringe Elitists' Table

SID: Yeah, the bloody Arts Council want to cut our grant, in real
terms so we only got what we got last year in real terms, when
what we need is more dosh just to stay alive in real terms . . . I
mean I'm alive, I'm very much alive but the poor fucking staff
have to eat, nay survive on the thrown-out sandies from the
brasserie next door. We need another million.

SYCOPHANT: Of course you do . . . your work is so . . . historic,
and so vital . . . it's so relevant, I mean you've got your stink
finger on the pulse of the monetarist society so to speak.

SID: We've got to have the right to fail . . . it's a God-given right, I
mean we're not here to try out wanky musicals on taxpayers'
money to line some investors' pockets . . . we're here to expose
alternative Britain. I mean we're their voice! If they don't give
me another mill I'm closing the theatre down!

SYCOPHANT: Oh God, that would be the grossest act of
philistinism if the government was to let that happen . . .
Look at Europe, France, you'd be honoured in France or
Germany . . . (*To* WAITER) Another Pouilly Fuissé '85.

Garry's First-Night Table

GARRY: So you think it went down well do you?
WOMAN: More than well, I mean for a First Night it was super . . . I

mean Garry it *was* your first night and the set didn't fall
down!

WOMAN 2: I noticed that! Usually it falls down on the first night
or wobbles precariously when you slam the door or the
revolver gets stuck and the poor actors stand there with egg
and have to make up the words, it's fabulous, but your set
was firm and erect, it was a beautiful set . . . (*Turns to man
nearby*) Well done Keith.

KEITH: Oh ta!

GUEST 1: Yah, congrats on set.

GUEST 2: Triffic design . . . a beaut.

GUEST 3: Oh I loved the way it scooped and twisted, its art
nouveau line but that dash of German Expressionism?

KEITH: Oh yes, I do admit . . .

GUEST 3: Little nibbles from Max Rheinhardt's Thirties
production of *Midsummer Night's Dream*?

KEITH: Spot on!

GARRY: (*To* WOMAN FRIEND) How was my last speech? (*Ignored*)

GUEST 4: Keith, correct me if I'm wrong but a dash, dare I say in
a moment of tongue liberating inebriation, of shades of
Gordon Craig!?

KEITH: Yes!!

TABLE: (*All clap*)
Bravo.
Triffic!!
You are clevah Tom.

GUEST 4: And if I'm not pushing the boat out too far, a mere
scintilla of the Kabuki?

KEITH: Yes, yes!

TABLE: Bravo.
Fab.
Cheers!
Bollacks!

GUEST 5: Yes, but I also thought I sensed a touch of Meyerhold's
bio-mechanics!

TABLE: Boo!
Bravo!

Fab!

Supaah!

Brill darling!

KEITH: I'm going for a piss. 'Scuse us!

GARRY: So how was my *last scene*! I'm not paranoid but I'm an
artist, not a butcher, or toss-pot director who learnt his trade
at Oxford directing from the stalls while staring up the skirts
of undergraduates or picking clinkers out of Sir's asshole!

WOMAN FRIEND: SHHH! Garry, you're a bit piddly!

GARRY: I'm not an animal, I'm a human being! I'm an artist! A
creative artist! Fuck the set! Fuck it! The audience come to
see me! Not the fucking set! Live human flesh, living tissue,
not John Wankers and his 3000 light cues! Human being!

TABLE: Bravo, bravo!

Cheers Garry, Triffic!

Well done mate!

Channel Four!

Left-wing Fringe Elitists' Table

SID: I swear I'll close the theatre unless I get more dosh to put on
artistic failures! It's my right to play to empty houses! How
many paintings did bloody Van Gogh sell, eh?

SYCOPHANT: You're absolutely right.

SID: I mean we're not Andrew Lloyd Webber!

SYCOPHANT: Thank God for that. Oh dear, he's actually sitting
across the way!

SID: Shit! You don't think he heard me?

SYCOPHANT: No, there's far too much noise.

SID: You sure?

SYCOPHANT: Positive . . .

SID: OK . . . I mean we're like pioneers like scientists and
explorers and must have funding.

SYCOPHANT: So you should!

SID: How many people were in tonight?

SYCOPHANT: Seven I think and three comps . . .

SID: That's five more than last night . . . ten! So we're up fifty per

cent on the night before! You know we should inform the
press about that! The only theatre in London up fifty per cent!

SYCOPHANT: That's right! Darling they're coming because you
are part of that great tradition and I beg of you that no matter
how hard you might fight and how tough things get, without
you it would be a cheap *commercial* success but with you it's a
fabulous *artistic* disaster!

SID: Darling . . . I've got a hard on! Darling . . . (*Look limpidly
into each other's eyes.*

THREE ACTRESSES *swan in. They pass Sid's table and stop for
those brief encounters.*)

3 ACTRESSES: Hi.
Darling!
Hello.

SID: Hello . . . how are you? I heard you're doing great stuff.

3 ACTRESSES: So exciting!
Fab!
Wonderful!

SID: So what you up to?

3 ACTRESSES: We're doing the *Three Sisters*!

SID: That's *so* unusually fantastic.

3 ACTRESSES: It's such a moving play.
Really, quite beautiful.
There's such depth, such real power.
I adore Chekhov.
I love Chekhov.
I always have.
He understands the human soul.
Its 'gravitas'.
Its sonorous humour.

SID: So you three are playing the *eponymous* heroines.

3 ACTRESSES: Yes, isn't it too fab.
It's simply wonderful!
Ecstatically exciting.
I adore playing Russians!
Oh I love the roles.
The way he writes for women.

He seems to *understand* women.

SID: Who's directing you?

3 ACTRESSES: You won't believe it.

It's just too brill for verbs.

He's God of course, who do you think?

SID: Apart from from . . . aah??? . . . Hmnn . . .

3 ACTRESSES: Who's the most talented director of their
generation?

The greatest exponent of physical theatre?

The man who lets the play 'breathe'.

Who doesn't stamp his director's boot in the face of the
author?

Who lets the lines speak for themselves?

Who? Who? Who?

(SID *looks baffled*.)

Leslie Ponce!!

SID: Oh my God! I thought he was touring China with a fifty-hour
version of *The Talmud*.

3 ACTRESSES: He was, but he's had to cancel it for political reasons
and he's come back.

Specially for us.

It's so . . . awesome.

(*They head off round other tables exploding their greetings here
and there*.)

SID: Shit! Leslie Ponce is back!

SYCOPHANT: So what darling!

SID: The press will hold him up like their saviour! He'll be in all the
bloody supplements plus the *Guardian*'s weekend feature.

SYCOPHANT: But darling, he's into bourgeois, revisionist
eclecticism plus middle-class ethnic romanticism . . .

SID: That's true . . . I think I'll take a piss . . . order another
champagne will you?

Terry's Table

TERRY: No, once I was off the 'A' list I thought sod this for a laugh.

FAT PRODUCER: You'll get back on it don't worry . . . a little jogging, a Cambridge Diet, a spot on the Johnny Carson show . . . you'll be up there with Kirk . . .

BILLY: Who's on the 'A' list?

TERRY: Well, Kirk for a kick off, Fonda, De Niro, Jimmy Stewart, Greg Peck, even Madonna . . . !

BILLY: My gawd! And they drop you, the wittiest, funniest, sweetest guy who ever filled a chair, and so who's who on the 'B' list?

TERRY: (*Almost weeping*) Tommy Lee Jones, Robert Duvall, Sydney Poitier, Jeff Goldblum!!

BILLY: Oh no! Don't tell me anymore . . . I can't bear it, you have to sit at the same table with Jeff 'The Fly' Goldblum . . . Uuuuuugh!

TERRY: Not only that . . . no . . . wait . . . I've got to tell you this . . . not only that my dear (*holding back the tears*) but, no VALET PARKING!

TABLE: Shit!

I don't believe it!

Disgusting!

Ugh the Cheapos!

TERRY: Right! No valet parking, so you're walking all the way back to the party from where you've parked . . . sometimes you walk a hundred yards in an *ordinary* street with *ordinary* people.

TABLE: Eeech! Ugh! Help! Oh no! . . .

TERRY: You know like ordinary people like those extras you see in movies for background who eat in their own canteen . . . I had to walk in the *same street*!

FAT PRODUCER: Am I hearing right!!! Is that what the bastards made you do!!!?? (*To* SYCOPHANT) Get me I.C.M. on the phone . . . !

TERRY: (*Bravely holding back tears*) Yeah, I try to look at the pavement and keep a low profile but they stared at me with those ordinary eyes!

BILLY: I feel sick . . . I'm going to the bathroom . . .

TERRY: Not only that, when I got in I was served *Californian* not French champagne!

FAT PRODUCER: Heads will topple for this . . . don't worry, heads will topple. Does Pepsico know about this?

TERRY: I guess it's all over town . . . Europe, Russia, maybe even China, there's not many places I can go . . .

FAT PRODUCER: Somebody will pay!

TERRY: But the worst is this (*Struggling*) . . . I was doing my impression of Marlon . . . you know . . .

FAT PRODUCER: Ach! You give too much of yourself . . . you're too generous . . . he's too generous . . .

TERRY: I don't mind, I was trying to adjust to a lower class, like mix in, show good will . . .

FAT PRODUCER: Oh my God, the man's a saint . . . heads will roll, believe me . . . I'll take it out on their skulls . . . Ron and Nancy will know about this . . . !

TERRY: So I was doing Marlon, you know . . . 'I coulda had class, you shoulda looked after me a liddle more' when Jeff Goldblum does an impersonation of a fly!

FAT PRODUCER: Tell me you're kidding! Please! Jest not!

TERRY: I swear, in the middle of my shtick. He buzzes around me as 'the fly' and everybody laughs and nobody pays attention to my impersonation.

FAT PRODUCER: The asshole! Did you say anything to him?

TERRY: I did, I said, 'Come on Jeff, give me a break . . . you'll have your moment when you're not an empty chair.'

FAT PRODUCER: So what did he reply?

TERRY: He said he was just being a fly in my scene . . . in *my scene*!

FAT PRODUCER: (*Shakes head, on mobile phone*) Hello, hello, I.C.M. OK give me the head of I.C.M., yeah that's right, look I don't care if he *is* working, wake him up! Heads will roll believe me.

(WAITER *passes by*)

Oh, do you have any more of that delicious pizza bread?

Linda and Steve's Table

STEVE: You don't think *Macbeth* has been done to death? I mean . . . it's *so* familiar . . .

LINDA: I'd love to see *your* Macbeth . . . I mean we've seen
Larry's, Ian's, Tony's, Brian's, Paul's and now the public
are *dying* to see yours . . . Don't forget you have *some* fans . . .

STEVE: So you think Macbeth is right?

LINDA: It's never been more right! Steve darling, you've got to
get your balls between your teeth and do it!

STEVE: (*Brainstorm*) You're right! Look, why don't we read the
play together at your flat . . . and get the *feel*.

LINDA: SUPAH!!!

STEVE: Then we can test it and you read Lady Macbeth . . .

LINDA: Hippopotamus!!

(STEVE *looks puzzled*)

I always say that when I am *hugely* thrilled!

STEVE: Aah?! So get out your filo and book a time . . .

LINDA: Lovely! (*Thumbing through*) Well, um . . . Monday I have
an audition, must keep my head clear that day, Tues, I've
got my Zen chanting group, Wed, my ex-husband's coming
to pick up Jeremy and God knows how long that will take.
Thurs, I go to *his* home to pick up Sally, you see we baby-sit
for each other. Friday, I do my stretch class and I'm useless
after that . . . Oh he's so fabulous, and you do feel *wonderful*
after, you really must come. Sat, we're off for the weekend
'Sleep in' to save the 'Rose' . . . Umm? Next week's
chocabloc with the kids' school play. What about Tues
fortnight at four p.m. for an hour? At least kick it about a
bit?

STEVE: (*Consults filofax*) Uuh . . . no, that day I'm seeing a new
agent so it'll be lunch at Groucho's, Wednesday I'm doing a
voice-over for 'Chockee Nuttees', Thurs I'm doing a re-
birthing session, oh that is something you should have a go
at, does get rid of birth trauma, Friday, my Mum's coming
over for her golden wedding celeb but I could shift that . . .

LINDA: You can't shift that darling, that's once in fifty years!

STEVE: Well, I s'pose not . . . then that weekend I'm doing a yoga
retreat in Suffolk. What about Monday in three weeks?

LINDA: Well, that lands *smack* in the middle of the kids' mid term
and we did promise we'd go to their father's cottage in the

Lake District . . . can't duck out of that . . . that's a week, then back on Sunday when I *did* promise to sell programmes for an anti-poll tax play at the Palace Theatre which would be bad politically to duck out of since the directors are doing a play about the Greenham Common Women which I'm dead right for, 'fingers crossed' so we don't want to muddy those waters. Right?

STEVE: Oh no . . . quite . . .

(*They continue to study their filofaxes.*)

Morris Welder's Table

WELDER: It was Marlon, definitely . . .

SLOANEY FEMALE: So what *did* he do in the stretch limo with his trousers down and the blonde bimbo . . . I can't wait for you to tell me!

WELDER: Mooning darling!

SLOANEY FEMALE: What on earth is that?

WELDER: She doesn't know what mooning is?

ALL: AHAHAHAHAHAHAHHA!!

WELDER: You can tell how young she is . . . Sweet young thing that you are, well mooning is baring your bum darling . . .

SLOANEY FEMALE: Baring your bum? My what exciting times you old hairy renegades had in the Sixties!

WELDER: He stuck his bum out of the window can you imagine . . . I mean in the street you would see two white spotty moons . . . and never guess it was Marlon's! HAHAHA! I mean he's incredible . . . brilliant mind you . . . a genius . . .

WOULD-BE PRODUCER: Ah definitely he is and was and will be and should be and will continue to be . . . and has been and really should always have been . . . unique . . .

SLOANEY FEMALE: Why did he bare his arse, I mean what a pointless Sixties thing to do, no wonder you made such awful spotty films!

WELDER: *Marlon* (pronounced with emphasis on both syllables) Said to me, 'Morris,' he said 'Morris, I love working with you . . . I feel released, open,' and in a moment of exultation he moons . . . it's a rebel's way of expressing himself . . .

SLOANEY FEMALE: I thought you meant that he wanted to crap out of the window!

WELDER: Oh she's so sweet and innocent, you see we were all rebels . . .

WOULD-BE PRODUCER: I have this screenplay about rebels I'd like to pass by you . . .

WELDER: (*Cut short*) He would say 'Morris' or Morry or sometimes Mo . . . yes in a good mood Mo!

WOULD-BE PRODUCER: (*Trying to be helpful*) Or even Moisher . . .

WELDER: GETOUTOFIT! *Never* did he call me that word, never. It would be Morry, but more than often as not, Mo . . . Morris on the set of course in front of the crew . . . but at Tramp's at night surrounded by our mates, Roman, Jack and Marlon, it was *Mo*!

WOULD-BE PRODUCER: (*Trying to be helpful*) In a way he was saying perhaps unconsciously that although the world sees him as some kind of God-like figure, in real life he's just another guy, with a spotty bum.

SLOANEY FEMALE: AAAAAAAAAH! I see, how awfully cute . . .
(DICK TONG, *the vicious drama critic, enters and the room echóes with his name.*)

Garry's First-Night Table

ONE: There's Dicky Tong!

TWO: Oh no.

THREE: He slaughtered my last play.

FOUR: Bastard, what did he say?

THREE: That it could have been written by an orang utang.

FOUR: That's not *so* bad.

FIVE: Tong! He nearly wiped my career off the map.

FOUR: What did he write?

FIVE: My Othello reminded him of Al Jolson singing 'Mammy'.

SIX: That's OK . . . He killed me.

SEVEN: What did he scribble?

SIX: Next time I decide to act, try not to do it publicly!

SEVEN: It could be worse, mine was.

EIGHT: How much worse?

SEVEN: Said I directed *Hamlet* as if it was *West Side Story*
performed by the Co-op's Amateur Dramatic Society?

EIGHT: Why Co-op?

SEVEN: Don't look for sense in his pathological eruptions, please!

EIGHT: Well he hates me.

SEVEN: Said I emptied theatres quicker than the bubonic plague!

NINE: Vicious bitch! I'd like to kill him, he once penned that my
presence on stage could cure insomnia. Imagine reading that
the next morning with your muesli?

FIVE: I could barely go on stage the next night . . .

SIX: I'm not surprised, I had to see a shrink!

SEVEN: We closed after a week!

EIGHT: I became unemployable for five years . . . five years until
the stink wore off.

NINE: He's just a vicious, nasty, jealous, sick, twisted . . .
(DICKY TONG *passes their table.*)

ONE: Oh hi Dicky.

TWO: How are you?

THREE: Great to see you.

FOUR: *Loved* your article on the state of lunch-time theatre in
Glasgow.

ALL: Yes, wonderful, needed to be said, so interesting,
fascinating, hmnnn.

FIVE: You're looking really well.

SIX: How are things?

SEVEN: Been to a show?

EIGHT: What did you see?

DICKY: *Richard the Third*.

ALL: Oooooooooooh!!

ONE: How was it?

DICKY: (*Pause for effect*) Memorable! . . . More at this moment it
would not be appropriate to say . . . (*He wanders in the
direction of the* THREE SISTERS.)

ALL: (*Screeching with laughter*) Hahahahahahaha!

ONE: Well, wait to read it!

TWO: I hope he crucifies him!

THREE: I want to see the blood dripping down the page.

FOUR: He deserves to get clobbered.

FIVE: Oh he will, he will.

SIX: Did you see the way his lip quivered on 'memorable'?

SEVEN: *I* saw it!

EIGHT: Very menacing quiver.

NINE: Sent a shudder down my spine.

EIGHT: I'd hate to be Brick Bergman tomorrow morning.

SEVEN: Horror, horror, horror . . . (*Sees* WAITER) Oh can we see the puddings menu *please*!

Left-wing Fringe Elitists' Table

SID *returns to his* SYCOPHANT *bird*.

SYCOPHANT: Hello darling, feel better . . . your flies are undone . . .

SID: Oh bollocks, I've just been through the restaurant saying hello to the three sisters . . . oh shit, I wonder if they noticed!

SYCOPHANT: Doesn't matter darling really . . . they understand . . . I mean geniuses are forgetful . . . it's really rather endearing . . . lots of directors go around with their flies undone, specially in Brighton.

SID: Yes, but I'm supposed to be the head of a vital revolutionary theatre . . . you don't go round with your flies undone . . . and I want them to be in my poll-tax play . . . !

SYCOPHANT: Do you want me to subtly find out if they noticed? They probably weren't staring at your crotch . . . Come on now . . .

SID: Can you mention it . . . like . . . subtly . . . don't make a thing of it . . . but casually like joking . . . you know . . . like sound them out . . . if they noticed anything, well unusual . . . just approach them on the way for a piss . . .

SYCOPHANT: Sid, please! Do not use that vile expression, women do not piss! Men piss! Women spend a penny or pee . . . but I'll pass them on the way to the loo . . .

SID: Come off it, you Sloane Ranger, you half-baked tart, poncing

off Daddy until he booted your supine lazy arse into a paid flat
in Ovington Square and threw in a BMW . . . you superrating
media whore, dying to get into Nigel's column, you star
fucker, don't you preach your Home Counties, *Sunday Times*
Arts Magazine morality to me . . . you bitch . . . before you
met me the only work you ever did was writing the occasional
rejected review for the *Good Food Guide*!

SYCOPHANT: Oh darling, you were quite wonderful . . . you're so
. . . Jimmy Porter!!

SID: Oh noooooooo!

Linda and Steve's Table

STEVE: (*Still looking through filofax*) Well next month looks fairly
clear, although that's the summer season and I am short-listed
for a couple of plays in Bexhill-on-Sea, fingers crossed, so I
don't want to say now just in case I mess you around and you
book it and then have to cancel . . . like you find you've got a
couple of hours one afternoon . . . give me a bell, jump in the
jam jar . . . that might be better . . . keep it casual . . . like oh
. . . I've got a couple of free hours . . . let's do *Macbeth* . . .

LINDA: Yes, let's keep it light, otherwise it gets heavy . . . I'll call
you or you call me . . . just tickle the play . . . read it over a
cuppa . . . no big deal. Any time.

STEVE: Exactly, don't plan it, let it happen . . .

LINDA: Very Zen, let it pop into your mind spontaneously . . .

STEVE: Yah! Like for example Monday you might find you've got
a couple of hours, it's Parkinson's Law, there's always
time . . .

LINDA: (*Consulting filofax*) Well Monday I have my audition
Tuesday I have my Zen Buddhist chanting group . . .

Brick's Table

BRICK: (*Still straining after the stool effect*) 'Now are our brows
bound with victorious wreaths' . . .
(TABLE *thumps*.)

'Our brui-sed arms hung up for monuments' . . .

(*Thump*.)

Hey it's definitely better . . .

SIR M.: You're getting the rhythm, the music, it's like playing an instrument, (*To* WAITER) Another large gin, you're an instrument, *you* . . . a living human instrument.

HANGER-ON 1: My tuna was awful, how was yours?

HANGER-ON 2: Mine was OK, a bit dry, mind you I'm getting fed up with tuna . . .

HANGER-ON 3: Mine was lovely, I had it with the sauce, that hot chilli sauce.

HANGER-ON 1: He never offered the sauce to me.

HANGER-ON 2: Nor me, I wonder why?

HANGER-ON 3: Had it made specially, Giovanni knows I like that sauce.

HANGER-ON 2: Cheeky bitch . . .

HANGER-ON 3: Well I used to work in the kitchens when I was just a young pretty ingenue . . .

HANGER-ON 1: That was centuries ago ducky, the restaurant wasn't even thought of then!

HANGER-ON 3: Don't be such a bloody cow just because your tuna's all dried up!

BRICK: You're right, you're right, I'm an instrument, I must learn to use my 'instrument'.

SIR M.: Aaaah you see, you are a humble player, playing your . . .

BRICK: Instrument! I see, I see, it's beautiful, I love my instrument . . . Oh Sir Michael (*takes hand and kisses it*) You are the conductor of my . . .

SIR M.: . . . instrument!

BRICK: Now I'm ready for Othello, Macbeth, Romeo, I can't wait to use this fantastic marvellous . . .

ALL: INSTRUMENT!

BRICK: I'll go to New York, I'll show them the new, renovated and baptised Brick Bergman (*to* SECRETARY) Get New York on the phone, I wanna talk to Joe Papp! Hey I wanna surprise Joe . . . We'll get Meryl for Lady Anne and Robert De Niro for Buckingham, yeah his career needs a kick in the butt! And if he don't get too self important like, 'the-sun-shines-out-of-my-ass-crap', we'll offer Gloucester to Pacino . . . I can't wait to show you Noo York, I know places where you get the biggest corned beef sandwiches you ever saw . . . your eyes will pop out of your head . . . huge . . . you can't even open your mouth . . .

Morris Welder's Table

WELDER: So Marlon said, 'Mo, I love you . . . I love you Mo,' because Marlon was a prince . . . mind you he's a genius, he is a genius and *I* allowed his genius to grow . . .

WOULD-BE-PRODUCER: Talking of genius, I have a play about genius that . . .

ACTOR: 'Hey, I'm gonna make you an offer you can't refuse, how come you don't come round for coffee, pay your respects . . . to the family . . . '

WELDER: He's wonderful, the kid's wonderful, I love impersonators . . .

ACTOR: 'OK, we'll make a deal that's honourable for the family, but drugs we do not do, prostitution, gambling, these are human needs but not drugs . . .' (*Switching movies*) 'You shoulda looked afta me a liddle more . . .'

WELDER: I love him!

ACTOR: (*Streetcar*) 'Take a look at yourself in that worn-out Mardi Gras outfit . . . What kind of queen do you think you are?'

WELDER: He kills me!

WOULD-BE-PRODUCER: I have a play in mind for him that . . .

WELDER: SHHH! Go on . . . go on . . .

ACTOR: (*Getting excited, stands up*) 'You gave it to Joey who was one of your own . . . I'm glad what I done to you . . . You hear me . . . I'm glad . . .'

WELDER: Marvellous!

Brick's Table

BRICK: (*On phone*) Joey, hey . . . how are ya? Yeah it was terrific
. . . Frank Bitch flew in . . . he was seen smiling at the end . . .
No I kid you not, we got witnesses . . . you going to Florida for
the weekend . . . no I don't miss New York, what you kidding
me! I miss the food, yeah . . . fly me over a few kilos of
pastrami . . . Thanks Joe . . . Now listen . . . (*adopts stool
position*)
'Now is the winter of our discontent
Made glorious summer by this sun of York'
How's that sound to you? It's my new sound? What, it sounds
like I'm taking a crap . . . you kidding me? It's the line (*telephone*)
. . . hey fuck you! You think I need you? You need me!

Three Sister's Table

They are joined by TONG (*the critic*).

SISTER ONE: I love what Chekhov says . . . the way that he says
it . . .

SISTER TWO: That's right . . . it's the way . . . it just seems so
right.

SISTER THREE: He lets you fly . . . it's somehow open . . . you
know . . .

TONG: Yaaah.

SISTER ONE: He loves human beings . . . you feel that love . . .

SISTER TWO: Oh yes, he allows you to love your character . . .

SISTER THREE: I mean you must love your character.

SISTER ONE: I want to reach the people with it . . . play it in
factories and schools.

SISTER TWO: And prisons, I adore playing in prisons . . .

SISTER THREE: They're a wonderful audience and *so*
appreciative . . .

TONG: I was in prison once . . .

SISTER THREE: Oh wonderful, did you give a lecture on theatrical
criticism?

TONG: God no, I did two weeks in Pentonville for flashing at
minors . . .

SISTER TWO: Oh, how horrid for you . . .

SISTER ONE: Prisons are the bourgeois way of dealing with the nonconformist . . .

SISTER THREE: (*As* WAITRESS *passes*) Excuse me can we have another champagne . . . same as before . . .

WAITRESS: We've only the Moet left.

SISTER THREE: Oh no . . . none of that lovely Chrystal?

WAITRESS: Sorreee . . .

SISTER THREE: Oh well, disappointment is good for the character . . . the Moet then . . .

Terry's Table

BILLY: Well it's been a fabulous evenin' . . . ah loved meetin' ya and I hope we'll get together real soon . . .

TERRY: Definitely, we're doing a charity concert for starving kids in Calcutta, there'll be a triffic party after, if you fancy bowling along . . .

BILLY: That sounds wonderful, do you have a pen?

FAT PRODUCER: I'll get the bill.

TERRY: No, I'll get it.

FAT PRODUCER: I'll get it . . . come on it's my treat . . .

TERRY: You're always getting it, (*Voiceover*: You fat adorable ponce!) Sit down, I'll get it . . .

FAT PRODUCER: Please Terry, please, I'll be offended . . . it's mine . . .

TERRY: Come on, *I'll* be very upset . . . (*Voiceover*: You wobbly mass of unpaid profits) . . . I'll do it . . .

FAT PRODUCER: I won't hear a word of it . . .

TERRY: Shut up, it's my treat this time, OK?

FAT PRODUCER: No way, I invited you . . .

TERRY: Just this once . . . you're too generous . . . (*Voiceover*: With all the money you thieved!)

FAT PRODUCER: It's my pleasure . . .

TERRY: Next time! (*Voiceover*: You vile boring and repetitive scumbag!)

FAT PRODUCER: OK, you get it next time, OK. (*To* WAITRESS) You take plastic . . . ?

WAITRESS: Sorry we don't take credit cards, only cheques . . .
  (*Voiceover*: We told you this last time! Asshole!)
FAT PRODUCER: Oooops, I have only my cards . . . you don't
  even take AMEX *Goldcard*!!!
WAITRESS: Money or cheque . . . Sorreeeeeeee . . . (*Voiceover*: Do
  you use shit for brains!)
TERRY: I've only got plastic too, I haven't seen a cheque book in
  years . . . !
FAT PRODUCER: Hey Billy, I'm sorry but . . .
BILLY: Sure I've got a cheque book . . . (*Voiceover*: (*Surly and
  cross*) Bunch of wankers! (*With a smile in voice*) Bore me to
  death and then I pay!)

Left-wing Fringe Elitists' Table

SID: (*Studying bill*) What a sodding rip-off, how many
  champagnes did we drink?
SYCOPHANT: Two bottles . . .
SID: Jesus Christ, you certainly knocked it back.
SYCOPHANT: I hardly touched it . . .
SID: You know, we've got to get a bigger grant . . .
SYCOPHANT: You should, it's the philistine government that puts
  a price on everything . . . even *art*.
SID: Bastards, look how much they pour away into that khazi
  down the road full of seriously overweight pasta noshers
  warbling their guts out. Can't give them *enough*!
SYCOPHANT: Of course the opera's a show place for the Tories to
  bring their Japanese investors . . .
SID: Still we'll rock the bastards with our poll-tax play! Those
  riots are like music in my ears . . .
SYCOPHANT: Terribly exciting!!!
SID: It's the pounding heart of the people!
SYCOPHANT: It's just like the French Revolution.
SID: Smashing all those capitalist shops!
SYCOPHANT: A surging mass of humanity, there's your audience
  Sid, if only they would come to your theatre . . .
SID: They can't afford theatre you idiot, that's why we're doing

the play . . . we're reflecting THATCHERITE
BRITAIN!!

SYCOPHANT: Sid, you're making me feel . . . terribly horny . . . !

Linda and Steve's Table

STEVE: I'll get it . . .

LINDA: You sure?

STEVE: Sure, you got it last time.

LINDA: No, you got it last time.

STEVE: You sure?

LINDA: Yes, I remember because we were at this same table . . .

STEVE: I don't remember that . . .

LINDA: Yes you do, we had tuna and you had this big obsession.

STEVE: I did? What about?

LINDA: Whether you should play Macbeth . . .

STEVE: Oh yes . . . (*Voiceover*: I don't think I'll have her in *my*
Macbeth – bitch!)

Garry's First-Night Table

GARRY: Sodden awful night and I've got to go on the next and the
next. . .

VOICE 1: Fabulous evening, keep it up and thanks for the dinner,
tuna was wonderful.

VOICE 2: Wonderful night Garry, all the best, must fly.

VOICE 3: Will you be safe getting home, you know what it's like
out there . . . it's a *jungle*!

VOICE 4: The rioters have gone home by now and my car's
outside.

VOICE 5: Love you, you were so good tonight . . . chin chin . . .

WOMAN FRIEND: Darling you are generous getting the whole
bill . . . !

GARRY: Tax deductable darling . . .

VOICE 6: If the critics don't simply adore it, then there's no hope
in this country!
(MANAGER *enters room and stands on step.*)

MANAGER: Excuse me ladies and gentlemen, no alarm needed but please leave by the back exit, the rioters have passed by and have been smashing cars . . . anyone own a silver grey Volvo parked just outside the door . . .

SID: Shit! That's *my* car!

SYCOPHANT: Oh NO . . . !!

MANAGER: Unfortunately it's been set on fire . . .

SID: Crumby, dirty, anarchist bastards!!

(RESTAURANT *leaves in a mild frenzy of excitement*.)

VARIOUS: Oh my God. How exciting. Let's go together. Form into small groups. My chauffeur's outside.

MANAGER: Please be careful.

VARIOUS: It's like World War Two.

BRICK: It's worse than the Bronx on Saturday night.

ACTOR: 'I'll take it out on their skulls.'

WELDER: I wish Marlon was with us.

VARIOUS: Billy come with us. We'll be safe down Tramp's. Let's link arms. It seems quiet out there now. Better be careful.

SID: You got money for a cab?

VARIOUS: Have I got time to go to the loo?

(*Restaurant slowly oozes its occupants out unrushed until only* STAFF *and* STEVE *and* LINDA *are left*.)

STEVE: So you do think I should play Macbeth?

LINDA: You'd be marvellous darling . . .

(*We leave them pondering the bleakness of their fate and dreams. She writes out a cheque*.)

DOG

AUTHOR'S NOTE

A day in the life of yet another strange beast whose energy still attracts one to define and examine. A man with his dog, but a pitbull, one of those creatures I had been reading about, or, should I say, had forced down my gullet as ravage after ravage appeared in the papers as the beasts tore into innocent young flesh. It seemed to go with the British low-class yob culture more prevalent in the Thatcher years as class-division widened and the social fabric decayed. It went with the pub, obsessive drunkenness, football and xenophobia.

So this is a comedy of manners if you like, performed by a simple direct, strong, unconfused guardian of British morality. The dog merely amplifies the insane and undirected energy of its owner. Curiously, his beliefs are not vague or confused but are held with dedication and conviction which makes him in a way repulsively ATTRACTIVE.

Dog was first performed (under the title *Pitbull*) at the Warehouse Theatre, Croydon, on 13th August 1993. The cast was as follows:

MAN ⎫
DOG ⎭ Steven Berkoff

Director Steven Berkoff
Designer Steven Berkoff
Lighting Brian Knox

A man enters stage appearing to be fulling a strong dog on a leash which we are made to imagine, by the stress the actor demonstrates, is huge and ferocious. It's called Roy. The man is dressed in the mandatory eighties weekend gear: a lurid track suit and what are commonly called 'trainers', a form of jogging shoe. His guts are sagging over his waistband.

MAN: Nah, e's alright, 'e gets a bit excited, that's all, e's got a bad press, 'snot 'is fault that kid stuck his nut between his jaws. (DOG *pulls on lead.*) Come 'ere, you little bastard . . .

ROY: (*Growling*) Stop pullin my lead, you cunt, or I'll sink my teeth into your fuckin leg!

MAN: 'Ere, come 'ere you naughty boy. Nah, 'e's lovely 'e is, arncha Roy? You can pat 'im! Go on, PAT 'IM!! 'e won't 'urtcha, don't provoke 'im. Well, that kid 'ad 300 stitches in 'is nut, looked like a patchwork quilt 'e did . . . Well, I was lookin for a tachometer and a second-hand petrol pump for me Ford Transit, so I jumped in the van, bunged Roy in the back and 'eaded down to the Paki who's got a garage off Stratford East, before Romford, just before the A25 turns into the A23 which turns into the A2. E's a good geezer, this Paki, 'We do a very, very good service, costs you half as much anywhere else!' but you don't wanna get downwind if he's eaten a chicken vindaloo the night before! Right, Roy's in the van and I'm chattin' to the Paki about gear boxes, petrol pumps and all that sexy stuff about engine parts when some little kid outside finks, 'Oh ho! The van door's unlocked, maybe that cunt's in their chattin, so let's see what we can 'alf-inch.' Opens the door . . . WALLOP!! Roy's out like a fuckin greyhound, kid's 'ead in a vice, blood spurtin everywhere, claret all over the van. 'ROY, GET THAT JAW OPEN, YOU BASTARD' . . . bless 'im 'e's got a bite like a steel vice. Well, eventually we 'ad to clobber 'im wiv a starting wrench to make 'im let go . . . didn't we, Roy . . . 'e 'ad a sore 'ead for a couple of days, didn't like that, did ya, old son?

ROY: GGGGGGGGGGGGGGGGGGGRRRRRRRRRRRR, STOP PULLING MY LEAD OR I'LL BITE YOUR

FUCKIN 'EAD OFF!

MAN: GGGGGGGGGGGEDAHDOVIT!! Well, I said sorry to the
kid's dad and all that and offered to buy 'is dad a pint and a
Mars bar for the kid, but 'e wasn't havin' any of it, 'e was
right choked, but I says you don't wanna mess about in the
back of a van 'alf-inchin or you may get somethin you
weren't expecting, right! I mean, am I right? I mean, 'e can't
help 'is nature, 'e sees a brown face peepin in where 'e
shouldna done. Right?! . . . well 'is dad saw the truth of that
'e was where 'e shouldna been and so I got the tachometer
and the second-'and petrol pump and was a bit upset with all
that blood messin up the van. So I thought let's bowl down
the pub and sink a few lagers, so off we went and the new
pump worked a fuckin treat and Roy's in the back of the van,
only I locked it this time . . . right. 'E don't like bein' locked
in the back of the van do yer, Roy? . . .

ROY: GGGGGRRRRRRRRRRRRRRRRRR . . . (*Leaps up
and down in agitation.*)

MAN: Anyway, cut to the fuckin pub: 'ALLO DEN, 'ALLO
DAVE, LAGERS ALL ROUND, PLENTY OF
CAKEY-BOO*, GRAB HOLD OF THAT (*Mimes
throwing money down.*) IT'S MY SHOUT, AS THEY
SAY IN THE POXY TV SERIES 'NEIGHBOURS',
ABOUT A BUNCH OF POXY FUCKING MORONS
IN OZZYLAND! Dave? Got somethin for Roy, he's
starvin, yeah, wot about one o' them pies you got in that
'eated cabinet with the glass front, Roy's 'ad his eyes on them
for ages, aintcha Roy?! Well, they've been there for at least a
year, so bung us 'alf a dozen . . . Nah, don't take the wrapper
off, it's all brown and crinkly. . . 'ere you go, Roy . . .
(*Roy is thrown the pies one at a time.*)

ROY: AAAAAAARRRRRRGGGGGH . . . CRUNCH,
CRUNCH, CHUNCHH

MAN: He loves that, look at that, 'e likes the crackling round it, 'e
don't know it's cellophane, finks it's bits o' crispy bacon,

*Money

dontcha? (*Drinks his pint and talks to barman.*) So, Arsenal kicked shit out of Spurs, right Dave? So now they're set to play Millwall, which is just my manor, so next week we're off to see 'em . . . liked that did you, Roy??? Eh, my little sweetheart . . . did diddums like his little pork pies . . . 'ere Dave, you're lucky you didn't sell 'em or you would of done time for manslaughter, fucking poisoning the public . . . MORE LAGERS! Plenty of cakey-boo, grab 'old of that!! (*Pulls out wad of money. Drinks*) So that night I downed thirty-five pints of fucking lager 'cause I was still upset about Roy . . .

ROY: GGGGRRRR! Stop pullin my lead, you maggot, or I'll eat your fuckin leg.

MAN: Nah, 'es alright, he gets excited but he's sweet as a nut really, I swear . . . look, 'e's got temperament, I mean you wanna dog wiv a bit of temperament dontcha, I mean, I live between Commercial Road and Whitechapel, say no more, well wot if your old mum, EH! Wot if . . . your old mum lived down 'ere, I mean she's bowlin down the road one winter's night, bless 'er, just been to the off-licence for some fags and a couple of Guinness to slurp in front of the telly, when out of one of them council estates steps 'alf a dozen bleedin Pakis, right, or bleedin' Irish yobs. I ain't prejudiced, name your particular poison, alright two Pakis, two paddies and two 'asidic Jews out for a night of robbery with violence so, you got six kids out to do some muggin, right, foggy evening and there's your old mum, bless 'er, trottin along all innocent for 'er nightly booze in front of *East Enders* . . . right? NOW, WITH ONE OF THEM AT THE END OF HER FUCKIN LEAD YOU DON'T HAVE TO FUCKIN WORRY MATE!! Eh, your mum's safe as houses, right, 'cause that's a fuckin tank wiv teeth! She can go out at midnight if she wanted but she wouldn't want to, 'cause the place is dead from 6 o'clock anyway and there's no fuckin place to go except yer dreary fuckin poxy pub with a fruit machine blinkin its pissin head off and two old-age pensioners sitting in there waitin to drop dead of boredom. Yeah, that's yer average pub round 'ere, mate. That's why I come all the way to Dave's . . . anyway, so I drank thirty-five pints that night and I was so sick I barfed all over the fuckin pavement . . . WHOOOOSH! Right skating rink it was . . . Course, Roy's not fussy, 'e's a bastard 'e is . . . and 'e likes chicken chow mein even if it's been keeping warm in my guts for four hours . . . you're disgusting, aintcha Roy!!?

ROY: Stop pulling my fuckin lead, this is the last time I tell yer!

MAN: (*To* ROY) Gertcha! 'E's a fuckin' vacuum cleaner, e'll fuckin eat the telly if 'e could, oh 'e's a wild one but 'e's good as gold, 'e's got a lovely nature if you show 'im a bit of love and attention, nah 'e's lovely. So we went to the match, course we got tanked up a bit first 'cause you can't drink at matches no more, you get caught wiv a bottle then some fuckin rozzer's gonna whack you wiv 'is truncheon, so you get right fuckin tanked up so as to combat the cold, right, and Millwall were kickin shit out of Arsenal and some Arsenal supporters were gettin the shit kicked out of them on the terraces, when Roy, who I sneaked in, took after the fuckin ball! He pulled the lead right out of my 'and and went for it. Course the place was in a fuckin uproar and the players all gave Roy a wide berth 'cause 'e was chewing the bloody ball . . . like . . . well, I called 'im and 'e came, I mean 'e's well trained, an' I was thrown out and banned for fifty years! Well, I'm right choked 'cause we used to go week after week and I only took Roy under my coat for protection 'cause that Arsenal mob can get fuckin stroppy. And now me and Roy stay at home and watch Rambo movies 'cause he likes them, but 'e barks when it's over and I have to play the bloody thing all over again . . . It's a right bore, and I can't get out to the pub as much 'cause 'e gets so restless and they won't give 'im those plastic pies . . . says it disturbs the customers and so I'm thinking of gettin' a babysitter . . . anyone want a part-time job? . . . 'e's lovely . . .

ACTOR

AUTHOR'S NOTE

I was, on the recommendation of my friend John Joyce, looking
for material for a one-man show. One doodles as the information
bubbles away in the unconscious and suddenly there is an
eruption which seems to be feeding from a deep current of energy
within. Years of struggle, unemployment, auditions, begging
letters, agents, directors who didn't re-employ, self-loathing,
disappointment, lack of courage, self-worth, self-pity leading to
paranoia, neurosis etc. – this is the life of an actor as he tries not
only to express the best part of himself but is condemned or
rejected as part of his daily life. It is a harrowing profession while
you are in the pleading position. So these thoughts store
themselves in what seem small compartments in your mind,
festering away like a compost heap and suddenly there is a break
in the soil.

I was partly inspired by a Marcel Marceau sketch where he
walks apparently on the spot forever and the world passes him by.
I performed this on the spot as the actor walks through his life
watching it slowly disintegrate. The player's life is a hard one and
the actor's present low status is further confirmed as neophyte
directors grab more media space for their 'conceptions' than
actors who have given many more years to their craft. However,
that is another story.

Actor was first performed at the Traverse Theatre, Edinburgh, on 31st January 1984. The cast was as follows:

ACTOR   Steven Berkoff

Director   Steven Berkoff
Designer   Steven Berkoff

ACTOR: Greetings, hello John, hello Richard and how are you?
. . . Hello Mike and how are you? . . . working? . . . really,
that's good . . . what are you doing? . . . a play . . . how very
nice . . . see you . . . have a nice day you . . . Hello Peter . . .
how are you? . . . I'm doing well too . . . working? . . . you
are? . . . that's good . . . Bastard, he couldn't act his way out
of a paper bag . . . the slag . . . still, I'll show them . . . those
out there . . . the faceless ones . . . the ones in the chairs . . .
the ones who say 'thank you – we'll let you know' . . . they
haven't the guts to get out there . . . Hello darling . . . you're
lovely . . . you really are . . . I think our fate's designed in the
stars . . . you're divine . . . Yes I do take this woman to be
really mine . . . Get the kettle on love . . . it's nearly nine . . .

Hello Ma, hello Pa, this is . . . going just great . . . getting on fine
. . . just watch this space . . . 'So why couldn't they get you a
commercial or two', Sorry Ma . . . that's not what I have in
view . . . for me . . . that's for the others . . . not men of
quality . . . 'I saw you last week on the TV . . . playing an
astronaut but couldn't see your face . . . I rang Aunty Betty
. . . my son on TV . . . she raced for the . . . but when she got
there . . . it was off the air' . . . Bye Ma, ta-ta Pa . . . Yes,
darling, of course I'm as happy as . . . how can you doubt . . .
I haven't kissed you in weeks? . . . sometimes you forget . . .
stop nagging, I'm trying to work on my text . . . if I don't
work soon . . . I don't exist . . . that's a feeling these days that
tends to persist.

Hello Paul . . . how are you? . . . you working? . . . oh . . . I'm
glad that you're pulling through . . . I'm glad to hear all your
efforts are beginning to bear . . . fruit . . . is that the word?
. . . I'm Fred, how are you? . . . you working, for TV . . .
directing . . . that's cool . . . then don't forget me . . . hah ha
ha . . . your old chum from school . . . How did he? . . . he
flogged his bum . . . succeed . . . that weed . . . joined the
club . . . the faceless ones . . . all rub shoulders in the bar . . .
the ones who can't do it . . . the ones in the chairs . . . the

ones who say 'thank you, we'll let you know, my dear . . .
Hello darling . . . yeah, I'm home . . . had a nice day . . .
yeah I did nothing . . . walked streets and sat in cafés . . . get
a job? . . . I'm an actor, you bitch . . . got to be free . . . got to
be fit, for the time when someone says 'you're it' . . . no one
phoned? . . . are you sure? . . . you were all day . . . at home
. . . Hello Henry . . . you working? . . . you are, that's good
. . . you'll go far . . . acts like wood . . . Hello Jack . . . you
working? . . . No! aah, tough . . . things will improve . . . the
going is rough . . . remember at RADA what they said, my
dear . . . if you want to be a star you have to persevere . . . if
you want to climb to the top of the shit heap . . . you mustn't
complain . . . if your shoes stink of turds at the end of the
day.

Hello darling . . . what's your name . . . you're lovely you are . . .
I love you for ever . . . you're what I'm looking for . . . Go –
you keep the TV . . . I'll keep the car . . . we'll sell the house
. . . can't stand no more . . .

Hello Roger . . . I'm doing great . . . up for a TV series . . . not
yet . . . short list . . . near as damn it . . . I'll get you a guest
spot . . . if you like . . . my agent's talking money . . . then
it's sewn up . . . Hello darling . . . sure I love you . . . hold
on, there's the phone . . . did I? . . . No . . . sure, there'll be
other parts . . . The bastards don't give me the shit from
their ass . . .

Hello Ma, hello Pa . . . how are things? . . . 'I've seen nothing but
rubbish on the TV . . . why aren't you there, son? . . . you
look like Paul Newman . . . doesn't he dear?' . . . Hello Dad
. . . 'Don't talk to me, you parasite . . . you bum . . . all you
can do is scrounge when you come' . . . Yeah! I'll be keeping
you one day, over my dead body, that's what I'd say . . .
'Don't talk to your father like that . . . be a son . . . that we
can be proud . . . whenever we speak' . . . I've got an
audition . . . I swear next week . . . To be . . . or not to be,

that is the question, whether 'tis nobler in the mind . . . to
bear the sling and arrows of outrageous fortune . . . Thank
you, that's enough . . . we'll let you know . . . we'll contact
your agent . . . please don't phone . . . Yes darling, I was
great . . . the money will flow . . . we'll celebrate . . . so what,
I've not made love in a month . . . what's in your head,
romance and bullshit, that's for the dead . . . then go . . .
fuck off . . . sorry I wed you . . . no, I didn't mean . . .

Hello Martin . . . you doing well? . . . you doing a movie . . .
fucking hell! No, I mean that's smart . . . you've got a good
agent . . . mine's just a fart . . . Anything going? . . . any
more parts . . . that require my stunning talent? . . . Oh, it's
all cast . . . Bastard . . . wouldn't give you the shit from his
ass.

Hello, did I get the job? . . . didn't think I was right? . . . Cunts, I
could act the pants off the slobs . . . theatre . . . it's full of the
dead . . . they rake the graveyards . . . the lousy shit-heads
. . . the walking corpses . . . little blind mice . . . rats in
armchairs . . . Hello? she hung up . . . Hello darling, I'm
back home . . . what's this? . . . Dear John . . . 'Sorry, I
really must go . . . sorry to leave like this . . . I just got so . . .
bored with the life . . . bored with the fight that must go on
. . . day and night . . . Don't forget to feed pussy . . . Please
don't write . . . I'll find better than you' . . . Go . . . you got
no guts . . . I won't shed a tear . . .

Hello Ted, how are you . . . working? . . . good! . . . He couldn't
fucking act an ape in the zoo . . . Hello Bill . . . you working?
. . . no? . . . good . . . I mean good you're not dead! . . . it's
good that you . . . hold on . . . hold on to your soul or take
arms against a sea of troubles and by opposing end them . . .
To die to sleep no more and by a sleep to say we end the
heartache . . . Thank you, we'll let you know . . . and please
. . . we do ask you not to phone . . . Excuse me, do I have a
chance? . . . tell me . . . you can tell me now . . . if I'm not

the right one . . . then I'd . . . We're thinking about it, we'll
let you know . . . call in the next as you go . . .

Hello Ma, Hello Pa . . . no, I got no dough . . . lend me a fiver just
to get through . . . I need a few bob . . . times will improve
. . . 'He looks like Paul Newman doesn't he, Al?' . . . 'He
looks like a ponce . . . go to hell' . . . I'll show them . . . I will
. . . I'll smash through . . . I'll show them what talent is . . .
I'll break fucking through . . . Hello Darling . . . you're
lovely . . . you look like a peach . . . you're divine . . . any
commercials even . . . will you be mine? . . . My wife ran off
with a dirty swine . . . there must be something! . . . I think
we're made for each other . . . like fate . . . no, I don't exude
hate . . . I love the bastards . . . I'm all sweet and charm . . .
all right, I'll lick ass . . . all greasy and smarm . . . She hung
up.

Hello Pat . . . you working? . . . you are? . . . where? . . . show me
. . . I'll be a star yet . . . Fuck you . . . you pigs . . . you
untalented shits . . . shit gather together in one bowl . . . I'll
flush you away . . . give me a role . . .

Hello Pa . . . what do you mean, cancer? . . . yeah, I'll try and get
round . . . yeah, that word has an ugly sound . . . Who would
fardels bear to grunt and sweat under a weary life but that
the fear of something after death . . . Yeah, OK – you let me
know . . . Hello darling, I'm home . . . course I love you! . . .
oh, leave me alone . . . I've got other problems . . . so sod off,
just go . . . you fed up with me? . . . women like you, they
grow on . . . Ma . . . don't die . . . don't go just yet . . . don't
leave me just now . . . I'm starring in . . . Hamlet . . . I think
. . . you'll be proud . . . What did she say? . . . her last words
. . . 'fore she passed away . . . You look like Paul Newman
and have a nice day . . . goodbye Ma and Pa . . . I'll cry at
your graves . . . but I've got an audition, I mustn't be late . . .
Whether 'tis nobler in the mind to suffer the slings and
arrows of outrageous fortune . . . 'Thank you very much . . .

we'll let you know . . . we'll call your agent . . . get the
fucking kid out of here . . . I'm on the phone' . . . She hung
up again . . . oh no!

Hello John . . . what's new . . . yeah, terrific . . . I do bits and
pieces . . . up for Hamlet . . . too old? . . . I'm an actor you
prick. Hello darling, I'm back . . . what's this? . . . 'Don't be
upset husband . . . don't be sore . . . just couldn't stand any
more . . . need peace for the kids . . . you can see them of
course . . . say once a month . . . we'll discuss it in court . . .
get a job and I'm sure you'll find . . . at the end . . . peace of
mind' . . . You're mad . . . I'm tough . . . I'm the tops . . . the
others are assholes and creeps . . . pigs at a trough.

Hello Frank . . . how's graft? . . . read your reviews . . . you're
doing good . . . you're smart . . . a good agent . . . that gives
you the start . . . yeah, feeling great . . . got an audition . . .
mustn't be late . . . To be or not to be that is the question . . .
whether 'tis nobler in the mind to suffer the slings and
arrows of outrageous fortune . . . outrageous fortune . . . to
die . . . to sleep . . . no more and be a sleep to say we end the
heart . . . ache . . . . . . Ma!